FIGHT ON,
MY SOUL

a biography

James E.C. Norris, M.D.

Published and printed in the United States of America by The Write Place. For more information, please contact:

The Write Place
599 228th Place
Pella, Iowa 50219
www.thewriteplace.biz

ISBN: 978-0-9800084-6-3
Library of Congress Control Number: 2009936126

Cover and interior design by Alexis Thomas, The Write Place

Copies of this book may be ordered from The Write Place at a cost of $14.95 each. Send check or money order to:

The Write Place
599 228th Place
Pella, IA 50219

For one to two books, add $3.00 shipping fee. For three or more books sent to the same address, shipping is free.

Dedication

This book is dedicated to my father's patients, for whom
he knew no bounds in compassion, kindness, and service;

to the citizens of Virginia, and particularly Lancaster
County, for whom his courage and perseverance to realize
his vision of a better society were without limits;

and to my mother, Theresita Beatrice Chiles Norris,
without whose unwavering support and unconditional
love, he could not have done so much.

My Soul, Be on Thy Guard

by George Heath, 1781

My soul, be on thy guard,
Ten thousand foes arise,
And hosts of sin are pressing hard
To draw thee from the skies.

Oh, watch, and fight, and pray,
The battle ne'er give o'er,
Renew it boldly every day,
And help divine implore.

Ne'er think the vict'ry won,
Nor once at ease sit down;
Thine arduous work will not be done
Till thou hast got the crown.

Fight on, my soul, till death
Shall bring thee to thy God;
He'll take thee at thy parting breath
Up to His blest abode.

Acknowledgments

In bringing this story to print, many persons helped in ways, large and small. There were those who agreed to a taped interview, those who talked or wrote about Morgan E. Norris and how he impacted their lives, those who read parts of the manuscript and some who read all six hundred pages of the first draft. Many persons gave advice on specific chapters, and friends and acquaintances shared information that enhanced the quality of the narrative and the accuracy of the legends to the photographs. To everyone, I will remain ever grateful.

If I did not heed some of the very solid advice or neglected to follow up on important tips, it was done at my peril. I accept full responsibility for shortcomings. And, after my many revisions, if I fail to convey to the reader the full measure of my father's life, it is a failure that I, alone, shall accept.

I must, however, single out individuals whom I pestered, annoyed, vexed, and may even have become a thorn in their sides. Mr. F. W. Jenkins, Jr., a former historical researcher at the Mary Ball Washington Museum and Library, helped kick off the story with oral history recordings and encouraged the writing of this biography. Mrs. Valencia Keeve, executive administrator, Mrs. Charlotte Henry, researcher and writer, and Mrs. Carolyn Jett, co-chairman of the Library committee, researcher and author, all of whom are associated with the Museum and Library, responded with cheerful efficiency to my numerous emails, letters, telephone calls, and requests for assistance. I am particularly indebted to the staff of three libraries in New York City where I spent many hours: the New York Academy of Medicine at Fifth Avenue and 103rd Street, the New York Public Library at Fifth Avenue and 42nd Street, and the Schomburg Center at 135th Street and Lenox Avenue. The staffs at these facilities were uniformly cooperative and never failed to offer assistance when needed. Especial thanks go out to two Academy staff members, Mr. Adrian Thomas and Ms. Arlene Shaner, assistant curator of the Rare Book Room and to The Schomburg's Assistant Chief Librarian, Mrs. Sharon M. Howard.

Three university archives, all at my father's alma maters—Hampton, Lincoln, and Howard—proved indispensable to my research. My deepest appreciation is extended to Mrs. Donzella Maupin, assistant to the archivist, Mrs. Andreese Scott, secretary, and Ms. Cynthia Poston, clerk typist of Hampton University's archives. Much of the correspondence used in this book having to do with the Piedmont Sanatorium, Hampton Institute, and the Hampton Institute Trustee Board came from the archives of Hampton University. I thank the archives for permission to use this material.

I am indebted to the Leyburn Library of Washington and Lee University for permission to use copies of the correspondence (1928-1964) of Mrs. Jessie Ball duPont with Dr. Thomas F. Wheeldon, Dr. H. Jeter Edmonds and Norris. Virginia Union University's archives department of the L. Douglas Wilder Library & Learning Resource Center was kind enough to give permission to use copies of Dr. John M. Ellison's correspondence with Norris during the 1940s. I thank the Library of Virginia for permitting use of copies of correspondence from the papers of Governor Colgate W. Darden, and the Library of Congress for access to the papers of Robert R. Moton. The University of Virginia's Albert and Shirley Small Special Collections Library gave access to the papers of Charles P. Wertenbaker and Governor Harry Flood Byrd.

Mr. Charles R. Pruett, certified land surveyor of Lancaster, Virginia, was of immense help with land records and maps, and Mrs. Donna Helmuth of Lancaster County, and formerly with the Mary Ball Washington Museum and Library, proved invaluable in the transcribing of records, in research, and in fact checking.

Marilynn Hawkridge, photo retoucher, of New York City, did a magnificent job of restoring the old photographs, particularly the Lincoln University Class of 1912, which was badly damaged. Carol Van Klompenburg, publisher, Donna Biddle, copyeditor, and Alexis Thomas, graphic artist of The Write Place, deserve accolades for putting up with a rather obstinate and finicky author.

My family members responded readily whenever I called, but I owe my youngest sister, Martha, and her husband, Robert Gilbert, of Richmond, Virginia, a special debt for the many stays, many meals, and many calls that interrupted the daily routine of their lives—and for their sage advice. I am particularly indebted to my nephew, Mark Norris Sims, and my grandniece, Caroline E. Jackson, who spent innumerable, tedious hours poring over the manuscript, helping to reshape it into readable form. And I must thank Patricia Hass and Daryl Cumber Dance, family friends, Richmonders, and writers, who reviewed drafts, gave critiques, and provided invaluable direction.

I would be an ingrate if I closed without a nod to my wife, Motoko, upon whom I inflicted profound dislocation and isolation when I brought into our apartment another desk, a word processor, printer, sheaves of papers, books, and all the paraphernalia necessary to write this book. God will surely reserve a special place in heaven for Motoko for her forbearance, endless patience, and tolerance.

Contents

Introduction

I started this book ten years ago with a modest objective. I set out to record for family consumption some of my father's adages, aphorisms, and anecdotes. "Dad," as I called him, had a saying for every situation. Regardless of the circumstances, he could reach into the deepest recesses of his mind and come up with a story, maxim, or proverb to fit perfectly the occasion. I began hearing the expressions in my earliest childhood, when I didn't have the foggiest idea what they meant. Among the first was, "Where there is no vision, the people perish." As a young child I pondered what a person's blindness had to do with other people dying. In August of 1953, just before entering medical school, I got the notion to drive 1,600 miles round trip to Montgomery, Alabama to bring my girlfriend back to Hampton Institute, Virginia, where she was to enter her sophomore year. I hadn't approached my father about my plan as I wanted to wait for a propitious time, but a schoolmate who was visiting my home at the time forced my hand. Dad's response was seven words: "When love steps in, reason steps out." When, as a pathologist's assistant in medical school, I inadvertently delivered the wrong body for an autopsy—and the pathology resident performed the autopsy—I knew I had committed a grave and unforgivable error. I asked myself how my father would salvage what could be a disastrous situation. One thing was sure; he would "take the bull by the horns." That is just what I did. When the director of pathology, Dr. Alan Moritz, walked into his office the next morning, I was waiting at the door for him. I explained to Dr. Moritz what had happened, apologized profusely, and offered to fall on the sword. He was noncommittal but neither did he throw me out of his office. The body was subsequently unclaimed, and I never heard another word from Dr. Moritz. When I would tell stories like these to my wife and son, they urged me to jot down my father's maxims and stories for the family. It helped that I had copies of some of my father's correspondence and that I had kept every letter that he wrote to me beginning with my college years. I felt that I had enough material to print a little monograph.

And then my project took an abrupt turn. I visited Hampton University's archives to review my father's school records. Hampton's archives are complete and well-ordered. I discovered there was a lot about my father that I didn't know. I then drove to Lincoln University in Pennsylvania and Lincoln's archives told me more and then I went on to Howard University. Howard University took some persistence, but remembering my father's dictum, "You must persevere," I learned even more. By the time I had completed the manuscript I had visited or contacted over thirty archives.

I found quite extraordinary facts about my father's life that I had, at most, only superficially heard about. My research is incomplete still, but I have pulled together a narrative that will give the reader not only insight into a remarkable character but insight into a remarkable period in our country's history.

This period, through which my father lived his entire life, is known as the Jim Crow era. Although I grew up in Virginia, spent four years in college there, and practiced medicine in Virginia and Florida from 1959 to 1962, I am embarrassed to say there was much for me to learn about Jim Crow, what it meant, and how pervasive it was. I had experienced segregation and discrimination in all its myriad forms. I even had a few raw experiences, something that was common to every Negro living in the South. Once, in the late 1940s, I was in Kilmarnock, Virginia, minding my business when a ten-year-old white boy walked up to me and exclaimed, "You're a nigger!" I did get to make that trip to Alabama in 1953 to bring back my girlfriend, but had to be chaperoned by an older sister who was unceremoniously evicted from a restroom in a Georgia service station. The restroom was for the white patrons. None existed for the colored customers. While practicing medicine in Melbourne, Florida, in 1960, I poked my head into the front door of the Melbourne Greyhound bus station to ask what time would the next bus arrive and was informed to "go around the back where you belong if you want that information." There were other humiliating episodes, but all were rather bland insults compared to what some Negroes experienced, and even what I might have experienced, given my rebellious streak, had lady luck not been my constant companion.

No one really knows where the term Jim Crow came from. It is thought to have come from a minstrel show written by a white fellow named Thomas Rice in the 1830s. The main character in black face was called Jim Crow, and the term appeared in the press for the first time in the 1890s. Until I began research for this book, I did not know that the integrated audiences at concerts at Hampton Institute's Ogden Hall in the early 1920s led directly to Virginia's General Assembly passing the notorious Massenberg Act of 1926. It barred whites and Negroes from assembling together in public places. I was poorly informed about post-Civil War Reconstruction. I had heard nothing about Virginia's Racial Integrity Act of 1924 and knew nothing about the Anglo-Saxon Clubs of Virginia.

Also, it seems preposterous that I could grow up under the same roof and have contact with my father for thirty-four years and yet know so little about him. I missed great opportunities, however, to learn more about him. My mother and my three oldest siblings, who would have certainly supported this project, had died when I began pulling together material for the manuscript. Another sister became ill and died shortly after I started. I do have an excellent taped interview from her. Two siblings who contributed earlier are now not well. The person who has been of most help is my youngest sister and the "baby'" of the family.

Fortunately, the Mary Ball Washington Museum and Library in Lancaster, Virginia, had started an oral history project. The museum has taped interviews of my mother; my father's first cousin, Martha Gibson; and two men that my father mentored, Julian Allen Ball and William Crosby.

After nearly a decade of work, I have crafted this biography of my father, Morgan Edward Norris, who was born in Jim Crow Virginia in 1883—some 125 years ago. He was classed as a mulatto when he was born, a colored laborer at age seventeen, and a Negro doctor in 1917. Labels are quintessential Americana. So was Jim Crow, a systematic suppression of blacks by whites, a suppression that could not be complete without those labels.

The arc of Norris's life transected just about every aspect of post-bellum American culture in the South. His life spanned the contentious period from post-Reconstruction to the relentless and inexorable erosion of civil liberties for Negroes, the encoding of segregation practices into law right into the first third of the twentieth century and finally the collapse of Jim Crow. Norris died just about the same time as Jim Crow, but when he died it was still illegal for a white to marry a Negro in Virginia, and the American Medical Association had yet to disavow local and state societies that discriminated against Negro physicians.

Norris died at age eighty-two in 1966, but he spent just about all eighty-two years of his life fighting against Jim Crow practices. Eighty-two years in the whole scheme of the universe is just a blip, like that little spike that shoots up from the wavy line of a seismograph. But for a human being it's a long time. It is far longer than the average man lived in 1883 when Norris came into the world, and it was longer than the average man lived in 1966 when he left. And it is a very long time for any man who chooses to spend his life fighting.

Norris might have chosen to go with the flow, not to rock the boat, to move to less conflicted environs, or even pass for white and abandon everything that he cherished and vanish into a vast anonymity. But for Norris, none of these choices fit. He chose to stay put in the South. Still, he didn't have to fight as long and as hard as he did. After his medical internship in Tuskegee when he returned to that remote, narrow slice of land called the Northern Neck, Virginia, he simply could have fulfilled the pledge that he had made to his dying father: to become a doctor and make sure that no one in his little insular community would suffer as his father had. Keeping that vow alone would have been commendable. But whenever the gauntlet was thrown down, he picked it up. It is no wonder that he once wrote: "The struggle is from the cradle to the grave." And because he was a warrior, he framed issues in a warrior's words, whether the foe was disease or discrimination. "I have no white flag," and "Fight on, my soul, till death," were among his mantras.

Norris's remedies for his plight and that of fellow Negroes in the segregated South evolved from the principles of the titans of his time: W. E. B. Du Bois and Booker T. Washington. In the manner of Du Bois, he let it be known that self-respect and dignity were not negotiable. He demanded what was rightfully his, and spared no sacrifice in lifting up his less fortunate brethren. And he embraced Washington's tenets calling for the pursuit of excellence, self-reliance, and economic independence.

Despite the onerous laws and the suffocating life of the South, Norris kept a deep and abiding faith in the goodness of mankind. He was, however, anything but naïve and fully recognized men's frailties and weaknesses. He once said, "If you took the entire wealth of the United States and apportioned it equally to every man in the country, in ten years those who had the wealth at the beginning would have it back, and those who were poor at the start would be just as poor." Yet deep down, he was not entirely pessimistic. He knew that the shackles of poverty and ignorance could be broken through education. His own life was testament to that.

This story is less about race and more about the man, although race defined many of Norris's daily encounters. It does illuminate the delicate balance between defiance of systemic racial practices and working within a system that stubbornly resisted change. It illuminates the role of whites as well as blacks in relieving suffering and educating the poor. How far could Norris have gone had not it been for the encouragement and support of George Bunker's family—the family that gave this nation the Ambassador Ellsworth Bunker? How far would he have gone had not Mary Alice Armstrong, the widow of Hampton University's founder, General Samuel Chapman Armstrong, mentored and tutored him? How much could he have done for the citizens of Lancaster County without the help of Jessie Ball duPont, widow of the industrialist, Alfred I. duPont, and one of his patients' main benefactors long before this country knew anything about Medicaid, Medicare, or a safety net?

This narrative is an account of strength and resolve set in the context of America's dual societies. It is about a man who refused to be marginalized in a segregated society. We have a portrait of a man who was a survivor or more artfully, a swimmer, though not always. When barriers were raised and obstacles thrown, his modus operandi would be first to try to wend his way around them, and failing that, to blast them down!

Self-confidence, self-assurance, and a marvelous philosophical approach to life's vicissitudes formed the triad of his unique personality. In some of his most trying moments he would reflect, "Things are not what we had hoped they would be, but we can console ourselves that they are not worse." The immutable principles of courage, decency, honesty, and generosity were his beacons. He did not look for scapegoats nor did he become consumed with hatred. And he was color-blind, both to the differences between the races and to the rainbow spectrum of his own race.

There is a powerful subtext streaming through this narrative, one as strong as an undertow. The title of the subtext could well be "Opportunities Lost." In no period in American history was there a greater opportunity to advance the nation by bringing into the mainstream a large segment of its population than during post-Reconstruction and the early part of the twentieth century. On so many fronts all that was asked by the Negro citizens of their states and the nation was "equal rights." That was not to be. This failure adds a special poignancy to many of Norris's battles, and the effects have reverberated through American society up to today.

CR

My nine nieces and nephews have been uniformly enthusiastic about the project, but several were bothered by the terms "Negro" and "colored," which I use interchangeably. One of my nephews sent this acerbic comment:

To make note that these ["colored" and "Negro"] were common

terms in the 30s or the 60s is appropriate and desirable. But to use these terms interchangeably with modern day terminology as in the very first sentence of your introduction, "This is the story about a colored physician . . ." is to suggest to the reader that the book fell out of a time capsule.

This view is understandable, although a bit harsh. Such a position by one who was born in 1955, however, demands an explanation on terminology. Most of my nieces and nephews were just toddlers at the beginning of the second Civil Rights era (1960s) when we called ourselves "Negroes." Sometimes the term "colored" was preferred as in the title, National Association for the Advancement of Colored People (NAACP), and in other places Negro was preferred as in the United Negro College Fund (UNCF), but "Negroes" and "colored" were the terms used throughout my father's life. We had pretty much accepted these appellations realizing that there were bigger issues than what we were called.

With the ascendancy of the "Black Power" movement in the late 1960s, "black" became the preferred term. Such a change was a seismic shift in attitude, for in my boyhood if any Negro or colored person was called black, it was a major insult. The inimitable cartoonist and satirist, Jules Feiffer, viewing the total absurdity in the lexicographically revolving door, published a marvelous cartoon in the 1960s. It showed six identical frames of a somber, rather resigned appearing fellow, looking out behind sunshades and lamenting the situation. The character bemoans, "As a matter of racial pride, we want to be called 'blacks'—which has replaced the term 'Afro-Americans'—which replaced 'Negroes'—which replaced 'colored people'—which replaced 'darkies'—which replaced 'blacks.' "

But the term "black" was not to be the end of the saga. Hardly had the ink dried on Feiffer's cartoon when the idea evolved that "African-Americans" would be a more acceptable term.

It is unfortunate that in America in the twenty-first century we have to debate the usage of such nomenclature, but for the purposes of this book about my father who lived in a time when it is utterly impossible to convey his struggles without a reference to race, I will use the terms "colored" and "Negro." If persons who prefer to be called African-Americans or blacks find my usage offensive, I apologize. I long for the day when we dispense with all labels and hyphens, and we all are called Americans.

FIGHT ON,
MY SOUL

CHAPTER 1

Primum non nocere
First Do No Harm

Morgan E. Norris was thirty-four years old and had completed his internship at the John A. Andrew Hospital in Tuskegee, Alabama. He had just returned home to practice medicine in a remote place called Lancaster County on Virginia's Northern Neck, the state's northernmost peninsula that juts into the mighty Chesapeake Bay.

The peninsula, eighty-five miles long, twenty-five miles wide at the bay and just five miles wide at the neck, is a flask-shaped piece of land sandwiched between the Potomac and Rappahannock Rivers. In 1917, the year that Norris returned, the best way to get there was by boat, and once one arrived, the best way to get around was by horse and buggy. Paved roads were still a decade away.

Norris spruced up the little unpainted clapboard house that he had inherited from his father, bought a horse and a two-wheeled buggy, hung out his shingle, and went to work. He was the only colored doctor in a county that had eleven white doctors. The population of ten thousand was about equally divided between the white and colored citizens.

His practice got off to a pretty rough start. Shortly after announcing that he was the new doctor in town, he was summoned to see three sick children. When he got to the home, he found a large family, quite poor, with three of the youngest seriously ill with diphtheria, a notorious baby killer at the time. Norris did everything he had been taught and more, but when he returned the next day, he found, to his alarm, that the children were no better. He tried different medications and returned the third day. When he knocked on the door, there was no answer. He could not hear anybody inside, but he knew that in such an impoverished family it was unlikely anyone would have gone away. He knocked again, waited, and then tried yet a third time. Finally, the door cracked open just enough for him to see one of the children who wasn't ill peering at him.

"Mama said to tell you one's dead and two's near 'bout dead and she done sent for a real doctor."

Not long afterward, the fledgling physician was called to a patient suffering from excruciating back pain. He went to the bedside of the emaciated elderly man. An examination disclosed a large, tender mass in the patient's upper back. It was unusual enough that Norris decided to have a more experienced physician take a look. When one of his senior colleagues examined the man, the elder physician dismissed the problem as "nothing but a wen," a harmless sebaceous cyst (a benign cyst containing oily, semisolid material) that sometimes becomes infected.

"Aw, Morgan, stick a knife in it, and give this fellow some relief," the elder doctor advised. Norris drew a long, narrow surgical knife known as a bistoury from his medical bag and cut into the mass. Blood spurted from the wound nearly to the ceiling, and as the physicians stood by helplessly, the old man bled to death. Norris's knife had punctured not a wen but a syphilitic aneurysm, an abnormal out-pouching of the patient's aorta, the main blood vessel carrying blood from the heart. The doctors were aghast and turned as pale as their doomed victim as the last drop of blood oozed from the gaping hole in his back. The callow young doctor had violated a fundamental commandment of medicine—a tenet that had been drummed into him since the first day of medical school: *Primum non nocere*.

Forty years later, in a subdued tone, he told me of those episodes, when I, too, faced a dispiritingly intractable case in my new medical practice. "Son, those were dark days for me, but I bounced back." Bounce back he did, for resiliency, a trait that was a defining imprint of his character, seemed so natural to him that he might have been born with it—though it was probably acquired. After all, life for him, in the words of Langston Hughes, had "been no crystal stair." For the first thirty or so years of his life, there had been not much to climb in the way of stairs at all. For him, life had been more like climbing the smooth side of a mountain.

CHAPTER 2

No Carpet on the Floor

"Life for me ain't been no crystal stair. It had tacks in it, and splinters, and boards torn up and places with no carpet on the floor ..."

LANGSTON HUGHES

"You don't get what you want in life; you get what life gives you." This was one of the favorite adages of my father, to whom life gave very little in the beginning. It gave him a country with a caste system. He was born colored in a predominantly white culture at the time when Jim Crow was beginning its malignant spread. It gave him a motherless childhood. His mother died when he was three years old. It gave him only a grade school education. It gave him poverty. It gave him tuberculosis, one of the most dreaded diseases of the nineteenth century. But the cruelest thing it gave him was a terminally ill father, Benjamin, who died at the age of forty-six when Norris was only seventeen.

Norris was born the second child of Benjamin and Elizabeth (Lizzie) Norris in a one-room cabin just outside the present village of Lancaster, in Lancaster County, Virginia, in a community with the proprietary sounding name of George's. The date was August 13, 1883. The child was named for the pious and venerated Lancaster County schoolteacher and music teacher, Morgan James Edwards. Edwards was assistant superintendent of the Sabbath School and conductor of the music class and choir at Saint John's Baptist

Church, the first church founded for Negroes in Lancaster County. He and
Benjamin were members of Saint John's, and were close friends. Benjamin
and Lizzie had evidently hoped that by naming their son after such a revered
man the child might turn out to be "somebody."

Norris's parents were mulattoes—the racial classification given to
descendents of mixed parentage (white/black) in the nineteenth century. They
had been born free persons in antebellum Virginia and were thrifty, honest,
hard workers. Their lives revolved around the community and the church.

Benjamin, although just a subsistence farmer, was something of a mover
and shaker in his own right. In 1884 he left Saint John's Baptist Church to join
with his sister, Athaline, her husband Joseph Nickens, and a man named Isaac
Harcum in founding the Willie Chapel Baptist Church in Lancaster. Norris
would later write of his father's founding of the church in a letter to a friend.

> I attended the builder in his death illness and he always related the
> very difficult time my father had in getting money for material and his
> pay. He [the builder], too, was white. The church has gone a long way
> in … being modernized since that time. The old nucleus still stands,
> with the graveyard behind in which my parents and family, who have
> passed, lay.

Norris was just a toddler when his mother died from tuberculosis at
age 25. He was much too young to understand the tragedy of her death. It is
said that he cheerfully rode astride the coffin as her body was borne to her
grave. Robert Koch, the German bacteriologist and physician, had just discovered the germ (mycobacterium tuberculosis) that causes the disease in 1882.
It is doubtful that the discovery was fully appreciated in the Northern Neck,
and even so, there was little anyone could have done. A physician in 1886 had
no way to test for tuberculosis. The skin test had not been refined. William
Roentgen did not invent the x-ray machine that could identify the disease
until 1895. Treatment in the nineteenth century, once the disease was diagnosed, was not much better than snake oil. Consumption, as tuberculosis was
popularly known, was a wasting, often lethal disease. It was called the "great

white plague," an antonym to the "great black plague" of Medieval Europe. Norris's life was intertwined with tuberculosis from the time his mother died, during childhood when he had the infection, and throughout his career as a physician battling the disease.

As a child, Norris had scrofuloderma, a tubercular infection of the skin resulting from the direct extension of the infection from the lymph nodes in the neck. Thick, cord–like scars are usually the end result of healing. Norris carried the neck scars for the rest of his life. The infection may have been a favorable roll of the dice for him. It undoubtedly conferred a degree of immunity against the disease and may have helped prevent him from becoming infected when he worked with tubercular patients. Physicians who treated tuberculosis patients during the period when Norris practiced were at a greater risk for contracting tuberculosis than members of the general population.

Few records exist of Norris's early life, and he seldom spoke of his childhood. Stories related by family and friends remain the only repository of those early years. One harrowing episode that occurred when he had just started walking is still part of family lore. Martha Pinn Gibson, his first cousin, told the story best in a recording of oral histories for the Mary Ball Washington Museum and Library in Lancaster County:

> Cousin Morgan was a little boy, I heard my Mama say it a many times. There was an old well, and that well is down there now [referring to Norris's birthplace]. Because it was bricked-up—you heard talk of a bricked up well? That well was bricked up and they weren't using that well and they had boards on it and those boards had rotted. One morning Cousin Morgan went out. He was a little boy, a little, small boy, and he walked out on those boards and sat down and scared all of them to death. They didn't know how to get him off there. They didn't know what to do. They were afraid to holler at him 'cause they were afraid he would jump up and down or something other, and they just coaxed him along and got close to him ... and snatched him off those boards. I have never forgotten it. They said he was a little, tiny boy.

Some family members thought the shock of this episode contributed to his mother's death. That may or may not be true. But Benjamin was left to rear the child largely by himself. His maternal grandmother apparently had some part in his early upbringing, but the role was minor. In a speech to the New Farmers of America at Hampton Institute in 1936 Norris related, "I remember distinctly that my grandmother started fire in the home with flint and steel when there were no matches, and I studied many a lesson by the light wood torch." But none of his surviving children recall any role that his grandmother played in his life. His aunt, Elizabeth "Betty" Wright Pinn, his father's half-sister, did help with his upbringing even though she had a large family herself, four boys and five girls.

Our mother told us about his resoluteness when he was but a tyke. Norris had just started the first grade. His father could not afford to buy trousers, so he had to wear a skirt to school. When he bounded into the classroom on that first day of school, the teasing and taunts from the other children were more than he could take. He returned home crying. He was not going back to school. His father told the boy that he had no choice—he had to wear the skirt to school. Norris settled the issue in a flash of anger. He ripped off the skirt and threw it into the open fire. His father found the money to buy him trousers.

In the late 1800s no such thing as a lunch program existed in Virginia's school system. The citizens counted themselves lucky if they had a school. Norris's father, not understanding a child's needs, would send him to school without lunch. Irene Pinn, Norris's classmate, reported to her mother, Hannah Pinn, that he had nothing to eat at lunchtime. From the day Mrs. Pinn learned of his predicament, she prepared lunch for two, Irene and Norris. He never mentioned Mrs. Pinn's generosity, but unquestionably, he shared a deep bond of friendship with Irene for their lifetimes.

Travis Robbins, a lanky, taciturn Lancaster County farmer, and a mentor to the young Norris, often told of the boy's little enterprises. He said that when Norris was a boy, perhaps about ten years of age, he sold packets of watermelon, cantaloupe, and turnip seeds for three cents each. Robbins related affectionately how he felt sorry for the little fellow trying to sell those useless seeds. "They weren't worth a hill of beans," said Robbins with a dismissive chuckle. "I would buy a packet anyhow, and as soon as that boy was out of sight, I'd toss them into the bushes."

But Norris's little enterprises did pay off. When he was fifteen, his father wanted to buy a parcel of land on the highway just below Kilmarnock, a village located at the junction of two main roads—now Virginia State Highway 3 and Highway 200. It was a prosperous little town and considered to be the center of commercial activity for the lower Northern Neck. It was desirable to live near Kilmarnock, for not only did the village have several stores, but a nearby steamboat wharf was planned. Most importantly, however, Benjamin was contemplating marriage, and he couldn't very well bring his bride to the shanty that they lived in. It was a little better than some shanties, with boards on the floor instead of dirt, but there was no carpet on the floor, not even a rug. It was as Spartan as it could be without living outdoors. One obstacle remained to the purchase of a new home. Benjamin was short $50 of the price. He told his teenaged son that he wanted "so badly to buy that place up on the road, but I don't have all the money." Norris had savings that he kept in a jar under a board in the floor of their cabin. Eagerly, he lifted a board, removed the jar of coins, counted out $50 in quarters, dimes, nickels, and pennies and gave the sum to his father to help purchase what would become the family homeplace. It remains in the family to this day.

CHAPTER 3

A Vow to His Dying Father

"Son, if you promise someone something, then do it!"
                                          MORGAN E. NORRIS

It was not long after the purchase of the new home site and the marriage of Benjamin to his second wife, Sarah, that tragedy struck the Norris household again. Benjamin became terminally ill. As Norris watched his father die a painful, agonizing death, he was forever changed. He made a solemn vow to his father: "I will go away, become a doctor, and return so that no one will ever suffer as you have."

Norris's father fell ill just at the turn of the twentieth century. The illness began with severe stomach pain and vomiting. The local doctor gave him medicine, but he got only temporary relief. Soon neither the pain nor vomiting let up. The doctor told the boy that he had to take his father to Baltimore for treatment.

Traveling to Baltimore was not exactly like going up the road to the nearest village. The city was located some 130 miles north up the Chesapeake Bay from Kilmarnock. The sick man had to go to the hospital by steamboat, the only way anyone could get off the distal peninsula. There were no roads and bridges to Baltimore. Although hospitals were located in Fredericksburg and Norfolk, sick people from Lancaster County, where Norris and his father lived, preferred Baltimore as most had relatives there. Besides, the hospitals in Baltimore were considered better.

The doctors in Baltimore examined the stricken man and decided that he had to be operated upon. The surgical diagnosis was grim—cancer. The prognosis was grimmer. Nothing could be done. The *Virginia Citizen*, a local newspaper published in Irvington (Lancaster County), Virginia, on December 7, 1900, carried an account of the tragic train of events in just two sentences: "Ben Norris, aged about 35 years and living near Kilmarnock, Lancaster County, was taken to a Baltimore hospital for a surgical operation from which he died. His remains were brought to his home Saturday morning and interred in Little Willie Chapel cemetery near Lancaster Courthouse that afternoon."

Benjamin's sister, Betty Pinn, described his last throes even more succinctly but considerably more dramatically: "When he passed his water, it was like you would pour coffee grounds in water. That was his liver. It was a cancer on his liver."

His wife, Sarah, Norris, a daughter, son-in-law, and granddaughter who lived in Yonkers, New York, and two siblings survived Benjamin.

After Benjamin's death, Sarah cared for Norris only briefly, as she had no resources to sustain a growing teenager. The boy was adrift. He had no skills and little education. He had known only subsistence farming. The 1900 federal census had classified him as a laborer. The youngster, about five feet and nine inches tall and on the verge of becoming a man, had grown to be a sturdily built fellow. He had black, curly hair, and was light complexioned with thin lips and dark eyes. His muscular forearms were like tree trunks—the kind of muscles that one gets from the rigors of farming and the strains of manual labor. But he had made up his mind; he wasn't going to be a laborer for the rest of his life. Furthermore, he had a promise to keep.

CHAPTER 4

Keeping the Promise

Not long after his father's death, Norris set out on his own. He took the steamboat to Baltimore where his father's younger brother, Elias, lived. But Elias had little to offer. After failing to find a job in Baltimore, Norris continued to Yonkers, New York, to stay with his sister, Mary Jane, who was married to Augustus A. Thornton, superintendent at the United States Sub-Treasury Building in New York City. They had an infant daughter named Alma.

Mary Jane helped him secure a job in Yonkers working for the prominent Bunker family. The patriarch of the family was George Raymond Bunker, a co-founder of the National Sugar Refining Company, one of the major sugar refining companies in the United States at that time. The Bunkers had two young sons, Arthur and Ellsworth, and a daughter, Katherine. On the Bunker estate, Morgan was a "houseboy." He did household chores, took care of the furnace, cared for the animals, and did yard work. But Bunker saw something in this youth that was different. The boy had a unique drive and ability, and deep down George Raymond Bunker knew it would be an injustice to hold him back. Bunker told Norris that he needed to get on with his education.

Norris took Bunker's advice. He decided he would go to Hampton Institute in Hampton, Virginia, a trade school that had been established for Negro youth in 1868. He had worked for the Bunker family for less than three years. It was hard to leave the Bunker estate. George Bunker had given the youngster something he had never had before—a secure home and a secure job. He was leaving this security to set out on a journey of chance, and as he departed the Bunkers he also entered manhood. He turned twenty-one in August 1904. Most men at that age either had a job or were looking for one. Here he was going back to school and to a training school, to boot.

Norris, with Bunker's support, left for Hampton Institute in September of 1904. He returned to the Bunker estate the following June for summer work, but never again after that. He did not, however, sever his relationship with the Bunkers. He kept in close contact with the family for the rest of his life.

Arthur, the younger son, became an electrical engineer and metallurgist and set out on his own in business and finance. During a varied and prolific career he was president of the Radium Company of Colorado, organized the United States Vanadium Company, was chairman of the board of the Colin Oil Company, served as chief of the War Production Board during World War II, was president of the Climax Molybdenum Company, and was chairman of the board of the American Metal Climax Company, a company that dealt in uranium and oil. He was responsible for a number of innovations in mining. Years after Norris left the Bunker fold, he would call on Arthur during his trips to New York, and sometimes he visited him at his retreat in Walpole, New Hampshire.

But Norris was closer to Ellsworth, who would become one of our country's leading statesmen. He thought so much of Ellsworth that he named me for him. Even after Norris's death in 1966, Ellsworth, then serving as the United States Ambassador to South Vietnam, continued to maintain close contact with the Norris family.

One of the reasons Norris favored Ellsworth may have stemmed from an incident that occurred while he was working in the Bunker home. He was in the basement tending the furnace, and Ellsworth, who was about seven years old, came into the furnace room and began tampering with the valves. Norris, fearful that Ellsworth might hurt himself, either pushed him or slapped him. Norris realized immediately that he had been too harsh. Contrite for his hasty response, he asked Ellsworth how he thought his father would respond if he found out that he had struck him. Ellsworth replied, already demonstrating his diplomatic bent, "My father doesn't have to know." It probably was well that his father didn't know. In 1903, for a Negro houseboy to corporally discipline

the scion of a wealthy white industrialist, even in New York, might have cost
Norris more than his job. He could have ended up in jail.

CHAPTER 5

"Kind Mother" - Hampton Institute

Norris had selected Hampton Normal and Agricultural Institute by a stroke of luck. While working in Yonkers, he heard that a talk was being given about Hampton Institute at the Armstrong League in New York City, a society that had been founded to perpetuate the ideals of the late founder of the school, General Samuel Chapman Armstrong, a Hawaiian native, a child of missionaries, a graduate of Williams College, and a Union general in the Civil War. Hollis Frissell, the white principal of the school, was the speaker. Frissell, a minister, had succeeded the general upon his death in 1893. Norris was so impressed with Frissell's presentation that he decided immediately to apply for admission.

Hampton Institute was a private preparatory school in Hampton, Virginia, founded in 1868. Its emphasis was on training Negro students in the trades and agriculture. It did have an academic program, which was expanded to four years in 1904, but all male students had to take courses in agriculture. The school consisted of sixty buildings built on a 188-acre plantation that was the site of Hampton Hospital, a Union military hospital during the Civil War. The site is a spectacularly scenic setting on the Hampton Roads, a broad channel where the James, Nansemond, and Elizabeth Rivers meet and flow into the Chesapeake Bay. Before the white man came to Virginia, the Indians had established a village there named Kecoughtan. The whites liked the site and pushed off the Indians. The federal government liked the site and set up a Civil War hospital. Like Norris's home, this place was located at the southern tip of one of Virginia's peninsulas on the Bay.

When Norris entered the school, enrollment consisted of about 900

Negro students and 100 American Indians. Indians were first admitted to
Hampton in 1878 and were enrolled until 1923. (The Indian experience at
Hampton is a little-known piece in the history of our nation's treatment of
Native Americans. While many whites during that period had great reservations about the educability of the Indians, they held no qualms about insisting
on segregation of Indians and Negroes. At Hampton Institute, the Indians
were assigned separate living quarters—two dormitories were built to house
them—and in many aspects of school life were treated separately and differently from the Negro students.) Hampton Institute's mission, as promulgated
by Armstrong was:

> To train selected youth who shall go out and teach and lead their
> people, first by example by getting land and homes, to give them not a
> dollar that they can earn for themselves, to teach respect for labor; to
> replace stupid drudgery with skilled hands; and, to these ends, to build
> up an industrial system, for the sake not only of self-support and intel-
> ligent labor, but also for the sake of character.

The Virginia Department of Public Instruction did not certify this novel
academy as a four-year secondary school until 1916.

There were modest charges for an entering student when Norris enrolled.
All students were required to deposit $15 upon entry. There was a book fee
of $5, and tuition was free to deserving students. Board was $10 a month.
The student could pay his board partly in cash and partly through work on the
campus. All male students were required to wear a navy blue uniform. Costs
of the uniform were $7.25 for a coat, $4.50 for trousers, $2 for a vest, and
$1 for a cap. Norris worked on the farm, in horticulture, and in the campus
museum to help pay his way through school.

Scholarship aid was available. If a student received assistance, the
student was required to write a thank-you letter to his donor. The Hampton
University Archives has in its possession such a letter written by Norris in
1905. That document is most likely a draft because of the impersonal salutation and the penciled comments in the margins. It is a lengthy and detailed

letter telling of Norris's experiences at Hampton and expressing his deepest appreciation for assistance.

Norris's entire performance at the institute was exemplary and was predictive of his future accomplishments. His farm chores, which consisted of "milking and care of the cow barn, over [supervising] other students," and his work record and deportment were graded "excellent." The evaluation read: "This student has been very earnest in his work, faithful, trusty, kind and done well in work and in teaching the other milkers, yet never above himself in any way." For the rest of his Hampton years, he received "very good" and "excellent" grades in all evaluations. His grades reflected a conscientious student who excelled even in mechanical drawing.

Norris graduated in 1908, at age twenty-five, and was already addressing public health problems. At graduation, he gave a speech at the YMCA at Hampton Institute, entitled "The Negro and the Liquor Problem." The text could not be located, but we can safely assume that it dealt with the adverse effects of alcohol consumption. Norris was a teetotaler all his life.

Years later, he related to me a poignant episode that he experienced at his graduation:

One of my classmate's parents had come from rural Virginia to the graduation exercises. They were kindly people whose clothes were threadbare and faded. They did not speak well, but their pride in their son's achievement was palpable. My classmate was so embarrassed by their appearance and speech that he rushed those poor people out of Hampton so fast, I doubt they realized that they had ever visited the school. I never in my life felt so sorry for anyone as I did for that couple. I would have given anything had my parents been living and able to attend my graduation.

Norris was forever grateful for his education at Hampton Institute and the manner in which he was treated. Up until his last letter about Hampton, he referred affectionately to his alma mater as "kind mother." Perhaps the institute became for him the mother that he never had.

Norris became a close friend of Armstrong's widow, Mary Alice, who was one of his teachers at the institute. He worked at her summer camp in New Hampshire during his student days and maintained contact with her until she died in 1958. The Hampton ideology and Mrs. Armstrong's guidance were crucial factors in Norris's development and he never forgot that.

Hampton Institute has been accused of having had a paternalistic attitude toward its students. After all, the students were all colored or American Indians, and the faculty was all white. Perhaps, an element of paternalism did exist at Hampton during those years, but not paternalism in the pejorative sense. Armstrong even addressed this issue in a report to the American Missionary Society in 1869:

> We do not believe in presenting the freedmen with occasional old clothes and intermittent dollars, accompanied by paternal "Bless ye, my children." Wages are a help, charity a hindrance. But America owes the black man a debt, whose arrears run back two hundred years. To give him schools and a chance of manhood is not to attempt payment, but only acknowledge the obligation.

The institute engaged its students from the beginning and kept in close contact with them after they graduated through the Department of Correspondence. The students responded with a reciprocal devotion. Norris had a fealty for Hampton that never relented and that he carried to his grave.

After he left Hampton in 1908 for Lincoln University and then Howard University, he wrote detailed letters to Dr. Frissell and two other members of the faculty at Hampton. He poignantly captured the essence of what Hampton meant to him in a letter written on January 10, 1909, to Dr. Frissell: "If my life amounts to anything in the way of usefulness, it will certainly be due largely to the training I received at Hampton."

CHAPTER 6

"A Broad Literary Training" - Lincoln University

After graduating from the Hampton Institute, Norris entered Lincoln University in Oxford, Pennsylvania, to obtain what he called "a broad literary training." He could have gone from Hampton Institute directly to a medical school, thereby obviating the need to spend four more years in college—an attractive alternative for an impoverished young man with no parents and with sparse financial support. At that time, just 16 of the 155 medical schools in the United States and Canada required two or more years of college work for admission. Howard University's medical school, where Norris would later enroll, required only a "high school course or its equivalent." The requirements would change shortly, for in 1910, Abraham Flexner, an educator and a reformer, reported in his study to the Carnegie Foundation that of the three medical schools in Virginia and seven in Maryland, only Johns Hopkins in Baltimore required a bachelor's degree for admission. The University of Virginia required one year of college work in the sciences, and the remainder of the schools required a four-year high school diploma or less. The Flexner Report, as the study has since been called, led to major reforms in the admission requirements to medical schools in the United States and Canada, revamping of the curricula, and the closing of many marginal schools and diploma mills.

In 1908, Lincoln was the premier college in the United States for colored men. Rev. John Dickey, the white pastor of the Oxford Presbyterian Church, had founded the school in 1854, "to bring the benefits of a liberal Christian education within the reach of worthy colored men." Dickey was a supporter of the American Colonization Society, which had the objective of sending emancipated slaves and free Negroes to Africa to serve as missionaries. The missionary bit may have been a guise. It appears that the American Colonization Society may have had a greater concern about integrating free Negroes into the larger American culture. Rev. Robert Finley, one of the founders, felt that methodical colonization of Negroes to Africa would both improve their condition and solve the larger problem of their future in America. Lincoln was originally named Ashmun Institute in honor of Jehudi Ashmun, a white theologian and agent of the American Colonization Society. He was the first governor of Liberia, the colony of Negro immigrants from America that had been established by the Society.

Oxford was a logical location for the school as the town had served as a way station along the Underground Railroad. It was no accident that the school was located deep in the cornfields of Pennsylvania. The founders of the school made an undisguised effort to remove young men from the "distractions of city life." Distractions of country life were removed as well. Even cigarette smoking was prohibited, a rule that would not have disturbed Norris as he never smoked. In 1866, the name of the school was changed to Lincoln University to honor the memory of Abraham Lincoln—the then recently assassinated president of the United States who had issued the Emancipation Proclamation in 1863. Lincoln was a small school by today's standards. In 1912, the year of Norris's graduation, there were 134 students: 33 seniors, 34 juniors, 35 sophomores, and 32 freshmen. There were 12 faculty members, including the president of the college—all male and all white.

The curriculum for an undergraduate at Lincoln during the period between 1908 and 1912 consisted of English, Bible, Study of Language, Latin, Greek, German, Philosophy, Rhetoric, Ethics, History of Philosophy, Logic, Economics, Astronomy, Psychology, Pedagogy, Lyceum, Geometry, Trigonometry, Analytic Geometry and Physics.

In Norris's junior year, he was awarded Special Honors in Bible study and he was in the "Second Group" of Junior Honor Men. He graduated with honors on June 4, 1912.

Excited about his work at Lincoln, Norris wrote to Miss Sherman in the Correspondence Department at Hampton Institute on January 24, 1909:

> The class work here is hard and a great deal of energy and push is required to keep in good standing. The school life is free from social attractions and is made inductive to study. There is a great deal of zeal among the students here to excel in class honors which makes the work go with a good deal of enthusiasm.

He was grateful for the opportunity to advance his studies, and he was determined not to let down those people at Hampton who had done so much to help him. He added in the same letter to Miss Sherman: "It shall ever be my aim to so direct my life, with the help of God, that Hampton may never feel ashamed of me as one of her graduates."

The liberal arts education at Lincoln would have a profound effect on Norris's communication skills. He grew eloquent in both the spoken word and the written language. His delivery was free of mannerisms and clichés. When he spoke in public, which was often, he spoke with confidence and clarity. "Damn" or "hell" would be as profane as he would get, and those words were uttered only on rare occasions. Scatological words had no place in his vocabulary, and he never referred to any ethnic group in pejorative terms. (Nor did he use the word "nigger." We were brought up in an environment where usage of the word "nigger" was a tripwire for a potentially explosive situation. When whites used it toward colored persons, it was demeaning in every sense of the word. It sent the message that the one on the receiving end was unadulterated trash, subhuman. When colored people used it among themselves, depending on the context, it often conveyed the same message that whites intended. Some colored people have contended that the word "nigger" used among each other was sometimes more a term of endearment than of derision, but Norris did not share that opinion. While it might be used among some colored men in a jocular, self-deprecating manner, he felt usage of the word was crass and uncouth.)

At Lincoln, Norris also honed his skills in letter writing, a passion he had developed at Hampton. His letters were written in a neat, cursive, clearly legible style, a skill that he apparently lost after becoming dependent on the typewriter. He gained access to a typewriter when he arrived at Tuskegee in 1916. Thereafter, nearly all of his correspondence was typewritten. Although he never mastered the touch technique, he could "hunt and peck" with remarkable speed and accuracy. Only once when a typewriter was available did he forgo its use for a fountain pen. In 1953, he was sailing for Paris on the ocean liner, The United States, when he was told a room was available where he could use a typewriter. Upon entering the room, he noticed that "most of the people wrote so rapidly, I thought I would not let them know how slow I was." In a concession to vanity, he decided to stay with the fountain pen.

While in his junior year at Lincoln he tried to join the national effort in the fight against tuberculosis. He wrote Dr. Charles P. Wertenbaker of the United States Public Health Service at Norfolk telling of his interest in the disease and offering to help:

> In a recent letter from Dr. Livingston Farrand of New York, he spoke of you as being very much interested in the preventure of tuberculosis among colored people. Dr. Farrand also said that I might be able to obtain valuable information regarding the matter.
>
> About a year, I have been studying the subject and seeing the great need for workers to prevent the spread of tuberculosis. I feel that I would like to enter the work and lend what help I could if such a thing is possible.

Dr. Farrand was then a New York City physician and chairman of the Department of Anthropology at Columbia University. He was also secretary of the National Association for the Study and Prevention of Tuberculosis. He became so renowned for his work in tuberculosis that he was sent to France during World War I to tackle the problem of civilian tuberculosis there. The *New York Times* in Farrand's obituary November 9, 1939, stated, "This disease was threatening to make more havoc behind the lines than the German shells did in the trenches." France awarded him an Officer in the Legion of Honor.

Neither correspondence between Farrand and Norris nor any record of Wertenbaker's response to Norris could be located. In 1911, there were no colored physicians working with the United States Public Health Service (USPHS), so it is doubtful that Wertenbaker had anything to offer him. Norris did not resume any serious effort toward the treatment and control of tuberculosis until he entered medical practice.

Norris gained wide latitude in thought and perspective from his studies— from the agronomy he learned at Hampton to the astronomy he studied at Lincoln. Additionally, the grounding in philosophy and the Bible that he acquired at Lincoln gave him great depth in discussions with whomever he met. He was as comfortable speaking with a farmer about crop rotation, soil conservation, and animal husbandry as he was speaking to a college president about the educational needs of the youth.

It is without doubt that upon finishing Lincoln, he was as well educated as any Virginia college graduate and better educated than most of the applicants to the medical schools in Virginia.

CHAPTER 7

The Making of a Doctor:
Not Quite Utopia – Howard University

In 1912, the year that Norris entered medical school, few white schools in the North and none in the South would consider a Negro applicant. Norris, while at Lincoln, had spoken of his intention to go to Cornell, but for reasons that could not be found, that plan went nowhere. Seven colored medical schools of varying quality existed about the time that he began applying, but the Flexner Report in 1910 consigned all but two to oblivion. That left Norris with basically two choices, Howard University's College of Medicine in Washington, D.C., and Meharry Medical College in Nashville, Tennessee. He chose Howard.

Howard's medical school, in existence since 1867, had had a roundabout beginning. A school of medicine had not been uppermost in the minds of Washington's Congregationalist Church members when they first met November 20, 1866, to found a school for the newly freed slaves. They had set out to establish a theological school to be named for General Otis Oliver Howard, one of their members who was prominent in national affairs, worked with the Freedmen's Bureau, and held strong convictions about freedmen having sufficient educational opportunities. Howard, a native of the picturesque town of Leeds, Maine, had been a general in the Union Army. He led a brigade at Manassas, and commanded the Army of Tennessee before the end of the Civil War. A veteran of thirty-six Civil War battles, he lost his right arm to the South at Fair Oaks in the Richmond-Petersburg campaign. James McPherson, the Civil War historian, described him as "a monogamous, teetotaling Congregationalist known as the Christian soldier." Another Civil War historian, Bruce Catton, described Howard's character in a more churchly tone: "He was a little too widely known as the Christian soldier, a major general who went to hospitals on Sunday to distribute baskets of fruit, which were welcomed, and religious tracts, which regrettably were not." Abraham Lincoln appointed the Christian gentleman to the post of commissioner of the Bureau of Refugees, Freedmen, and Abandoned Lands. Congress had established the bureau to furnish supplies to the destitute newly freed slaves; to supervise contracts between the freedmen and their employees; and to protect the civil rights of the freedmen.

At a subsequent meeting the founders felt that there ought to be a normal school as well, so the name then became the Howard Normal and Theological Institute for the Education of Teachers and Preachers. After further meetings and discussions, the group felt that the objectives should be enlarged and that a medical department should be established. At a meeting on January 8, 1867, the trustees of the Howard Normal and Theological Institute voted to change the name to Howard University. On March 3, 1867, President Andrew Johnson signed Senate Bill 529 into law, incorporating Howard University in the District of Columbia.

General Howard, though responsible for obtaining the site for the school and directing over $500,000 from the Freedmen's Bureau to the support of the school, was not its first president, but the third president. He had envisioned a university that would be race-blind in its admissions. The first medical school graduates completed their course in 1869, and of the five graduates, three were white and two were colored. This racial ratio would not last long. By the end of the century, Howard University had become a *de-facto* Negro institution and remains so today. Howard is one of the largest universities among the Historical Black Colleges and Universities, a list designated by the Higher Education Act of 1965.

From Howard's catalog, Norris must have thought that he was bound for utopia. The facilities available at Howard's medical school were impressive by the standards of 1912. Howard's own Carnegie Library had 25,000 books. The Surgeon General's Office that was overseer to the U.S. Public Health Service contained 150,000 works in its library. The Library of Congress had 800,000 books and 15,000 pamphlets. Museums such as the Army Medical Museum and the Museum of Hygiene, which were located in Washington, D.C., were open to the students. The university's 300-bed Freedmen's Hospital, where the Howard medical students and graduates would receive their training, was described as having the latest in equipment and facilities. A hospital report dated June 30, 1912, stated that 3,093 patients had been admitted during the year. Two hundred and ninety-two obstetrical deliveries took place and 1,922 operations were performed. The "out door department," now called the Out Patient Department, recorded just over 5,700 visits.

According to the 1912 medical college catalog, the school was open to "all persons, without regard to sex or race, who are qualified by good moral character, proper age, and suitable preliminary education." But these admission criteria would soon change. The following statement was made in a special notices section in the catalog: "Beginning with the session in 1914, the Medical College of Howard University will require of all matriculants two years of college work in physics, chemistry, biology, and a reading knowledge of one modern language besides English." Apparently, these requirements were introduced in response to the Flexner Report of 1910.

Howard University was given favored status by Flexner who was candid about his vision of the role of Negro medical schools in training Negro physicians. He stated: "The practice of the Negro doctor will be limited to his own race, which in its turn will be cared for better by good Negro physicians than by poor white ones." He felt "the future of Howard is assured; indeed, the new Freedmen's Hospital is an asset the like of which is in this country extremely rare."

If Norris had any illusions that he was about to enter Utopia, he was in for a dismaying revelation when he came upon item V of Special Notices:
> There are no funds available for helping students in the School of Medicine. The faculty does not advise prospective students to come to the school until they are able to pay their tuition in full, without having to depend upon outside employment.

This statement was a marked departure from the benevolent policies of Hampton Institute and Lincoln University. Fortunately, Norris had ample opportunity for summer employment through his contacts at Hampton. He worked summers in New Hampshire at Camps Rockywold and Deephaven, family resorts owned by Mary Alice Armstrong, widow of Hampton Institute's founder, Samuel Chapman Armstrong. Norris had started working at the camps while at Hampton and continued during the summers until his junior year at Howard University's medical school.

The work at Mrs. Armstrong's camps provided a reasonable stipend plus full board and lodging. Tips were frequent and particularly generous for extraordinary work. A guest died during one of the summers he worked at Camp Rockywold. The body was kept overnight, as it was not possible to transport the remains to the train station. Someone had to stand guard during the night to prevent animals from violating the corpse. Norris was the only person who agreed to keep watch. The payment was breathtaking for a poor, struggling student. He was given $100 for the night! He said it was the easiest money he had ever made in his life. He also said: "I never had a better night's rest!" Norris remained a lifelong friend to Mrs. Armstrong. She died in 1958 at age ninety-four, and as testament to the affection and esteem that the family acknowledged she held for her former student, he was seated with the family at the funeral.

Norris required only five hours or so of sleep at night, and this had its advantages, particularly for jobs where working late and rising early were prerequisites. While in medical school, he secured a winter job banking furnaces for a number of homes in northwest Washington. In the early part of the twentieth century, homeowners who could afford central heating had coal-burning furnaces located in their basements. The furnaces heated water so that either hot water or steam—depending on the type of furnace—circulated through a network of cast iron radiators in the homes. It was important to prepare the fire at night so that it would burn at a minimum. This process was called "banking the furnace." In the morning, the furnace would be fired and the heated water or steam would flow into the radiators. Norris's job was to go by each home on his route in the late evening and bank the furnace; then early in the morning he would return and stoke the furnace so that the occupants would wake up to a warm house. Norris made his rounds on foot, and it was not uncommon for his shoe soles to wear through. Having shoes soled was too costly for a student chronically short of cash, so he lined them with newspapers. With his summer jobs and night chores, he was more than able to meet his expenses at Howard.

This was not the whole story of how he survived at Howard. He had no compunction about engaging in shenanigans to help ease his way. Henry A. McAlister, a student in Howard's dental school, was his roommate and best friend. They were partners in survival tactics. McAlister later practiced dentistry in Hampton, Virginia. He often visited Norris and conducted dental clinics in Norris's office. After the clinic was done, they would relax over dinner and regale each other about how they crashed wedding parties, dinner parties, or any party to garner a meal or how they wheedled the local grocer out of an extra can of beans. Reuben Burrell, the renowned Hampton University photographer, recalls Norris speaking to his freshman class in 1938 about his days in medical school. Norris told the class that he and McAlister had one dress suit between them, so they could never go to a formal occasion at the same time. By the time Norris finished medical school in 1916, he had $1,500 in his savings account and no debt.

During Norris's years at Howard, total enrollment in the medical school was about 200 students, yet there must have been an appallingly high attrition rate because there were only sixteen graduates in his 1916 class. Lack of money was a major factor in the high dropout rate. Poor preparation for a rigorous medical school curriculum could also have been a factor in the dropout rate, as the requirements to enter medical school could hardly have been called rigid in 1912.

CHAPTER 8

Going Nearly Full Circle: Hampton to Tuskegee

Norris's formal education began at Hampton Institute and ended thirteen years later and 750 miles away at Tuskegee Institute in Alabama—Hampton Institute's ideological twin. He completed a one-year internship in medicine and surgery at Tuskegee's John A. Andrew Memorial Hospital.

Norris did not have a great deal of options available for an internship. In 1916, white medical school graduates had hundreds of places in the United States where they could intern, yet Negroes, even if Harvard-educated, were limited to only four hospitals: Freedmen's Hospital in Washington, D. C.; John A. Andrew Memorial Hospital; George W. Hubbard Hospital in Nashville, Tennessee; and Frederick Douglass Memorial Hospital in Philadelphia, Pennsylvania.

Norris elected to go to Tuskegee's hospital through his Hampton connections, primarily Robert R. Moton, Tuskegee Institute's new principal, whom he had known at Hampton. Moton, who had just succeeded the late Booker T. Washington as the school's principal, encouraged Norris to study under John A. Kenney, M.D. Kenney, a Hampton alumnus, was gaining renown for his work at Tuskegee. A native of Albemarle County, Virginia, he had graduated class valedictorian from Hampton Institute in 1897. He graduated from Shaw University's Leonard Medical School, Raleigh, North Carolina, in 1901. (Leonard Medical School fell victim to the Flexner Report and closed in 1918.) Washington had recruited Kenney to Tuskegee in 1902 for the specific purpose of developing a hospital and a nurses' training school. With $55,000 donated by Elizabeth Mason, granddaughter of the Honorable John Albion Andrew, Massachusetts' war governor from 1861 to 1866, Kenney delivered.

A 65-bed hospital built by the students of Tuskegee Institute opened in 1913.

Norris may have had other compelling reasons to enter Tuskegee, but no one can dispute that he brought the same enthusiasm to the wards of the hospital that he had shown in the cow barns at Hampton. His mentor, a wiry little man, was known for his indefatigable energy, but so was Norris. Kenney was at the bedsides of patients at 4 a.m.; Norris was at his side. Kenney, in 1916, had just taken over as editor-in-chief of the *Journal of the National Medical Association*, counterpart to the journal of the white American Medical Association, and he got a lot of help from his intern. Kenney paid Norris a fine tribute in the journal:

Dr. M.E. Norris who has spent one year as Interne at the John A. Andrew Memorial Hospital, Tuskegee Institute, Alabama, left on the 15th of June, going directly to Virginia to meet the Virginia State Board of Medical Examiners. Dr. Norris has greatly assisted the managing editor with the business affairs of the Journal for the past year, and we wish, in this public manner, to acknowledge his valuable service.

Norris observed firsthand Kenney's annual clinics where generalists and specialists—Negro and white—came to Tuskegee to engage in a clinical marathon of training, treatment, and surgery. The physicians got exposure to a virtual pathology text of illnesses and surgical conditions, and the patients, brought in from near and far, got sorely needed treatment. Kenney had hit upon the idea for the clinic in 1911 while attending a meeting of the National Medical Association at Hampton. He invited the association to convene at Tuskegee the following year. It was during that meeting of the association that Kenney held the first John A. Andrew Hospital Clinic. Over four hundred patients were seen and nearly forty operations were performed. Norris would later bring the concept of the clinics to the Northern Neck. Norris's clinics, of course, were on a far smaller scale and were solely for treatment of illnesses, and orthopedic and surgical conditions.

Before leaving Tuskegee in the spring of 1917, Norris joined with Kenney and ten other colleagues in founding the John A. Andrew Clinical

Society, an outgrowth of the John A. Andrew Annual Clinic that had been started by his mentor five years earlier. The foreword to the program for the thirty-eighth Annual Society Meeting in 1956 stated that the object of the society was to ensure "permanency of the clinic and to develop the program for increasing the effectiveness of the practice of medicine through sharing professional knowledge, skills, and experience. ..." In the ensuing years, the society developed a strong and progressive clinical teaching program to help colored physicians keep abreast of the scientific advances in the practice of modern medicine. The conference was the premier annual postgraduate training program for colored physicians for nearly fifty years. Claude Organ wrote in *A Century of Black Surgeons*: "This clinic was the basic activity of the prestigious John A. Andrew Clinical Society, which offered the first post-graduate course in medicine and surgery for Negroes in the South in 1921."

The Clinical Society did not have a social arm. There was no wives' auxiliary. The physicians met to work and learn at a four-week long session. Prominent specialists of both races from major medical centers were invited to the meetings as lecturers and demonstrators. At a time when membership in the American Medical Association was closed to virtually all colored physicians, and before the term "continuing medical education" was coined, these doctors pursued assiduously the study of new ideas in medicine and new clinical approaches.

Both Moton and Kenney implored Norris to stay on at Tuskegee. He declined. He was determined to return home. But spiritually, he never left Tuskegee, Kenney, or Moton. Thirty years after he left Tuskegee he wrote to Kenney:

> I say without any flattery that I deem it one of the finest things in my life that I came under your teaching, discipline, and guidance. Of all my teachers, none has given me more enthusiasm than you. Your personal example has not only been for me, but also for many others.

After Norris left Tuskegee in 1917, he often returned for the society meetings.

For the next thirty years, he traveled to Tuskegee by railroad in segregated cars, suffering the indignities and humiliation that were the given lot of colored travelers in the South. The Supreme Court outlawed segregation on interstate carriers in 1946. Few people now can imagine the abuse a colored person had to endure when traveling into the deep South in the first half of the twentieth century by car, bus, or train. The rail cars were segregated, and the dining cars were closed to Negroes. Colored passengers had to bring their food in a box or a brown paper bag. The colored sections in the train stations and the restrooms for "colored only" were often dirty and unkempt. Traveling by bus or car was not much better.

Traveling from Virginia to Alabama in segregated railroad cars was not the only discomfort for Norris. The logistics of getting from Lancaster County to Tuskegee by train could prove taxing and arduous. Travel time to Atlanta by train from Richmond was about twenty hours. In Atlanta, he would board a Western Railway of Alabama train. In 1916, the 136-mile trip from Atlanta to Chehaw, Alabama, a rail stop near Tuskegee, would take Norris 4½ hours. He then would transfer to the Tuskegee Railroad at Chehaw, Alabama. This trip took thirty minutes to cover the five miles to Tuskegee Institute, allowing for a stopover in the town of Tuskegee.

Norris's attendance at the meetings in Tuskegee continued until 1963. In that year, the president of the John A. Andrew Clinical Society was Dr. Eugene Dibble, a surgeon who was also the director of the John A. Andrew Hospital. A dispute developed between the men. Norris wrote a terse letter to Dibble on December 8, 1963, from Ft. Pierce, Florida, where he was vacationing. He asked that his name be removed from the mailing list of the John A. Andrew Clinical Society: "The clinic is a closed book to me. This decision has been made after very careful consideration." It will never be known what transpired with Dibble that prompted Norris to resign from the society that he helped found and for which he was such an ardent supporter. I found no correspondence between the two other than this letter. Whatever occurred, a forty-six-year association with Tuskegee came to an end.

Norris went to Tuskegee for an intensive one-year clinical medicine course. He got more than that. He got to know life in the deep South, an experience not necessarily desirable for a Negro in those times, but one from which he could not exempt himself. He also got a re-immersion in the philosophies of Hampton's General Armstrong and his protégé, Booker T. Washington.

Washington, the founder of Tuskegee Institute, was the foremost colored educator at the turn of the century. Washington's philosophy, begun at Hampton and burnished at Tuskegee, would shape Norris's approach to life in the South for the rest of his life. Moton, in a letter to Norris in 1917, put it succinctly when he referred to Washington's philosophy as "The Tuskegee Spirit."

Washington never wavered in promoting General Armstrong's principles of industrial education, self-sufficiency, and community service. Publicly, Washington eschewed political involvement and felt that skilled labor, land ownership, and businesses should take precedence in the endeavors of Negro women and men in America. Norris was acutely aware of the views of Washington's political polar opposite, W. E. B. Du Bois.

Du Bois was one of the leading intellectuals in this country at the turn of the century. He was a founder of the National Association for the Advancement of Colored People, a sociologist of renown, an author, and a relentless campaigner for racial equality, political involvement, and civil rights. He felt that in education, Washington stressed the trades to the exclusion of the liberal arts.

Rather than being drawn into the schism between the Washington faction and the Du Bois accolytes, Norris found great benefit from a synthesis of the positive aspects of the policies of both men. Though an unabashed admirer of Washington, he found common cause with Du Bois, who had called on the "talented tenth" among young colored men and women to disdain material possessions and devote their lives in service to the masses of the colored population. Du Bois said, "Willingness to work and make personal sacrifice for solving these problems was of course, the first prerequisite and *sina qua non* (the essential element)."

If any person belonged in Du Bois' class of the talented tenth, Norris would have been valedictorian. But he was far from alone in heeding Du Bois' call to shun self-aggrandizement and to devote his life to the uplifting of his fellow citizens. Many colored professionals did just this, but few surpassed Norris in their enthusiasm and resoluteness. Though some of his colleagues, and even some of his closest friends, drove Cadillacs and Packards, Norris was perfectly content with his V-8 Ford. While a young man whom he had helped establish a successful small business boasted of having over a half dozen pairs of the finest footwear, it is doubtful if Norris ever had more than two pair of shoes at any time in his life.

Norris recognized early on the importance of independence, of not being beholden to any man. He could attack discrimination without fear of reprisal from an employer. Following the edicts of Washington, he owned his own home, he had farming skills, and he was self-sufficient. And following the pronouncements of Du Bois, through his professional training he strove mightily to lift up his fellow citizens through leadership in civic affairs.

Norris remained, to his death, a devout apostle of Booker T. Washington. He took Washington's mantra and made it his own: "Where there is no vision, the people perish" (Proverbs 29:18).

CHAPTER 9

Capturing a Proper Richmond Belle

Norris was bound for Kilmarnock, but with a minor detour—he had to meet a proper Richmond belle.

While serving his internship at the John A. Andrew Memorial Hospital, Norris had been invited to dinner by the Institute's comptroller, Charles Hanford Gibson, and his wife Maggie. In an array of photographs on the Gibson's piano, Norris spotted a stunning sepia-toned portrait in profile of a fetching young woman. He asked about the photograph and was told that it was a portrait of their niece, who was attending Hampton Institute's Summer School. When he left the Gibson's home that evening, he carried an introduction from Maggie Gibson to her niece, Theresita Beatrice Chiles.

He arrived in Richmond in June of 1917 with two objectives: to take the Virginia State Board Examination in Medicine, and to meet Miss Chiles.

He dispatched with the examination and then went to Miss Chiles's home in Richmond, a two-story brick house on a tree-lined, cobblestoned street with sidewalks. He knew little about the Chiles family except for what he had learned from Maggie Gibson. He would soon learn more.

According to family history, Theresita's grandfather, Richard Chiles, was the messenger who, on Sunday, April 2, 1865, delivered the portentous message from Confederate General Robert E. Lee to Confederate President Jefferson Davis, while he worshiped at Richmond's Saint Paul's Episcopal Church, that the city must be evacuated.

After the Civil War, Chiles worked as a janitor at the Capitol. (The Capitol was the building designed by Thomas Jefferson and completed in 1789 to serve as the Capitol of Virginia.) He and his wife, Martha, were parents of three sons and four daughters. One son, John R., became a postal clerk, an envied position for a colored man in 1890. Another son, James Alexander, was among the first colored persons to graduate from the University of Michigan's Law School in 1889, and on February 24, 1891, became the first Negro lawyer to argue a case before the Kentucky Court of Appeals. Richard, the third son, was a clerk in the Treasury Department at Washington, D.C. The daughters were Marietta, a schoolteacher, Maggie, Julia Jeter, and Maria Brooks.

John R. Chiles married Lucy Turner in 1889, when she was a student at Hampton Institute. Lucy came from an accomplished family as well. Lucy's brother, Ulysses "Tap" Turner, owned a tobacco factory in Richmond. John R. and Lucy Chiles had ten children in the brick home that he had built. The first child, a boy, John R. Chiles, Jr., died at age 9½ months on November 2, 1891. The second child, Theresita, was born July 10, 1892. She was named after the daughter of a Latin American guest at the Chamberlin Hotel in Old Point Comfort, Virginia, where Chiles had once worked. Chiles was so enamored of the name that he decided if ever he had a daughter, her name would be Theresita. In Spanish, the suffix "sita" means little, thus, little Theresa.

Theresita's father kept a daily log of every penny he earned and spent. Part of that record is still in the family. He emphasized that it was not what was earned that mattered, but how much was saved. He was on the board of directors of the colored Mechanic's Savings Bank in Richmond. The bank failed in 1922 due to malfeasance of some of the officers, but he was not involved in the schemes. The directors were forced into insolvency, but he refused to declare bankruptcy. Theresita was always proud of that. At the time of his death in 1936, he owned real estate in four states: Virginia, Maryland, New Jersey, and New York.

All this family history was not of any great interest to Norris on that June day when he went to 316 West Leigh Street to ask for Miss Chiles. He was told that she was attending school at Hampton Institute. He went to Hampton Institute. Nearly fifty years later, Rosa, one of Theresita's schoolmates, recalled the day that he came on campus. She wrote in a letter of condolence to Theresita upon Norris's death:

I know this is a surprise, but when I read in the paper of the home going, my mind immediately bounced back to the summer of 1914 [actually the summer of 1917] when Mr. Norris came across the campus at Hampton asking for Miss Theresita Chiles saying your aunt at Tuskegee had asked him to contact you. Do you remember that? Inasmuch as I saw the beginning I had to express my sympathy at the ending.

Theresita did remember that day, for no "beginning" could have been more awkward. Norris had contacted a former schoolmate at Hampton, Charlie Williams, to arrange an introduction. They found Theresita seated on a campus bench overlooking the picturesque Hampton Roads, a broad channel where three rivers meet and flow into the Chesapeake Bay. As Theresita rose to be introduced by Williams, an errant cyclist collided with her, and sent her sprawling, rag doll fashion, across the lawn. Norris rushed to her aid and helped her to her feet. After she had regained her composure, and they had gotten beyond the perfunctory greetings and obligatory small talk, Norris asked if he could see her in the evening.

On their first date, he talked of her aunt and uncle at Tuskegee. She asked what he did at Tuskegee. He replied, "I do whatever is necessary—cleaning, scrubbing, anything that needs doing." She told him that he seemed intelligent, and she inquired about his ambition to "make something of himself." He responded that all honest work well done was worthwhile. She was flabbergasted the next day when she was told by Williams that "Dr. Norris" was very impressed with her. She had not the foggiest notion that she was talking to a physician. Norris wanted to know if she were interested in the man or the degree. Theresita unwittingly had to pass one other test. He asked if she would like a piece of chewing gum. She declined. She did not chew gum. Had she accepted the gum, the relationship might have ended right there. Norris disdained the chewing of gum all his life.

The courtship was carried on largely by letter. After the first meeting,

Norris saw Theresita only three times before they were married. There was one matter, however, that threatened to derail his carefully made plans, and it was of no minor import. On April 6, 1917, the U.S. Congress had declared war on Germany. President Woodrow Wilson believed that he could field a volunteer army, but he soon realized the futility of this idea. Men would have to be drafted. Congress passed the first Selective Service Act May 18, 1917. Early that summer the War Department made an "urgent appeal" for physicians to enlist in the U.S. Army Medical Reserve Corps. Norris went to Fort Monroe, Virginia, in December 1917, and volunteered to serve in the army. He was commissioned as First Lieutenant in the Medical Corps of the U.S. Army January 23, 1918.

Mary Jane Thornton, his sister, wrote to him that she was

... quite surprised to hear of your readiness to enter the medical section of the army. I suppose you don't know if to go or not, but if they get in much tighter straights [sic] you may have to. And it is considered much better to enlist than be drafted.

His sister need not have worried. He was never called to active duty. The Army awarded commissions to a "small quota" of colored physicians. Norris was not part of that quota. Setting a quota for colored physicians was a charge not denied by the military. The Armed Forces defended its position because of what it called "practicality," that is, caving in to the prevailing societal prejudices against Negroes, the Army being merely a reflection of the greater American society.

White physicians who responded to the government's appeal to enlist were commissioned immediately and assigned to active duty. Yet only one-third of the 300 colored physicians commissioned were ever called to active duty. Incredibly, those physicians who were drafted through the Selective Service Act were inducted as privates with no chance of being assigned to the Medical Reserve Corps. The policy was enunciated in clearest English in a letter from Colonel R. B. Miller of the U.S. Army Medical Corps to New Jersey's United States Senator David Baird.

It is impossible to assign Negro medical officers to organizations in which the line officers are white. Only one Negro division [the 92nd Division] has been organized. In this division the company officers are white and the department has assigned Negro medical officers to the regiments. All the other Negro medical troops who have been called under the Selective Service Law have been utilized in stevedore regiments or other organizations of that character in which all the line officers are white. It is therefore impractical for this department to assign any more Negro physicians to active duty except as vacancies occur in the 92nd Division.

The department regrets that men who may be professionally qualified for this commission should be required to serve as enlisted men on account of their color, but there seems no way out of the difficulty, and there are, of course, many educated men of other professions serving in the ranks.

Norris never spoke of the fact that he had been commissioned in the Army, but not called to active duty. Since he spent so little time dwelling on unpleasantness, he may have made the decision just to let go of the issue and move on. He proposed to Theresita the next time he saw her, in the fall of 1917. He saw her again Christmas of 1917, and Easter of 1918—just twice between proposing to her and their marriage in June 1918.

Theresita's marriage to Dr. Norris on June 24, 1918, was the social event of the month in Richmond's colored community. It was front-page news for the popular local colored paper, *The Richmond Planet*. The owner and editor, John Mitchell, a suitor of Theresita's aunt, Marietta, had no qualms using hyperbole to describe the country boy moving into Richmond society: "The groom is a graduate of Hampton Institute, Lincoln University, [and] Howard University, has been a successful physician at Tuskegee, Ala., and now is located at Lancaster where he enjoys a lucrative practice."

Norris and Theresita were a study in contrasts. He had been born poor, had been orphaned by age seventeen, and had to work his way through three schools. No one else in his family had gone to high school, let alone college.

Theresita's family, on the other hand, was decidedly middle class. All of her sisters and a brother had finished or would complete college. Her brother, James, would be among the first Negroes to graduate from dental school at Tuft's University, Boston. One brother died in Gary, Indiana, while working in the steel mills at age twenty-one. Her aunt, Marietta, was a schoolteacher and a political activist, having been co-founder of the Women's League in Richmond, Virginia. At the end of the nineteenth century Marietta had played a major role in freeing three black Lunenburg County women who were wrongly accused of murdering a white woman.

Norris took his new wife to Washington, D.C., for their wedding trip. It turned out to be one of the most unusual honeymoons in the annals of the ritual: he brought along one of his ill patients who required treatment at Freedmen's Hospital. Theresita never forgot this episode! Nor did she ever forget that during their honeymoon, he deposited her daily with her relatives in Washington while he went on medical rounds at Freedmen's Hospital. It was a brief honeymoon, all of six days.

On July 1, 1918, Norris took Theresita to Lancaster County despite major obstacles to establishing himself in a medical practice. There was the lingering uncertainty of being sent to that devastating war on the European continent. (In a little over four years, from 1914 to 1918, nearly eight million men were killed.) Norris had to register for the draft, and it is not clear why that was necessary as he already had a commission. And many of his friends and relatives doubted that he could succeed in the county, given the esteemed reputations of the white doctors. The most favored physicians among the Negroes were Doctors Chichester T. Peirce, Maryus C. Oldham, and George H. Steuart in upper Lancaster County; Henry Jeter Edmonds in Kilmarnock; and Benjamin H. B. Hubbard in White Stone. Doctors Hubbard and Edmonds had God-like status in the colored communities. Undaunted, Norris pressed on.

CHAPTER 10

The City Girl Goes to the Country

For Theresita Beatrice Chiles Norris, Richmond, Virginia, was a long ways from Kilmarnock, Virginia, and not just in miles. Where there had been romance, there now was reality. The city girl went from indoor plumbing to outdoor privies, from gaslights to kerosene lanterns, from cobblestoned streets to dirt roads, and from trolley cars to horses and buggies. Virtually no rural homes had a bathroom, just an outdoor toilet euphemistically called an outhouse. Running water was virtually non-existent. Water had to be drawn from a well with a bucket on a rope, and if it could be afforded there might be a pulley instead of having to pull up the bucket hand-over-hand. Electricity could be found only in the towns. Outside the towns the people had to make do with oil lamps and wood stoves. Few homes had telephones. The dirt roads turned to mud following a rainstorm, and clouds of choking dust followed any activity on the roads in the summer heat. If a fellow's finances were good, he drove a horse and buggy. If the family were really poor, then there would be no horse at all; they walked.

The only industries in Lancaster County were tied to fishing and farming. Many of the colored men were employed in the menhaden fishing industry. The menhaden is a small, oily fish that is valued for the production of fish oil and fertilizer. Processing plants were based along the coasts of Lancaster and Northumberland Counties, and men fished in waters that ranged along the coast as far north as Maine and as far south as Louisiana. Men who did not work on the boats or in the processing plants worked in pound net fishing, oyster tonging, crabbing, or farming. The women worked in the processing plants, and oyster houses and crab houses shucking oysters and picking crabs.

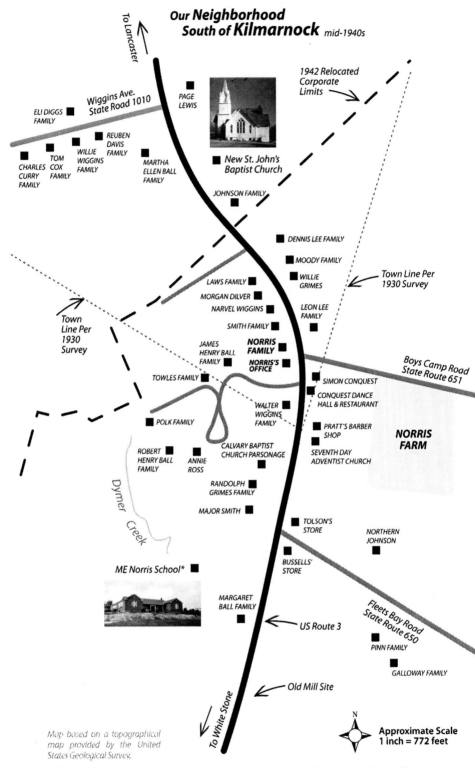

Our Neighborhood
South of **Kilmarnock** mid-1940s

To Lancaster

Wiggins Ave.
State Road 1010

ELI DIGGS FAMILY

PAGE LEWIS

1942 Relocated Corporate Limits

REUBEN DAVIS FAMILY

CHARLES CURRY FAMILY

TOM COX FAMILY

WILLIE WIGGINS FAMILY

MARTHA ELLEN BALL FAMILY

New St. John's Baptist Church

JOHNSON FAMILY

DENNIS LEE FAMILY

MOODY FAMILY

WILLIE GRIMES

Town Line Per 1930 Survey

LAWS FAMILY

MORGAN DILVER

NARVEL WIGGINS

LEON LEE FAMILY

Town Line Per 1930 Survey

SMITH FAMILY

JAMES HENRY BALL FAMILY

NORRIS FAMILY

NORRIS'S OFFICE

Boys Camp Road State Route 651

TOWLES FAMILY

SIMON CONQUEST

CONQUEST DANCE HALL & RESTAURANT

POLK FAMILY

WALTER WIGGINS FAMILY

PRATT'S BARBER SHOP

NORRIS FARM

ROBERT HENRY BALL FAMILY

ANNIE ROSS

CALVARY BAPTIST CHURCH PARSONAGE

SEVENTH DAY ADVENTIST CHURCH

RANDOLPH GRIMES FAMILY

MAJOR SMITH

TOLSON'S STORE

NORTHERN JOHNSON

Dymer Creek

ME Norris School*

BUSSELLS' STORE

MARGARET BALL FAMILY

Fleets Bay Road State Route 650

US Route 3

PINN FAMILY

GALLOWAY FAMILY

Old Mill Site

To White Stone

N

Map based on a topographical map provided by the United States Geological Survey.

Approximate Scale
1 inch = 772 feet

*Photo of school, circa 1933, courtesy of the superintendent's office, Lancaster County Schools.

Herring was also fished and distributed to local canneries. The one other major industry was tomato canning that had started in the late nineteenth century. A few families had businesses, mainly mom and pop stores.

Hardly any colored people had year-round work, nor did most white residents. Farming and fishing were seasonal occupations.

Starting a rural medical practice was a bold undertaking for any doctor, colored or white. A white physician wrote in the *Virginia Medical Monthly* in 1923 that the "deplorable, damnable conditions of the roads," the small fees, poor school facilities, and the absence of entertainment were hardly inducements to come to the country. Nor could a physician expect to find professional enrichment in the community. There was no chance to work in a hospital. And to compound matters for the colored physicians, they were not welcome at the local medical society meetings.

Norris did have a few assets. He had a home and a small savings by the end of his internship, and he had no student loans—they didn't exist. Nor did he have a mortgage to pay off. He did, however, have a medical practice to start, and he expected his share of adversity at the outset. What he did not count on, however, was Theresita's dissatisfaction.

The idyllic country life that the Impressionists so gloriously captured in their watercolors and oils at the end of the nineteenth century and the beginning of the twentieth century hardly reflected the harshness of rural living. Theresita had to make do in a cramped space above Norris's little medical office. To get to a store was an exercise in frustration. She said her most difficult adjustment was using the outhouse, located about a hundred feet behind the dwelling. The inconveniences of a wood stove, the lack of electricity, and the outdoor toilet taxed her resolve. She did what any bride would have done under, what to her were, nearly intolerable circumstances. She voiced her discontent to her new husband, but his response was hardly what she expected. He exploded. She immediately sat down and wrote to her father that living conditions in her new home were beyond her endurance and asked him to send for her. She gave the letter to Norris to mail, and he tucked it into his inside coat pocket. He hadn't the slightest idea of its contents. Several days later, while preparing his clothes, she found the letter still in the pocket. By then, she had had time to reconsider and with great relief, tore it to bits.

Theresita's difficulties in adjusting to rural life persisted, however. She felt that she lacked the necessary skills to function in such a rustic setting. She returned to Richmond and had a frank discussion with her father. She tearfully told him that she could no longer put up with life in Kilmarnock. His advice was blunt and brief: she must return to her new home and endure. He reminded her that she had skills that were not in abundance in the country—sewing, playing the piano, and teaching. She had graduated from the Virginia State Normal School in 1911 and had taught home economics in a Richmond high school. She returned to Lancaster County, but she did more than endure. She got involved in the community, the church, schools, and Norris's manifold projects. And she got pregnant, the first of her nine pregnancies.

Sometimes she was amused by incidents that brought home to her the lack of sophistication of her new surroundings. Once, she hired two young boys to do chores, and thinking that she would reward them with something "very nice," she prepared cups of hot cocoa for them. Neither boy touched his cup, and they began giggling between themselves. When asked why they weren't drinking their cocoa, they replied with all the innocence and sincerity of country boys who had never tasted such a drink, "This is slop water you are serving us."

Theresita found a very different community in the country than the one that she left. Her Richmond neighborhood was only a few city blocks and could have fit easily within the three-acre Norris homestead. Her new community was along a meandering road that ran through roughly a two-square-mile area just south of the village of Kilmarnock, an unincorporated township. The village consisted mostly of white homes bunched around a few stores. The homes of the colored families in Theresita's new environs were scattered along the main road running toward White Stone with a few families clustered around several pipe stems. By neither plan nor design, Norris's place was just about center in the community. Woods and farms separated the homes. The isolation and the seemingly interminable darkness of nighttime, with the screeching of owls and howling of dogs, could unnerve the most stalwart of souls. The outhouse, dirt roads, and oil lamps were all new experiences for her and added to her disquiet with her new landscape.

Over the almost fifty years that my parents lived and reared their children, the number of families in the community would peak to about thirty. Fifteen families plus five families of Balls, three each of Lees and Wiggins, and two each of Smiths and Grimes were scattered about, and more often than not, the families were unrelated. A few families moved in, some moved away, many children were born, and some adults and children died.

Changes did come to the area with the paving of the main road, and the installation of telephone and electricity lines. But over all, the area remained relatively stable. With a school, a church (two during the 1930s), two stores, a dance-hall/beer-garden/restaurant, an auto repair garage, and a doctor's office, a certain self-sufficiency reigned. So much so, that Chiles Lee, who grew up in the neighborhood and left at age eighteen in 1939, said he never really experienced discrimination. (Lee is now a successful Los Angeles businessman.) Incredulous? Yes. Beyond the realm of possibility? No. After all, as in so many colored communities in the south—and ours was no different—an infant could be delivered of colored parents by a Negro doctor or midwife, go to colored schools to be taught by colored teachers, worship a color-blind God at a colored church with a Negro minister, and go to colored civic and social functions where the Negro National Anthem would be sung. It was entitled "Lift Every Voice and Sing." Inspiration was found in the poetic phrases and the soulful melody. Work could be found in a colored environment, goods bought at a colored store, and at death, a funeral held in a colored church, with burial by a colored undertaker in a colored cemetery.

The community was one of mutual support and cooperation. For many years Norris had the only telephone in the neighborhood, and the task of delivering Western Union messages to the neighbors fell on the Norris children.

Also, the Norris family had the only radio in the community until the late 1930s. I still recall the neighborhood boys crowded around the Philco radio at our home to listen to the famed second brawl between the dethroned Negro boxer, Joe Louis, and the world heavyweight champion, Nazi Germany's Max Schmeling, on June 22, 1938. Louis won by a knockout, and pandemonium erupted in our dining room.

All homes had shallow wells, and if one neighbor's well ran dry, he could depend on help from the other neighbors. Foodstuffs were freely exchanged between neighbors.

The division between the village of Kilmarnock, which was inhabited primarily by whites and our community, was well demarcated. The stately New Saint John's Baptist Church and a few families including Martha Ellen Ball anchored the community to the north (See map).

Mrs. Ball's six children were left fatherless by the sudden death of her husband in 1925, just before her twins, Almetia and Julian Allen, were born. A thin, energetic, and indomitable woman, she saw to it that all of her children got advanced training and degrees. Two of her children were valedictorians of their high school classes. Allen, her younger son, a scrawny kid of sixteen, moved into our home in February 1941 when their home was destroyed by fire. He was so cadaverous in appearance that Norris dubbed him "Skully." The moniker stuck. From the day Skully moved into our home, he and Norris developed a symbiotic relationship—he got a home, and Norris got a willing hand to help with his farming. Skully served in the U.S. Navy during World War II, graduated from Virginia Union University, married a local girl, Ruth Caster, and returned to Kilmarnock. He became a leading educator and politician in the county and the person most responsible for the placement of Norris's portrait in the Lancaster County Courthouse. And through it all he remained pencil thin.

Just as in every neighborhood, we had our share of tragedies and successes, although sometimes it seemed as if the tragedies overshadowed the successes. Teeny and Ben Johnson lived with their family just south of

New Saint John's Baptist Church. Their fifteen-year-old daughter, Pearlina, and sixteen-year-old son, Morgan (named for Norris, as were many of the babies that he delivered), were electrocuted by a downed light pole following an ice storm in March 1934. Morgan died during the night, and when his mother came outside early in the morning, she saw the body sprawled over the wires. She screamed, and Pearlina, alarmed, ran to her brother's aid not realizing he was already dead. She was promptly killed. The father tried to rescue his daughter and received a terrible jolt of electricity, but his heavy rubber boots saved him. Norris and his colleague, Dr. Jeter Edmonds, were called to the frightful scene, but Pearlina was dead when they arrived. The family was granted a settlement of $3,500 from East Coast Utilities. No word was mentioned in the Rappahannock Record about the culpability of the utility company, but the community knew that negligence was a factor. Narvel Wiggins, a farmer, school bus owner, and insurance agent, who lived diagonally across the road and slightly south of the Johnsons, had notified the utility company the evening before that the lines were down.

Just south of the Johnsons were two large families, that of Dennis and Grace Lee and Rueben and Lucy Moody. The Lee family suffered a monumental tragedy in 1946. A teenage son, our schoolmate, died in early May from "galloping consumption" as rapidly fatal tuberculosis was called. Thirty days later his sister, a best friend of our sister Alma and a recent college graduate, died of the same illness.

The home just to the north of our home belonged to the Smiths. They had two daughters, Edith and Catherine, who married brothers—Ball brothers. Edith, whose life spanned the entire twentieth century and four years of the twenty-first, was mentally sharp to the end. She told how Norris, when he returned from Tuskegee to practice medicine, would kill chickens and bring them to her mother, Rebecca, to cook. As a young girl, Edith often helped Theresita and recalled how Norris would sit on the front porch of his home and sing lullabies to his firstborn child, Alice.

There was a meandering lane just south of our home that ran west through the woods and up a hill about 200 yards to a plateau where five homes were scattered about. Also, on that plateau was the remnant of the two-room school that the neighborhood children attended until Norris spearheaded the building of the brick school. Among the residents of this area were the Towles and Polk families. Charlie Towles was one of the signatories with Norris to the deed for the land for the new colored school in the community. The Polks had five children, three of whom they lost to tuberculosis. Two daughters survived. One moved to Baltimore, and we never heard much from her again. The other daughter, Mary Susan, was mentored by our parents. She always considered herself their sixth daughter. Mary Susan graduated from A. T. Wright High School in 1936, studied nursing at Virginia's Piedmont Tuberculosis Sanatorium, became a Certified Tuberculosis Nurse in 1938, and then completed nurses training at Saint Philip Hospital in Richmond, Virginia, in 1940. She became a registered nurse and served in the U.S. Army Medical Corps during World War II and continued in the service after the war. She retired with the rank of Lieutenant Colonel.

Across the road from our home lived Leon and Lucretia Lee (no relation to the Dennis Lee family) and Annie and Simon Conquest. Lee, a master carpenter, was one of the builders of our home. He had a large family. They moved to Baltimore during World War II and left standing a majestic but uncompleted two-story home that gradually succumbed to the elements and the weeds.

Simon Conquest was a complex and colorful fellow. "Mr. Simon," as we addressed him, was an illiterate, gun-toting businessman who would unabashedly announce to anyone within earshot that "I couldn't read my name if you put it up on that Coca-Cola sign," pointing to a Coca-Cola billboard at the corner of his restaurant, "but geordjammit, I can count!!" And count he could! He had a cinder block and well curb manufacturing business, a dance hall, a restaurant, a well digging operation, and a farm. Nearly every sentence that fell from his mouth was punctuated with goddamn, but because he had an articulation problem the word always came out sounding something like "geordjam." Though he was profane, he never once used vulgar or scatological language. He didn't consider "goddamn" profane language, at least not the way he pronounced it. He once told me that he got into the habit of cussing when he had to drive oxen as a boy, "the dumbest geordjam animal that God ever made."

Mr. Simon never set foot in a church. He felt most churchgoers were hypocrites and he did not suffer hypocrisy. Nor was he the least bit reticent about letting churchgoers and even some ministers know his mind. He had no problem letting anyone know what his thoughts were, and with his strong tenor voice he didn't need a megaphone.

Race, gender, or religion did not render anyone immune to Mr. Simon's tirades. During the 1940s, a time of strict segregation of the races, no business in the town of Kilmarnock would serve alcoholic beverages to colored adults. Once, a car filled with young white men drove into Mr. Simon's parking lot, and one of the youngsters yelled, "Hey, Simon, you got any beer in there?" Mr. Simon replied, "You geordjam right I got beer and plenty of it, but you ain't gonna get a geordjam drop. Go up to Kilmarnock and get your beer."

Although Mr. Simon never spent a day in school, he brought an excellence to his endeavors that any trained person would envy. His formula for making cement blocks and well curbs produced the highest quality products in the region. They were also the priciest, and he didn't engage in bargaining. When anyone protested that his products were too expensive, he would tell the disgruntled shopper to get the cement blocks or well curbs where they were cheaper, but he was not going to reduce his price.

Mr. Simon's scrupulously clean restaurant, which became a beer garden on Saturday nights, was known throughout the state for deliciously prepared and appealingly presented food. His fried chicken was considered the best anywhere in the state. Mr. Simon boasted that he didn't tolerate flies in his restaurant. If, while eating in his place, a fly lighted on your table, he would refund your money. Nor did he permit the staff that prepared the food to handle the money.

The dance hall was a cavernous room where dances were held every Saturday night, always with a live orchestra. On Sunday nights the place became a movie theatre, and ten cents bought a seat on an empty Coca-Cola case for the show—for the most part, grade B westerns.

What would unite Norris and Mr. Simon, both from impoverished backgrounds and yet so different? One was highly educated, the other illiterate; one was refined, the other coarse; one never owned a gun, the other always carried a gun; one was a deacon in the church, the other contemptuous of churchgoers; one never spoke in a profane manner, the other used profanity in nearly every sentence; one routinely wore suits, the other routinely wore bibbed overalls. A common bond united them—self-respect, self-discipline, self-reliance, high self-esteem, and a commitment to serving the community. They respected and genuinely liked each other but even Norris was not exempt from Mr. Simon's temper. They were both overachievers, so it was inevitable that two strong men would eventually clash and on at least one occasion, clash they did. Oddly, the imbroglio was over something so minor that it could hardly be taken seriously. One of Norris's cows had jumped a fence and gotten into Mr. Simon's garden. Norris never maintained his fences in the best condition and was rather solicitous toward his cows anyway. Quite naturally, the cows sometimes ended up in someone else's pasture or garden. Mr. Simon and Norris had some words about the cows invading Mr. Simon's garden. Norris had a short fuse about his cows, and Mr. Simon had an equally short fuse about his garden. What started out as a discussion quickly spun out of control with an outburst from Mr. Simon. He yelled at Norris: "Don't you put your geordjam feet on my property as long as you live!"

Shortly after the incident between Norris and Mr. Simon, representatives from the Virginia State Alcohol Control Board tried to close Mr. Simon's beer garden and dance hall on the pretense that the place was a public nuisance. It did create a problem on nights that dances were held, as the road in front of the dance hall became clogged with traffic. The agents for the Alcohol Control Board needed only a signature from Norris to an affidavit they had prepared affirming that the place was a public nuisance. Early one morning, the agents came to Norris's office with the document and implored him to sign the paper so that they could close down the dance hall. The agents did not know that Norris felt Mr. Simon's dance hall was an important recreational asset to the community, and no one could dispute that Mr. Simon's operation was among the best run in the Northern Neck. Furthermore, Mr. Simon was one of Norris's staunchest supporters in his projects—holding the fairs, building the elementary school, and forcing the town of Kilmarnock to retract its southern corporate limits. The agents had asked the wrong person to sign the affidavit. They were politely but firmly informed that under no circumstances would he sign the papers.

Overall, Norris and Mr. Simon had a congenial relationship. Theresita was a late riser, something all the neighbors knew. They could tell what time she had arisen simply by observing the plumes of smoke coursing out of the chimney in the morning. The neighbors also knew that she was afraid of guns. Mr. Simon was aware that Theresita's late rising was a source of minor irritation to Norris. He would tease Norris by telling him he had the perfect solution to the problem. He offered Norris one of his pistols to put under Theresita's pillow in the morning: "Geordjammit, that'll get her up."

Fights between young men attending the dances were common, and Norris spent many a Saturday night sewing up knife wounds on the Saturday night gladiators. One Saturday night, there were so many young men requiring sutures to their cuts that he used up all his suture material and had to send over to our home for spools of thread from Theresita's sewing box. Never once did Norris protest about the disruptions to his rest and time caused by the altercations at Mr. Simon's. He would calmly go about repairing the lacerations to the best of his ability. He was patient with the young men, gently telling them: "Son, it might hurt a little, but I try not to hurt you anymore than I can help." Lack of anesthesia was not a major problem, for most of the fellows' blood alcohol levels were high enough to keep them numb. The young men were unfailingly mannerly toward him, never using foul language or in any way acting disrespectful, but when it came time to pay something for the doctor's services, their pockets were often empty.

Norris's daughter, Alma, when in high school, assisted him every Saturday night. She says she saw him become rattled only once. Nearly a dozen people with cuts and bruises poured in from a huge pileup of cars in front of Mr. Simon's. Agitated confusion ruled in the little office as the injured clamored for treatment. Norris became annoyed by the disorder, and with clenched teeth and an authoritative tone in his voice, demanded: "Please be patient. Can't you see I am doing the best I can!"

Mrs. Elsie B. Coleman, one of the first teachers at the Morgan E. Norris Elementary School and a Lancaster native, once told me, "Your father loved Mr. Simon." And justifiably so. Both Mr. Simon and his wife, whom we affectionately called "Miss Annie," were unfailingly kind to all of the Norris children. Not a Christmas passed that Mr. Simon and Miss Annie did not have Santa Claus leave a present for each of the little Norris children.

Mrs. Coleman related that in his later years Mr. Simon began having seizures. The family would send for Norris, and he would immediately give Mr. Simon an injection. But on April 20, 1950, he had a seizure and Norris was not available. Before another physician could be summoned, Mr. Simon died. Mrs. Coleman said, "It was one of the few times that I have seen your father cry." More than five hundred people attended the funeral services that were held at Mr. Simon's home. It was reported in the Rappahannock Record that remarks at his funeral were made by "Dr. M. E. Norris, a lifelong friend of the deceased."

South of Mr. Simon's place, Norris's cousin, Luther Cox, built a Seventh-day Adventist Church in 1929. The church had a short life span. Few colored people were Seventh-day Adventists in the Baptist-dominated communities in Lancaster County. The only one I personally knew outside of our cousins, the Coxes, was Mrs. Sadie Ward, a pious, thin little lady who helped Theresita and sometimes took care of us when our parents were away. Though Mrs. Ward abhorred the eating of pork, she never once complained

1111111

about preparing meals with pork for us. No greater distress could have been inflicted upon this devout woman than when the Seventh-day Adventist Order closed the church. Mrs. Ward then attended the white Seventh-day Adventist Church in Kilmarnock until she died. She loved her tiny church and lamented to Theresita about the condition of the vacant structure and how the bad, rock-throwing children—"chaps" she called them—were breaking the windows. The church and adjoining property were eventually sold to another one of our neighbors, James Moody, who remodeled the church, landscaped the grounds, and turned it into an attractive country cottage complete with a prolific garden.

Further south lived Norris's first cousin, a World War I veteran and a dapper bachelor (he never married) named Rossie Tolson, who had returned to Lancaster County from Baltimore. In 1940, he built a gas station and general store on Route 3 right across Fleets Bay Road from the store of George Bussells, a white businessman. Bussells, who until then had the only store in the neighborhood, lost a lot of his trade to Tolson, but never seemed to resent him. The men remained on good terms until Tolson died in 1960. Bussells was the only white in our neighborhood. (He did not live there. He is remembered as being kind and courteous to the colored residents.)

Down Fleets Bay Road were three families: the Johnsons, the Galloways, and the Pinns. Northern and Dora Johnson had acquired Tolson's parents' homeplace and about sixteen acres belonging to Norris. Theresita had so badgered Norris to get rid of the property that he sold it to the Johnsons, but he never really wanted to give it up. The parcel had been the site of his childhood homeplace. The Johnsons eventually sold it back to one of the Norris children, and it remains in the family. The Pinn family lived across the road from the Johnsons. Spencer and Ophelia Pinn lost both of their sons, one at age fifteen and the other at age twenty-two. These were stunning losses not only for the Pinns, but also for our entire community. The loss of the younger son was a tragedy for Norris as much as the Pinns.

Frank Pinn was a handsome high school student who chauffeured

Norris and helped with the farming chores. He was an industrious and studious youngster. He scored highest in the county-wide seventh grade intelligence test. Frank was one of the most popular teenagers in the county. On a cold, wet December morning in 1938, Norris gave him an assignment that would have a profoundly tragic ending. Frank was to drive the car about two miles to an area called Black Stump and pick up Theresita's helper, Bessie Johnson. Norris had planned to take Theresita to Richmond, Virginia, to visit her ill sister. Frank, while returning with Bessie to our home, lost control of the car. The automobile careened up an embankment and rolled onto its top. Bessie immediately found a telephone and reported the accident. She assured Norris that neither she nor Frank was injured. Norris told Theresita to continue with her plans to go to Richmond. He would check on Bessie and Frank and then stop at Crowther's Ford dealership in Kilmarnock to pick up another car. He had hardly left the house when Theresita received an urgent call. Frank was dead. Theresita, in total disbelief, told the caller that it could not be! Bessie had just called and assured her that neither she nor Frank was injured. The caller replied, "Yes, Mrs. Norris, Bessie is alright, but Frank has just killed himself." Frank, in an apparent panic, had gone to a lady's home, calmly told her that a mad dog was menacing the school children, and asked if he could borrow her shotgun. The unsuspecting lady gave him the gun, and as calmly as he walked into her home, he walked out, went behind her house, put the muzzle of the barrel under his chin and pulled the trigger. He was fifteen years old.

We will never know why Frank killed himself. He need not have worried about Norris's reaction to the damage to his car. Norris would have been so thankful that no one was hurt that he wouldn't have given a second thought about an automobile. He never spoke of this incident to me, but I can gauge his reaction to this tragedy based on another tragedy to which he responded. Four years earlier on September 3, 1934, he, along with four white physicians, was called to the scene of a bus-truck accident near Farnham, Richmond County. Six people were killed, and twenty children and adults were injured (all colored and all from Lancaster and Northumberland counties).

Among the dead were two thirteen-year-old boys, sons of his close friends, W. H. Dudley, the agriculture teacher and his partner in the fair, and Floyd Clark, a Lancaster businessman. In a moving letter of appreciation that he wrote to the *Rappahannock Record* thanking everyone for help, he expressed that the accident site was "one of the most pathetic scenes" he had ever witnessed.

Five years later, James W., the older Pinn son, died from tuberculosis at an army camp in Lake Placid, New York. During World War II, he had been drafted out of Hampton Institute into the army. Despite this immense double tragedy, Mrs. Pinn never lost her kindly disposition and cheerful smile.

Margaret and Frank Galloway lived just east of the Pinns on Fleets Bay Road. Frank was a farmer and waterman, and Margaret was a gifted milliner. Every Sunday, Mrs. Galloway cut a stylish figure as she entered church with a different hat. She was secretary and record keeper during the building of the Morgan E. Norris School. For years, she assisted Norris in his office and his clinics, and she was in attendance at the birth of his son Thornton's two daughters. All four of the Galloway children moved north and became accomplished in their endeavors.

The family of Walter and Clara Wiggins lived in a small house on a high hill just south of the boundary with the Norris property. Walter was tall, muscular, and laconic with an ever-present corncob pipe, and he was a bit of an eccentric. My brother Morgan swore that he buried jars of money in his backyard. We all thought it was Morgan's wild imagination, but he was vindicated fifty years later when the new owner of the property discovered a jar filled with silver coins.

Wiggins claimed a massive pine tree that sat on or near our common property line. Norris was confident that it was on our property. A surveyor's transit could have settled the issue, but Norris said, "Let him have the tree." He knew that Wiggins never would have believed the surveyor or the transit.

South of the Wiggins's was the Calvary Baptist Church parsonage. It was a two-story house built in 1929 on a scenic hill. As times changed and ministers preferred to commute rather than live in the community, the dwelling was allowed to fall in disrepair. Now all that is left is a vacant lot. Just northwest of this site was a wooded area that has now become the final resting place for my parents and other members of Calvary Baptist Church—a four-acre cemetery donated to the church by the Norris children in 1990.

Just south of the parsonage stood the home of Randolph and Henrietta Grimes. They had several children including a handsome son, Randolph, Jr., who as a high school student chauffeured for Norris. Randolph, Jr., succumbed to tuberculosis in the army during World War II. Major and Janie Smith lived just below the Grimes family. Smith served with Norris on the Calvary Baptist Church Deacon Board. Every Sunday after the minister's sermon, Smith would lead the congregation in singing the hymn, "Hold to God's Unchanging Hand."

The last family on the southern perimeter of our neighborhood was that of the widowed Margaret Ball. She had two daughters and two sons. Her sons were named Charles and James. James was nicknamed Bozo. Before a year had passed after Frank Pinn's death, Bozo, who had started working for Norris, was killed driving Norris's V-8 Ford, a fabulously fast car. During a Labor Day event at the fairgrounds in 1939, Bozo was given the job of shuttling Theresita and the children from home to the fairgrounds. On a return trip to our home, Bozo, traveling alone, could not resist giving the throttle to the V-8. Hurtling down the highway at an incredible speed—one witness described the ominous roar of the speeding car as though an airplane were flying low—Bozo failed to make a curve just north of Kilmarnock. According to witnesses, the Ford became airborne and then rolled three times before tumbling to a stop. Bozo was pulled unconscious from the wreckage and died shortly afterwards in Richmond's Saint Philip Hospital.

Norris was devastated by these losses, for Frank and Bozo were in and out of our home just like my brothers and sisters. But however pained Norris was, he surely suffered silently; he never once discussed these boys' deaths with us. Sixty-nine years after their deaths, I interviewed Chiles Lee, our former neighbor and a schoolmate of Frank and Bozo. I asked why he thought that Norris would let these young boys drive his cars and how Norris reacted to their deaths. Lee recounted the deaths in poignant, painful detail, once breaking down in sobs. He said Norris was like a father to him and that Norris wanted to help the young fellows grow up and develop confidence. On the matter of never once discussing these tragedies, he said, "Your father carried everything inside, as there were few people that he could relate to on his level in the community."

CHAPTER 11

The Homeplace and Family Life

For the first nine years of their marriage, my parents lived in the three small rooms above Norris's office. Five children were born in that little place. In 1927, the family moved into a large, new home. The house was built about a hundred feet north of the office. The buildings were located on a three-acre site in the center of our community, along the main road. The southern half of the property was flat and was used for farming and where Norris had a garden. Enough potatoes were raised every year to feed the family from one summer to the next. The northern half was a gently sloping hill that in the summer was used for grazing the cows and in the winter, whenever there was a snowfall, became the neighborhood children's paradise—the best and safest place in the area for sledding.

A large walnut tree sat on the north property line between our place and the adjacent Smith property. A burial ground located under this tree served the Smith family and was the gravesite for my parents' deceased child, Benjamin. Though there were only a few graves, the setting had a morbid, ghostly quality. The gravestones and the enormous tree with overhanging branches set against a thickly wooded area was eerily disquieting to a youngster, particularly at night. The older children in the family created hair-raising stories around this graveyard that the kept us younger siblings on edge.

Norris's farm was not limited to the homeplace. He owned a large field about two hundred yards from our home on Boys Camp Road where he grazed his cows and where grain such as wheat and corn were grown. Neighbor Allen Ball recalls that Norris used two other places for farming. One site was about twenty acres within a 55-acre parcel in the community of Black Stump that had been willed to Norris by a patient. Norris even used the fairgrounds when fairs and recreational events such as baseball games were not being held, and he sometimes farmed plots on his relatives' land.

In farming, as in every facet of his life, Norris wasted nothing and recycled everything. The leftovers from the table and any milk that soured were fed to the pigs. The manure from the cow barn and the chicken house was used as fertilizer. Every Saturday morning, my brother, Morgan Jr. and I could look forward to cleaning out the stables and chicken house and spreading the manure on areas where crops were grown. The recycling that took place on the farm was extended to the home as well. Newspapers and cardboard were saved and sent to Richmond to the recycling plant. Every stick of wood was used in wood burning stoves, and the empty gallon medicine jugs were washed and returned to the pharmaceutical company in Richmond. We got ten cents each for those.

Norris loved his cows and his cows loved him. I learned early on that cows not only recognize people, but also can be spoiled just as children. Nothing was more disconcerting for us children than to see the cows start mooing instantly when our father drove up. He would become annoyed immediately because he sensed the cows needed something. "Son, don't you see the cow needs water," or "The cow needs to be moved to a new grazing area," or "The cow needs to be milked." Once, he returned from one of the Hampton Institute trustee meetings and learned that one of his cows had died, mired in the mud in the grazing field. He was inconsolable. Allen Ball says he will never forget the day he found that cow. He said he had no desire to tell Norris; he told Theresita and let her be the bearer of the bad news.

Norris kept three to five cows, but the mainstays were a Holstein, a Guernsey, and a Jersey. We called the Holstein "Black and White." Her name was a precise description of the color of her coat—patches of pure white mixed with patches of jet black. Black and White was about as mean an animal as one could encounter. There was the ever-present danger of being kicked by her. Rather than get rid of her, Norris, with the assistance of his mentor and friend, Travis Robbins, designed an ingenious way of restraining her while she was being milked. We would throw a rope across her back, completely encircle her waist at hip level, and tighten the rope. The trick was to place the rope around her waist without her kicking out our brains. Norris had a solution for that, too. He recognized there was a correlation between a contented cow and the amount of milk given, and nothing would make the cow happier than to be fed bran, a mixture of grain and sorghum. We can attest to the tastiness of the bran, as we enjoyed handfuls of it ourselves! While Black and White was ecstatically devouring the bran, we would put the rope in place. She could then be safely milked. One might wonder why Norris did not simply send this ill-tempered beast to the slaughterhouse. Well, this cow was a champion producer of milk. She produced more milk than the other cows combined.

There were many lessons to be learned on the farm, and Norris knew that. What Norris could never understand was that not everyone shared his enthusiasm for raising crops and tending livestock.

∽

Norris had two families when he started out in Kilmarnock—the extended family and the immediate family. The extended family consisted of many, many cousins. He probably had enough cousins to sustain a physician's practice. Our cousins were white and colored, but we rarely talked about the whites. We also called many people in the lower Northern Neck "cousin" without the slightest idea how they were related. Among the known kinfolk were the Jordans, Nickens, Carters, Pinns, Jenkins, Tolsons, and Coxes—all large families. Norris was deeply devoted and intensely loyal to his cousins, sentiments that were reciprocated.

Martha Gibson, Norris's first cousin, once told me that Norris delivered nearly all of her children. She had ten—four girls and six boys. She said on one occasion, he was away when she went into labor. A white doctor in Lancaster, Virginia, came to deliver her child. He made her stay in bed during her entire labor. She lamented, "Cousin Morgan would let me walk around and sit until the child was ready to be born. That doctor would have none of that. Oh, I was so sorry Cousin Morgan wasn't there for that baby. I was just miserable."

Norris's immediate family in Lancaster County in 1918 consisted of his stepmother, Sarah Tucker, and his new bride, Theresita. (On November 2, 1904, Sarah had married Rev. Daniel Tucker, founder of the Sharon Baptist Church in Weems, Virginia.) Norris remained in close contact with his step-mother after he left Lancaster County in 1900. After her marriage to Rev. Tucker, Sarah moved from the homeplace and made no claim on the property. She was supportive of Norris throughout his long studies. When he would return to Lancaster County for visits, some of the older folk would question why he was spending so much time in school. She told him, "Boy, don't pay attention to what those people are saying. Finish your studies." "Cousin Sarah," as she was known to the Norris children, gave each of us a party on our fifth birthdays. When the youngest child, Martha Anne, was born in April 1938, she told my parents that she would not "live to give this child a birthday party." Perhaps she had a premonition. Cousin Sarah died May 17, 1939.

Over a span of nearly twenty years—from 1919 to 1938—nine children were born to my parents. Having so large a family and so many responsibilities and projects afoot, the division of labor in rearing eight disparate personalities (one child died) was imperative. So Norris left the girls to Theresita, and he took responsibility for the boys. This did not mean that he adopted a laissez-faire attitude in the rearing of his daughters, but that matters of discipline and decisions for the girls were relegated to their mother. Theresita, in her calm and disarmingly charming manner, was a taskmaster in her own right. She was the one who kept all the children in line and was determined that no daughter of hers would become an unwed mother and no son would become a teenage father. She succeeded. She disciplined more by guidance, explanation, and caring than by the hairbrush or switch.

Norris exerted his influence more by warmth and mentoring to his five daughters. A mutually deep love and a mutually solemn respect existed between him and each of the girls. From their earliest years, he treated them as ladies. Perhaps he did have his favorites—his oldest daughter, Alice (1919-1990), and his youngest child, Martha, whom he called Pasie's Gal—but he dispensed his affection equally for Elizabeth (1923 -1981), Alma (1925-2004), and Fannie (1927).

The girls did not brook criticism of their father. Nor did he tolerate mistreatment or humiliation of his daughters. He could get downright ornery if he felt one of his daughters had been slighted. I always felt that one of the reasons he admired President Harry S. Truman beyond Truman's stance on Civil Rights was the vigor with which Truman defended his daughter, Margaret, against criticism.

Once, Alma was on the receiving end of blatant discrimination in Kilmarnock. She was a teenager and had gone to a small clothing store in the center of town to buy a hat. She returned home in tears, without the hat. The sales lady had refused to let her try it on. Norris happened to be sitting at the kitchen table reading the newspaper when she walked in and told him how shabbily she had been treated. He leaped from his chair, grabbed the befuddled teenager by her wrist, got into his car, and drove straight to the store. He walked in with Alma in tow and asked to speak with the owner. When he appeared, Norris omitted the preliminary exchange of courtesies, got right to the point, and said: "My daughter came here to buy a hat, and your store refused to let her try on one. Well, I want you to know that her hair is as clean as that of any white girl who enters your store!" He took from his pocket a crisp white handkerchief, wiped it across Alma's hair, and held it in the proprietor's face. He then turned and left behind a startled, speechless, flushed storeowner. Leaving the store, he exclaimed over his shoulder: "And you will never have to worry about a member of my family or me coming into this store again!" and he meant it. No one in our family ever entered that store afterwards.

Norris was a master psychologist, and he was a lot more aware of what we were up to than we suspected. He would apply his brand of psychology evenly to the girls and boys, although he could be quite explicit in letting the boys know what he expected of them. He communicated his attitudes on issues to the girls by subtle and sophisticated forms of innuendo, and he made liberal uses of adages, anecdotes, and maxims with the girls and boys. Our father did not spend very much time with us in extended conversations, but there was one place where we would interact and get counsel, and that was when we drove him on his house calls.

Fannie, the sixth child and fourth daughter, recounted Norris's reaction upon learning of her plans to marry:

When I decided to get married in 1950, I told Mama first, knowing that Papa was decidedly not interested in a daughter aged 22 getting married. Mama and I were in the kitchen, and as Papa came through, Mama announced that I was planning to be married. I had a bad cold at the time and went into a coughing spell. Papa said, "What Fannie needs is a dose of cough syrup," and with no mention of the marriage, exited out of the back door.

Norris disdained smoking and the drinking of alcoholic beverages. He didn't want his children to smoke, but never once did he say to any of us: "Don't smoke." During the Second World War, Elizabeth, who was about twenty-two years old and was at home recovering from a foot operation, had begun smoking Kools, a popular mentholated cigarette. Theresita knew she was smoking but was careful not to let Norris know. One day while Elizabeth, Fannie, and Theresita were talking in the kitchen, Norris entered, and to Elizabeth's astonishment, handed her a carton of Kools and went upstairs without a word.

Alice, Fannie, and Martha graduated from Hampton Institute. Alice became a high school teacher and an associate in her husband's businesses; Fannie became a math teacher; and Martha was a specialist in early childhood education and a state agency coordinator. Elizabeth graduated from Virginia State College and Northwestern University in Illinois, and became a medical records librarian. Alma graduated from Howard University, and became a research librarian—the first colored person to hold that position at Reynolds

Metal Company in Richmond.

Thornton (1921-1990), the first boy, was passionate about poetry and literature and was an aspiring baseball player. He found farming the antithesis of everything he liked. He detested milking cows, shoveling manure, hoeing the garden, and anything having to do with farming. He went to his grave hating cows. Norris felt that boys should work on the farm. There was no choice in the matter; there was not even any discussion about having a choice. Norris extolled the virtues of balance in work, recreation, and education. Farm work is hard work and does not leave much time or energy for recreation or reading, a fact that Norris surely understood but did not apply to his sons. And none of us boys had the seemingly inexhaustible supply of energy that he possessed.

Thornton had another passion from earliest childhood—cars. (This passion led to his life's vocation—a taxi business in Richmond, Virginia.) His love affair with cars and, in his youth, fast driving, once proved costly. It was a bitter cold night in mid–winter in the 1940s. Thornton had borrowed Norris's only car, a V-8 Ford, to go out for a while. While rounding a curve at a high rate of speed, the car hit a patch of ice, skidded off the road, and plowed head-on into a tree, propelling Thornton through the windshield. Thornton's face was cut to ribbons. I don't recall how he got home. All I remember was seeing him standing, pitiful and dazed, at the kitchen door with blood streaming down his face. Norris dutifully took him to his medical office, cleaned his wounds, and sutured his lacerations. I don't remember my father uttering one word of admonition or scolding. Perhaps, he knew too well how much worse the situation might have been. As described earlier, our neighbors, Frank Pinn and Bozo Ball, did not fare as well following accidents with his cars.

I don't think my father ever understood Thornton. At the beginning of World War II, Thornton dropped out of Hampton Institute and answered the siren call of Chicago. There, he worked on the railroad as a Pullman porter for a while. In the summer of 1944, he sent word that he was coming home. He had a symptomatic inguinal hernia and had been deferred from military service. He returned home to have it taken care of. Norris, thinking this would be a great opportunity to literally bring Thornton back to the soil and figuratively back to earth, bought a John Deere tractor. About seven o'clock on a warm, humid summer evening, the Greyhound bus screeched to a stop in front of our driveway, and Thornton ambled out with his tattered baggage. He had barely entered the house when Norris proudly announced: "Son, I bought a tractor for you." Thornton, known for his affability and good nature, did have a temper, and this was certainly not the homecoming he had expected. In a flash of anger, he growled at Norris: "You didn't buy me any damn tractor!" This was certainly not the response Norris had expected. It was one of the few times in my life that I saw my father cry, and it was the only time I witnessed any of us challenging him.

After Thornton's hernia repair at Freedmen's Hospital, Washington, D.C., he was drafted into the Navy in November 1945. He served briefly because World War II had ended and the United States armed forces were being rapidly demobilized. While waiting to enter college, he had a taxicab business in Lancaster County—Kall-A-Kab. (Thornton had a talent for coming up with slogans.) He briefly enrolled again at Hampton Institute and then attended West Virginia State College, where he learned barbering. He returned home in 1950, and Norris turned over the service station that he owned at the time to Thornton and also did some matchmaking. Norris had gone to the annual meeting of the National Medical Association in Philadelphia in August of 1951, and at a dance, encountered the only girl that Thornton had ever loved, Gwen Cockrell. Gwen was pretty, petite, and feisty. Her family's origins were in Northumberland County, but Gwen had grown up in Philadelphia. Thornton met her when they were teenagers during the Cockrells' summer visits to the country. Norris knew how to manage almost any situation, and this one he managed admirably. Thornton and Gwen were reunited and shortly thereafter married. My parents even built a home for the newlyweds—less than a hundred feet from our home. Thornton was the only child of the eight for whom they built a home.

Benjamin, the third child and second son, died at birth (1922).

Morgan, Junior, the seventh child and third son, was a New Year's baby. He was born January 1, 1931. An exceedingly bright child, he marched to the beat of his own drum. He was probably the most talented of the eight children, and farming was decidedly not among his talents. He had two passions—playing the guitar and American Indian culture. His interest in American Indians could have been in his DNA. Theresita was 1/8th Cherokee, and we weren't sure about Norris's Indian ancestry, but more than one person has remarked about Norris's resemblance to Sitting Bull, the great Sioux chief. Morgan had an encyclopedic knowledge of American Indian culture and history, particularly that of the Powhatan Nation of Virginia. Today, the state of Virginia recognizes only seven tribes of the Powhatan nation. Two of these tribes—the Mattaponi and Pamunkey—are on reservations, which Morgan visited on occasion. (In a sad commentary on Virginia's educational attitudes about Native Americans mid-twentieth century, I learned about these tribes from Morgan, not from school.)

My parents clashed incessantly on the direction of Morgan's education when he was in high school. They were constantly at loggerheads whether Morgan should go away to a more challenging educational environment or attend our local high school. Theresita was adamant that he ought be in a milieu where his interests could be cultivated. She once arranged for him to study in New Hampshire at a private school, and for the school year in 1945 he lived with Rev. and Mrs. George S. Russell in Hampton where he was enrolled in a stronger school program at Phenix High School. The high school was the laboratory for Hampton Institute's teachers' programs. Norris felt there was nothing wrong with the local high school, A.T. Wright. After all, five of his children had graduated from A. T. Wright, and a number of other children had finished A.T. Wright and had done well. The bickering between my parents over Morgan and his studies was unrelenting, with Norris telling Theresita in a constant refrain: "Leave the boy alone; stop nagging him!"

Norris didn't nag. He told us what to do and expected that it would be done. Unfailingly it was. I am not sure that he understood Morgan any better than he understood Thornton, and I am not even sure he was aware that when it came to his sons, and to farming, that he was trying to force a square peg into a round hole.

My father did encourage us in entrepreneurial endeavors, as long as they didn't have the stigma of subservience. When Morgan, as a teenager, wanted to join his friend working as a pinsetter in a Kilmarnock bowling alley (all white except for the pinsetters), Norris handed him an unequivocal, "No, you will not!"

Morgan and I got into trouble with our father over another little enterprise. One summer afternoon when we were about twelve and thirteen, we got the novel idea that we would go to Kilmarnock and earn money by shining shoes. Norris did not object to our working. He had plenty of work for us on the farm, and he encouraged us to have newspaper routes. We sold the papers published by the Negro presses, the *Journal and Guide* from Norfolk and the *Afro-American* from Baltimore and Richmond. It was all right for us to work for Norris's friends (white and colored), and he did not object when we cut Christmas trees from our property and sold them in Kilmarnock, but our shining shoes was something that he would not tolerate. To him, his sons shining shoes was an unacceptable form of servitude when he knew they could do better.

Norris had returned from a house call and not seeing us, asked Theresita, "Where are the boys?" She replied that we had outfitted a shoebox and had gone to Kilmarnock to shine shoes. He hurried to town and found us busily putting a buff on a white man's shoes. Without a word, he jerked the shoebox from beneath the hapless man's foot and shepherded us into his car. He told us if we wanted to work, he had plenty of work on the farm. Within minutes he had gotten hoes and put us to work chopping weeds in his cornfield.

Morgan did graduate from A. T. Wright and then served in the U.S. Army in France during the Korean War. During his service abroad, he wrote warm, detailed, and informative letters to his parents and siblings and always sent part of his monthly pay to help out at home. After the military, he studied briefly at Hampton Institute, but decided to pursue a technical career in television and radio repair. This work served him well during the days of the old tube sets but quickly ran dry upon the advent of solid-state circuitry in the 1970s. Morgan then spent the rest of his career at Bellwood, the U.S. Government Defense Supply Center in that city. He married a nurse graduate of Saint Philip Hospital, and they reared their family in Richmond.

I was born in 1932, the fourth and last son and less than seventeen months after Morgan. I did not share my brothers' antipathy toward farming. I enjoyed milking the cows, raising pigs and chickens, and had a prolific vegetable garden while in high school. I am not sure that my interest in farming influenced my father's attitude toward me. I felt he treated us boys equally, but I had no dissent with him on the issue of farming.

I did have some rather challenging experiences while growing up, and I am sure my father's response helped mold my character in a positive direction. One of my most memorable adventures was around smoking, and although my father did not give me cigarettes—I was only 12 at the time of this incident—his response on discovering my errant venture was as shocking to me as his bringing home the carton of Kools must have been to Elizabeth. The event remains indelibly etched in my memory even to the time of year and kind of day. It was a clear, late autumn afternoon with the cool crispness and the long shadows that are so much a harbinger of the coming winter. Several of my comrades and I had gathered in the woods behind our home to try smoking for the first time. It was not a particularly pleasant experience, drawing into our lungs the noxious tobacco smoke, but we were all game, for nothing better assured a youngster's move up the ladder to manhood than to be able to confidently blow smoke. The pungent first taste of tobacco and the nearly suffocating fumes would be a small price to pay for entrance to the club. We were not long into our little experiment when one of the fellows became disgruntled over a minor event that I have long forgotten. He bolted from the party and made a beeline to my home to tell my parents about the illicit activity going on in the woods.

I felt quite literally between the woods and a piece of wood; at least that is what I feared. Paralyzed with the dread of having to face my parents, I stayed in the woods until dark. It was my first realization of how quickly darkness descends after sunset. Even the early chill of the evening was not as discomforting as the hooting of the owls and the varied sounds that wafted through the woods after dark, some real and many probably imagined. Besides, I was getting hungry. There was not much of a choice left, so with great reluctance and even greater foreboding, I headed home. A child of twelve, gripped with terror, gets the wildest, most irrational ideas. Somehow, I came up with the notion that I could furtively slip into the house, taking the back stairway to the upstairs, and go to my bedroom. As I stealthily planted my foot on the first step of the stairway, from the kitchen came that stentorian voice, so revered but also feared: "Son, come get your dinner." I sheepishly entered the kitchen, sat at the table, and ate what was and has remained the longest meal of my life. Not one word, then, or ever since, was said about my smoking, and from that day on no cigarette has ever hung from my lips. Out of the eight children, four became smokers, probably not a bad percentage for the 1940s and 1950s, but the effects of smoking on the four were devastating. Two had lung cancer. Two had other cancers, which occur with higher incidence in smokers.

I was afraid of my father when growing up. I am not sure how this came about, but I think my mother programmed us to fear him as a means of controlling us. After all, she had eight children to manage and was invariably pulled into her husband's many projects. She always admonished us that we had to do our chores "before your father comes." We were fearful of his coming home and finding things out of order, so we made sure everything was kept shipshape. There could be no paper on the lawn, trash or chicken droppings on the sidewalk, and the steps and porches had to be scrupulously clean. If a light was not being used, it had to be turned off. If a faucet was dripping, it had to be tightened.

When he came in for the day, Theresita always told one of us, "Get your father his slippers." We jockeyed as to who would do the task. The trick was for one of the children to beat the other to the command and say loudly in front of our father, "Hurry and get Dad his slippers." No way was the recipient of this directive going to protest.

Norris did have a temper, and that knowledge alone helped keep me in line—as well as Theresita's admonishments. As I was younger than Morgan, I could benefit from the results of his crossing my father—such as the time when we were youngsters and my father told Morgan to sweep the back porch of our home. (We started working at about the age of six or seven.) Morgan brushed the porch and apparently, in a hurry to get back to play, swept the trash under the linoleum floor covering. When Norris came in, he stepped on the linoleum, lifted it, and saw what was underneath. He called, "Morgan, come here!" (Our father gave us all nicknames: Thornton—"Thornty," Morgan—"Junior" and myself—"Jeemes." When he called us by our first names we knew something wasn't right.) When Morgan responded, Norris showed him what he had done, picked up an unshucked ear of corn in a basket on the porch, and began to flail Morgan. Morgan skirted away. I learned from that experience to never sweep anything under a rug.

Although my father was consistently kind, if we wanted something, we usually asked our mother, not our father. It was not until after I finished medical school that I developed a better understanding of my father and realized what a remarkable person he was on many levels. Nor did I realize until I was much older that it was my mother and not he who was holding me in check.

He was supportive of all the boys' interests. During World War II, I built model airplanes as a hobby. Cellophane, which was essential to make the cockpit windows, was in short supply. Yet, despite all the work he had to do, he would try to find cellophane for me. When I was about twelve years old, I acquired a small printing press to print tickets for various organizational and school functions, for a fee, of course. Once I needed a special piece of type. Norris went to the owner of the *Rappahannock Record*, our local newspaper, in an unsuccessful attempt to procure the type for me.

When I got into trouble with the law, which happened once, he was magnanimous toward a mortified fourteen-year-old. In Virginia during the 1940s, a fourteen-year-old could have an unrestricted driver's license. I had borrowed my brother's taxicab and was racing through Kilmarnock, when all of a sudden I spotted in my rear view mirror a police car gaining on me. For a brief moment, I considered trying to outrun him, but I knew even the V-8 Ford was no match for the policeman's souped-up Chrysler engine. It took no leap in logic to realize the futility of such an adventure. I pulled over to the side of the road, and the patrol car rolled up behind my car, with its red light mounted atop the Chrysler pulsing in synchrony with my heartbeat. Out stepped Clifford Jett, a gigantic, red-faced, former lumberjack whose counte-nance seemed as if it had never been graced with a smile. He was as taciturn as one could be without being congenitally mute. After asking for my driver's license, without another word he wrote out the traffic ticket listing the charges and the court date. I immediately plotted to go to court without my parents' knowledge. I hit upon what I thought was the perfect solution! I would get Jack Taylor, a graduate of Hampton Institute's auto mechanic school, who was running my father's service station, to take me. I made a deal with Jack: "Take me to court; I have the money to pay the fine—just don't tell my parents." Jack consented to the ruse. The morning of my court appearance, I bounded down the stairs with my book bag under arm, ostensibly on my way to school. Norris was sitting at his typewriter. When I said goodbye to him, he replied: "Son, I'll take you to court."

He did not utter one word on the drive to the courthouse. After arriv-ing, we had to wait in line before going before the judge. I can now imagine the humiliation my father must have felt standing in that line. My case was called, and the judge, hardly acknowledging my father, muttered: "Guilty or not guilty." Norris instructed me to say "guilty." The judge then grumbled some inarticulate words about the responsibility of driving (I was not hearing anything) and announced a fine of $40. I did hear the "forty dollars" clearly. Norris paid the fine. We left the courthouse, and he drove me to school. He said not one word about the ticket, the court, or the $40.

Norris once became more than agitated with me about Morgan, and it had to do with my almost giving Morgan a lifelong disability. Morgan was about to shoot a bird with his powerful BB gun, and as he bent over to cock the rifle, I pulled the trigger. The BB shot exploded from the barrel and struck Morgan in the root of his nose, dead center between the eyes. I shall never forget my father's facial expression as I cowered behind my brother. My father had to remove the BB shot. I waited for the blows that never came.

രു

We three boys, though with vastly different personalities and divergent interests, remained close throughout adulthood. That alone is a tribute to something our parents did right. And whatever faults Norris may have had in rearing boys, there was no lack of love and affection. That we all knew.

The reader should not get the impression that our parents, and particularly my father, were parents in absentia. They both were there for our needs. Despite my mother's involvement in the church, community affairs, and nearly all of my father's manifold projects, she prepared and served just about every meal we ate when we were growing up. And when we came home from school or from trips, we could be assured that "Mama was home."

Our family sat down for two meals a day, breakfast and dinner. Breakfast was always hurried, and after finishing the morning chores, the children were off to school, and Norris was off to see his patients. Saturday mornings were far less chaotic than the weekdays as there was no school. Cereal, eggs, bacon, and toast were the reliable breakfast menu items Monday to Friday. The children drank milk, and my parents had coffee. Saturday mornings, pancakes were added, and on Sunday mornings, particularly during the "R" months, oysters were standard breakfast fare. (It was traditional during those years to harvest oysters from September to April. This probably came about because of fear of oysters spoiling in the summer months.) Salted herring, codfish cakes, corn bread, and molasses were also staples. The bacon, eggs, and milk usually came from our farm, although with a large family and frequent guests from the city, the pantry often had to be supplemented with food items from the local farmers and grocers. Norris had a penchant for patronizing the colored businesses and would augment the family's food supply with canned goods and dried beans from their country stores. The items were a bit more expensive than those at the Sanitary Store (later known as the Safeway), but Norris felt the good will was worth more than the difference in price.

Dinner was served around six o'clock in the evening or whenever Norris could be there. We never sat down to eat until he arrived. The entire family sat together for dinner every day, and we always ate in the kitchen—a large room that had a wood stove and then an electric stove (early 1940s); an icebox until 1936, then a refrigerator; a sink; a kitchen cabinet; and a table with leaves that seated easily ten people. Dinner was never rushed, and much direct and incidental teaching took place at mealtime. At the beginning of dinner, Norris sat, but no one began eating until Theresita took her seat and grace was said. Lively conversation among family members dominated the meal. It was not uncommon for these animated sessions to be interrupted by someone calling on Norris to see a sick relative or friend, or the patient might appear in person. If someone arrived at our kitchen door while dinner was in progress, the visitor, regardless of his station in life, was invited to join us. On occasion, the invitation would be accepted. Any misbehavior at the table was quickly suppressed with a glare from Norris. He never scolded us at the table; just a stare and the horseplay would cease immediately.

There was never any shortage of food, but Norris did not take kindly to our leaving food on the plate. The dictum was: "Take all you want, but eat all you take." There were other dicta, and they came from Theresita more often than Norris: "Do not put your elbows on the table while eating; do not use your thumb as a 'food pusher;' do not scrape food from the platter onto the plate; do not slurp the soup; do not chew with your mouth open." At the end of dinner, if Norris did not have to return to his office he would turn to the daily quiz in the *Richmond News Leader* ("Test Your Horse Sense"), and we would all share in answering the questions. Then came the jockeying among the children as to who would wash the dishes. If Norris was going to the office, Alma would inform the table in earshot of Norris, "I am going to help Papa in the office," and that got her out of the kitchen work. No one, including Theresita, was going to say: "No, you cannot go help your father."

Our family was remarkably free of internal strife and placed a premium on family loyalty, but we were brutally frank with each other. Once my oldest sister, Alice, who assumed the role of surrogate mother (and father, too!) at times, began barking orders to me. I exclaimed to her, in one of the rare occasions that I used profanity toward a sister, "Goddammit Alice, every time I turn around you have me jumping through hoops!" She replied," You're darned tooting—that's what you're supposed to do."

In later years family gatherings were great fun and the time for rehashing of memories, much to the profound boredom of the in-laws. My father enjoyed these mini-festivals—something that fate had denied him in his childhood.

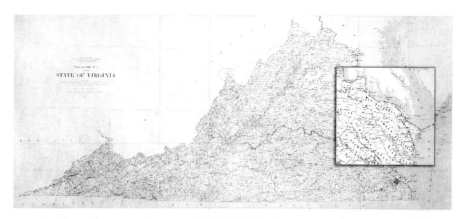

Above: *Map of Virginia
(1928), showing the
Northern Neck (area of
detail).*

Right: *The Northern
Neck, (from the collection
of the Geography and
Map Division, Library of
Congress).*

*Elizabeth Jane Tankersley Norris,
Norris's Mother, circa 1882, (copy
of tintype, courtesy of Morgan
Norris Jackson, M.D.). Born at
White Stone, Virginia, February 17,
1854. Married Benjamin Norris,
May 20, 1880. Died at Kilmarnock,
Virginia, September 1886.*

Willie Chapel Church, as it now stands (photo by James E. C. Norris, M.D. 2003). The church was founded on this site in 1884. A white landowner, George Cornwell, donated the two-acre parcel of land with the condition that the founders would name the church for his son, Willie. For many years, the church was called Little Willie Chapel Baptist Church. The church now—125 years later—has a congregation of 500.

Ellsworth Bunker, Businessman, Statesman and Diplomat, and Norris's Longtime Friend (photo property of James E. C. Norris, M.D.). Bunker left the company his father built to become a leading diplomat and statesman. On March 16, 1967, his appointment as ambassador to South Vietnam was reported in the New York Times. *The article described Bunker as presenting a "spare and slightly forbidding appearance. His hair has turned almost completely white, and he normally holds himself ramrod straight. He is slim and nearly 6 feet 2 inches tall."*

Hampton Institute Students at Rockywold-Deephaven Camps, 1907 (courtesy of Archives, Rockywold-Deephaven Camps). Norris is in the front row, second from left. Mrs. Mary Alice Armstrong, widow of Hampton Institute's founder General Samuel Chapman Armstrong, and Alice Mabel Bacon, a teacher at Hampton, founded the family camps at Holderness, New Hampshire. Mrs. Armstrong was teacher, mentor, and friend to Norris. At the camps, the students earned stipends to help defray school expenses and they made contacts that were invaluable to the development of their careers.

Class of 1912, Lincoln University (Norris family photo). This is a restored copy of the original. The author donated the original and this copy to Lincoln University Archives. Arrow points to Norris.

Class of 1916, Howard University College of Medicine *(Norris family photo). Norris is in top row, second from right. The author donated the original to the College of Medicine, Howard University.*

Henry A. McAlister (1892-1967), Norris's Roommate at Howard (courtesy of Mary McAlister Powell). "Mac," as Norris affectionately called him, was a graduate of Howard University's School of Dentistry, 1916. He shared part-time jobs with Norris during their Howard years, and they worked together at the Rockywold-Deephaven Camps. McAlister served for ten years as the school dentist at Hampton Institute and for years conducted a monthly dental clinic in Norris's office in Kilmarnock.

The Trustees, Faculties and Graduating Classes
Howard University
request the honor of your presence at the
Forty-seventh Annual Commencement
at which degrees in Arts and Sciences, Pedagogy,
Theology, Medicine, Dentistry, Pharmacy and Law
will be conferred
Wednesday, June seventh 1916 at four-thirty o'clock
University Campus
Washington, D. C.

Invitation to Norris's Commencement at Howard University (courtesy of Hampton University Archives).

John A. Kenney, Sr., M.D. 1874-1950 (courtesy of Linda Miller Kenney). Dr. Kenney, Norris's teacher and mentor at Tuskegee, fled Tuskegee in 1924 under death threats from the Ku Klux Klan because he vociferously supported placing Negro staff at the new Tuskegee Veterans Hospital. He located to Newark, New Jersey, and in 1927 built the first hospital in Newark that was open freely to Negro physicians, nurses, and patients. (The building was made a National Historic Site in 2005.) Kenney invited Norris to join him in Newark, but Norris's commitment to the Northern Neck was too great for him to leave.

John A. Andrew Hospital, Tuskegee Institute, Alabama, circa 1913 (courtesy of the National Medical Association). The hospital was built with a gift of $55,000 donated to Tuskegee Institute by the granddaughter of the Massachusetts war governor, John Albion Andrew. Dr. John A. Kenney wrote in 1913: "The building is largely [the] result of students' work from the digging of the clay, the making and laying of bricks to the installation of the electrical work, plumbing and steam fitting."[1]

The John A. Andrew Memorial Hospital

BOOKER T. WASHINGTON, Founder

Tuskegee Institute, Alabama

Open for the accommodation of colored patients from all parts of the country. Every kind of disease, except contagious ones, is treated in this hospital, and patients are afforded the very best facilities by skilled physicians and nurses. Persons desiring to enter the hospital should address

DR. JOHN A. KENNEY, Medical Director

Tuskegee Institute, Alabama

[1] *Journal of the National Medical Association* 5, no. 2 (1913): 89-94.

Photograph of Attendees at the John Andrew Clinical Conference, 1928. *Arrow points to Norris. (The author wishes to thank the Crisis Publishing Co., Inc., the publisher of the magazine of the National Association for the Advancement of Colored People, for the use of the image captioned The Annual Clinic of Negro Physicians, first published in the June 1928 issue of The Crisis.)*

Theresita Beatrice Chiles in her early 20s
*(Brown's Studio, Richmond, Virginia, Norris
Family photo). This is the photo that
Norris probably saw on the Gibson's
piano in 1917.*

Mr. & Mrs. John R. Chiles

request the honor of your presence at the marriage

of their daughter

Theresita Beatrice

to

Dr. Morgan Edward Norris

Monday evening, June the twenty-fourth, nineteen

hundred and eighteen

6 o'clock

316 West Leigh Street

Richmond, Va.

At Home July 1st, 1918
Kilmarnock, Lancaster, Co. Va.

*Invitation to the
Wedding (courtesy of
Hampton University
Archives).*

*Norris's office (1953)
(photo courtesy of the*
New Journal and Guide,
*Norfolk, Virginia). The
house had three rooms
downstairs and three
rooms upstairs. The
structure was demolished
by the family in 1990.*

Three Norris Children, circa 1925. (Brown's Studio, Richmond, Virginia, Norris family photo). From the left are Thornton, Elizabeth, and Alice.

Jaehn Benjamin Charlton, M.D., (1917-2004) (photo courtesy of archives, Meharry Medical College Library). Charlton was thirty-four years younger than Norris. He was a graduate of Meharry Medical College and interned at Harlem Hospital in New York City. He arrived in Northumberland County in 1947 and practiced successfully as a family physician for nearly forty-seven years. He and Norris worked closely together in the Rappahannock and Old Dominion Medical Societies.

JAEHN BENJAMIN CHARLTON
ROXBURY, VIRGINIA
3.S. Union University; Kappa Alpha Psi

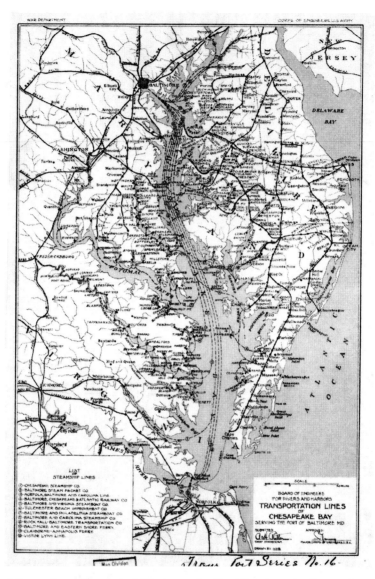

Map of Steamboat Routes of Chesapeake Bay Serving the Port of Baltimore, Maryland, 1926, (from the collection of the Library of Congress). Steamboats were the lifeblood of the Northern Neck until 1927 when the Thomas J. Downing Memorial Bridge was built across the Rappahannock River at Tappahannock. Until then, Baltimore was the most accessible and desired city for commerce and for medical treatment for the residents of the lower Northern Neck.

***The House Norris Built
for Theresita and Four
Children in 1927,*** *circa
1953, (courtesy of the*
New Journal and Guide,
*Norfolk, Virginia).
Fannie, the fifth child,
arrived four days after
the family moved in.
Three more arrivals
would swell the Norris
household to ten persons.*
*My parents built the little Cape Cod cottage to the right for their oldest son,
Thornton and his family, in 1953. The parcel where these homes are situated
has been in the family since 1898.*

The Morgan E. Norris Family, 1960, *(Broadnax Studio, Richmond,
Virginia, Norris family photo). Front row, from left, are Fannie, Norris,
Theresita, and Elizabeth. Back row, from left, are Morgan, Alice, Thornton,
Martha, James, and Alma.*

The Norris Family With In-laws and Grandchildren, 1960, (Broadnax Studio, Richmond, Virginia, Norris family photo).

The New Saint John's Baptist Church and its Founder and Minister, Dr. Daniel Harrison Chamberlayne (photo of church by James E. C. Norris, M.D., 2004). Dr. Chamberlayne with a group of members left Calvary Baptist Church in Kilmarnock to found the church in 1910. The first church building, built a year later, was destroyed by fire in 1922. The present edifice was completed in 1927. Steptoe Lee, Dr. Chamberlayne's brother-in-law, and Lee's son, Leon, built the church. Dr. Chamberlayne was pastor of New Saint John's for forty-seven years.

Northern Neck Baptist Association, 1923, (Brown's Studio, Richmond,
Virginia, Norris Family photo). Norris was active in the association until his
death. Norris is shown seated, first row, second from the right. His friend,
John Malcus Ellison, is seated in the second row, second from the left. The
Northern Neck Baptist Association was organized in Richmond County (the
county adjacent to Lancaster County) on September 29, 1877. Member
churches were the Baptist churches of the five counties of the Northern Neck.
Rev. Levi Ball, Calvary Baptist Church's first minister, led the association
for seventeen years. Under his leadership, the Northern Neck Industrial
Academy (NNIA) was founded in 1898. Until Albert Terry Wright led the
building of a high school for Negro children in Lancaster County in 1918
and the Julius Rosenwald High School was built in 1917 in Northumberland
County, the NNIA was the only school beyond grade school for the Negro
students in the Northern Neck.

CHAPTER 12

Norris's First Great Challenge: The Great Influenza Epidemic

Norris had hardly gotten his practice started before he was attending to the victims of the great influenza epidemic of 1918. It remains the greatest pandemic in world history and was the first worldwide epidemic since the Black Plague of the Middle Ages. It is estimated that in the United States alone during the years 1918 and 1919, 675,000 deaths were directly related to the pandemic. At that time no nationwide system existed for collecting data, so it is not known precisely how many died. It is estimated that worldwide, fifty million people died, and that figure may be too low. It is entirely possible that as many as 100 million people died, but the exact number never will be known.

The epidemic came in three waves: a mild but widespread outbreak in the spring of 1918, a devastating onslaught in the fall of 1918, and a less severe wave in the spring of 1919. The medical field was woefully unprepared for the impending disaster. Vaccines had not been developed for the influenza virus, and there were no antibiotics to counter the bacterial complications that followed the viral infection.

Remote places, such as the Northern Neck, were not so remote that they would be spared the spread of the disease, and the people were particular vulnerable because of lack of communications, inaccessibility to medical care, and poverty. The entire Northern Neck, with an estimated population of 45,186, had a single small hospital in its upper reaches at Fredericksburg. (Fredericksburg is in Spotsylvania County just over the border from King George County, the northernmost county in the Neck.) It is doubtful that the hospital would have helped very much as it had only sixteen beds.

Many of the victims succumbed to bronchial pneumonia. The most ominous sign was the heliotrope cyanosis (a progressive cyanosis beginning on the lips and ears, then spreading over the entire body, accompanied by widespread bleeding into the tissues and the coughing up of copious thick, yellow phlegm). Pete Davies in *Catching Cold* recounts Dr. Herbert French's frightening but gripping description of the patients he treated in England:

Hospitals filled within a day or two as temperatures rocketed to 103 degrees or 104 degrees, tongues coated, faces flushed, eyelids drooped, and voices became hoarse interrupted with hawking coughs. People ached all over and grew so sore that they couldn't swallow or speak; frothy liquids welled up in their throat. [*sic*] Nosebleeds were incredibly common—sometimes just enough to stain a handkerchief, in other cases a flood so heavy it would soak the sheets. Most did at least sleep well, and just wanted to be left alone with a cold drink; after three days or so, many then got better fairly fast. Others developed pneumonia; among these came the heliotrope cyanosis, the "dreaded blueness." It appeared in under half the pulmonary cases but when it did, French estimates that 95 percent of the time it was a death sentence. On the other hand, he said, any and every case could be fatal anyway. A patient might be mildly ill for a day or two, and seem to be improving—then his condition would abruptly alter for the worse, and in twenty-four hours he'd be dead.

In an interview with Theresita by a writer for the *Rappahannock Times* of Tappahannock, Virginia, October 21, 1976, she gave a startlingly clear and accurate account of the epidemic that occurred during the first year of their marriage. The interview took place fifty-seven years after the epidemic.

We didn't know what to call it, she says, remembering the suffering. Victims would begin with a high temperature and sore throat, causing them to come to Dr. Norris's office, which he maintained in his home. Then the illness would confine them to bed and Dr. Norris would have to visit them.

Mrs. Norris tells how a woman brought a girl in one day and that her husband (Dr. Norris) told her to keep the girl away from the rest of the children. Within days, two of the family's children had died and both mother and father were stricken with the flu. "Somebody died nearly every other day," says Mrs. Norris. "He got so discouraged." She adds that it took a long time for the fortunate to recover. "People were sick for a while with the influenza they had at this time."

Remembering the frustration of doctors who had to carry and give out their own medicine, Mrs. Norris notes how the Health Department sent out information to the rural areas. It seems that all the doctors could do was to give something to break the fever. She remembers, "We read papers and found it was happening throughout the state."

Mrs. Norris can still describe how her husband set out in a horse and buggy to visit flu victims and stay all day long. She says that Norris himself came down with the disease about three weeks after most people had had it, and that he, like everyone else took a long time to recover. What may be important, she remembers that the flu struck more children than adults, a fact verified by modern medicine.

In 1917, the year that Norris started his practice, 450 people died from influenza in all of Virginia, a rate of 20.7 per 100,000 residents. By the end of 1918, the number dying in the state from influenza had shot to 345.2 per 100,000, translating into an astonishing 7,839 persons. And the calculation did not include military personnel! The epidemic abated to some extent in 1919—still, there was a death rate of 168 per 100,000 for a total of 3,858 dead, and less in 1920 (99.8 per 100,000 or 2,311 deaths), but not yet at the pre-epidemic levels. By 1921, Virginians, the nation, and the whole world could literally breathe a sigh of relief—the great epidemic had run its course.

CHAPTER 13

The Country Doctor

There happens to be a waiting list of sick and suffering people, wholly rural, who are treated by the country doctor. Though in some instances he may be considered a back number because of the lack of hospital affiliation, group practice, laboratory diagnosis, and etc., yet when his horizon is at the right elevation and his vision not impaired, he fills a very important place in the life of the people. Whether for much or little, this is where I have cast my lot for the past quarter of a century.

MORGAN E. NORRIS, APRIL 7, 1942

In the early and mid twentieth century, the practice of rural medicine was one of the most demanding of human endeavors. Norris's practice as a country doctor would have tested the resolve and stamina of the most stalwart of men. As a solo practitioner, he was on his own seven days a week, twenty-four hours a day. He developed a sharpened awareness of how swiftly a supposedly normal event could turn to disaster. The patient with an asthmatic attack whose bronchial tubes clamp down like a vise letting no air in or out, and who, despite the frantic administration of medications, proceeds to profound air hunger, cyanosis, collapse, and death; the uneventful pregnancy that in the last hours of birth develops a trickle of blood soon becoming an unstoppable torrent as the physician tries vainly to stem the hemorrhage, his patient fighting desperately for breath as a deathly pallor settles in from blood loss; the heartburn that lingers, then becomes a crushing chest pain, the patient telling the doctor one minute that he feels "like a truck with a ton of bricks is setting on my chest" and the next minute begins convulsively jerking, his eyes rolling back as he dies.

Ambulance service in the Northern Neck did not exist at the time. In dire circumstances Norris sometimes turned to the undertaker who would lend his hearse to take an ill patient to the hospital, nearly a hundred miles away. The imminent childbirth, the broken arm, the throat abscess, the bleeding laceration had to be attended to immediately. Norris could not so readily bundle up his patients and put them on a steamboat to Johns Hopkins, or put them in a car and send them to Richmond.

For nearly half of a century he practiced in a small clapboard structure. For the first ten years he was limited to just three rooms downstairs—a waiting room, a treatment room, and a room for storage of medicines. A screened-in front porch extended the width of the building and was complete with wicker chairs, straight-back chairs, and a rocking chair. The porch served as an airy year-round complement to the waiting room. It seemed like a communal gathering place with the patients and their families trading stories about their aches and pains. His family lived upstairs in three rooms.

The storage room was about ten by twelve feet in size. Brown gallon jugs that contained the full gamut of liquid medicines available lined the shelves with military precision. White glass jars filled one shelf and contained just about every known salve. Additional shelves were lined with bottles of tablets, boxes of empty 3- by 5-inch envelopes, and cartons of empty 3-, 4-, and 6-ounce bottles. Norris could enter that room and instantly put his hands on any pill, salve, or liquid that he needed. He could have done it blindfolded, if necessary.

Norris dispensed most of his medicines, not for profit, but for practical reasons. A trip to the drugstore was impossible for most of his patients. Few had the means of getting around, and many could barely afford to pay the doctor, let alone the druggist. In those days, insurance plans did not exist, nor were federal or state funds available to help defray the costs of medication.

After Norris moved his family into a new house in 1927, the three upstairs rooms over his office were used as recovery rooms during his clinics, for the occasional complicated illness, and for maternity cases from the surrounding counties and the upper reaches of Lancaster County. It was Theresita's lot to prepare meals for the patient and the patient's caretaker and do the laundry. Expectant mothers, while awaiting the onset of labor, sometimes took their meals with our family. Norris attempted to create a permanent maternity unit, but it proved too costly.

Norris made house calls until the end of his career. His cousin, Effie Jenkins Stroud, recalls that he started out in a buggy with "two great big wheels" instead of the usual four. When he progressed from the horse and buggy to the automobile, Norris developed a preference for Ford cars. In the 1930s he briefly owned a Studebaker in addition to his Ford sedan with the rumble seat. (At about age four, I fell out of the rumble seat of the moving car onto the soft shoulder of the road. Luckily, I didn't land on the pavement. I was none the worse for the fall except for a few bruises. Shortly after that episode Norris traded in both cars for a Ford V-8.) In 1951 he bought an Oldsmobile "rocket 88," but he was not happy with that car. Too much power.

He usually had someone to drive him on his house calls, and often took advantage of the break from driving to get a quick nap. He also used the opportunity to dispense sage advice to the younger men and women and his children who drove for him. He taught all of his children how to drive, and as soon as we were old enough, we drove him on his house calls. Once, I drove him to see a mortally stricken patient. As we were speeding along the highway, we came upon a tractor pulling a disc in a no-passing zone. We slowed to about five miles per hour. Norris said: "Son, pass the tractor." I replied in a smart-alecky manner, "Dad, don't you see the double yellow lines?" Norris uttered a gentle rebuke: "Son, that which is lawful is not always expedient." I passed the tractor.

On his house calls, Norris carried the requisite black satchel that was a virtual miniature pharmacy. It was a leather, compartmentalized bag with foldout units containing smaller compartments with syringes, needles, ampoules of injectable medicines, tablets and liquids. The essential drugs were morphine for pain, digitalis for the heart, chloroform for deliveries, a barbiturate for convulsions and sedation, and aminophylline for heart failure and bronchial asthma. The sulfa drugs (prontosil, sulfathiazole, and sulfa-diazine) were added in the 1930s and early 1940s. Penicillin, the first true antibiotic, did not become readily available until the early 1950s.

Norris's routine was to make house calls in the early morning hours, just after sunrise. He wasn't fazed by Theresita's objection that no woman would want him calling before she had chance to make herself presentable. He wasn't going to a fashion show; he was going to see someone ill. He was meticulous about his own appearance, however. He always shaved before he left the house in the morning, using a straight razor that he sharpened on a strop; donned a clean shirt; preferably white, and made sure his fingernails were always trimmed and clean. So careful was he about his appearance that the summer heat often caused him to change shirts twice in a day.

When calls came in for the doctor, Norris had to go. The phone rang at all hours. Once, he was called out five times during a single night. On long trips for home obstetrical deliveries he would invariably stay over at the patient's home until the baby arrived.

Fortunately, he had a superb assistant, a midwife named Sarah Eliza-beth Campbell who was the leading midwife in the lower Northern Neck. "Cousin Sarah Lizzie," as she was affectionately known, had an extraordinary heritage. Her father was the legislator, Armistead Nickens, who represented Lancaster County in the Virginia State Assembly from 1871 to 1875. His portrait now hangs in the Lancaster County Courthouse. Armistead Nickens's ancestors were free men and a number of them fought in the Revolutionary War. Cousin Sarah Lizzie was the wife of William (Billy) Mack Campbell, the first colored undertaker in Lancaster County. Their son, Quentin, was the only licensed embalmer in the county for many years. (A little known fact was that Quentin embalmed whites as well, as the white undertaker in Lancaster County at that time was not a licensed embalmer.) It can be accurately stated that during much of the first half of the twentieth century, if you were colored and lived in the lower Northern Neck, a Campbell would bring you into this world and a Campbell would take you out of it. Cousin Sarah and Norris worked hand-in-glove for over thirty years. She was in attendance when each of the nine Norris children was born.

Norris helped to train midwives as well. He was responsible for helping train a young woman, Claudine Smith, who succeeded Cousin Sarah. Smith cut her first umbilical cord under Norris's supervision and went on to become a midwife in her own right. She delivered over 500 babies without assistance and earned the trust and respect of all the doctors in Lancaster and Northumberland counties. Smith chronicled her midwifery experiences in two books.

Norris never had a full-time secretary, although Martha Jones Lee assisted him in later years. Nor did he ever have a steady assistant in his medical practice. Carrie Bean Smith, a midwife and an artistic quilter, and Margaret Galloway, a talented and creative milliner, were particularly helpful during the clinics in the late 1930s and 1940s, and later Vivian Corbin, a granddaughter of Armistead Nickens and niece of Cousin Sarah Lizzie assisted him. His children who had an interest in medicine, Alma and I, also often helped him.

There was little in the practice of medicine that Norris could not handle, from broken bones to severe lacerations to difficult childbirths. There were two practices, however, that Norris would never engage in: that of abortions and the dispensing of narcotics to drug addicts. I never asked my father why he was opposed to abortions. I guess it was pretty stupid not to ask, but I rarely questioned him when he made pronouncements. Furthermore, in 1959 (the year that he "asked" me not to do abortions) a physician convicted of performing an abortion could look forward to a long period of contemplation behind bars. And everything would go down the drain—his career, his life's work, his family, his home, and everything that he had accumulated including his reputation. I must have thought the answer was pretty obvious in 1959. Norris was a pragmatist, and though he was a most decent person, I simply am not sure if career concerns or a moral imperative or both drove his stance.

Once, while working in the supply room of his office, I overheard a conversation he was having with a lady begging him to do an abortion. She pleaded tearfully with him, "Please help me out." He told her that there was simply no way he would do an abortion, but he could arrange for her to have the child, and he would assist her in placing the child for adoption.

He supported a number of desperate women through childbirth and adoption. One of the most appreciative letters he ever received was from a lady who had begged him for an abortion. He refused, but he did arrange for her to go to Baltimore, Maryland, to have the child. Two decades later, the grateful mother wrote to tell him about her life. She went through with the pregnancy and kept the child. She had become an invalid and the child became her sole emotional, physical, and financial support.

Norris was also instrumental in placing a number of children for adoption in the lower Northern Neck. Our community was a close one, and just about everyone's business was for general consumption. When a couple adopted a baby, everyone knew. What they did not know and would never find out was where the child came from. Norris was as discreet about the background of the child as any modern-day adoption agency.

Norris's attitude on narcotics was driven by ethics. Drug dealing had not reached rural areas at the time. There was no market in illicit drugs. He never locked his car or his office for fear of theft of narcotics. It was not necessary. The rare addicts were not stereotypical junkies, but rather the upright citizens of the community. He knew that to prescribe narcotics to those people, or any addict for that matter, was to go down a path that could be as distasteful as it was dishonorable.

CR

How could a man with such a passion for the practice of medicine find time to apply himself to other needs that he felt must be addressed in his community—those of education, recreation, business, and health? Above all, Norris had an edge over the average man due to his remarkable level of energy. He began his days at 4 a.m. Typically he would read the medical journals, type a few letters, check on his cows, and then make house calls. Yet, having to provide for a wife and children, serve as a Hampton trustee, organize the annual fairs, help young men in their business ventures, and work statewide to improve education and the health of the citizens of Virginia seemed not to dilute the quality of his medical practice.

Many couples had large families. One lady had eighteen children, including three sets of twins, all delivered by Norris. Another Kilmarnock resident, Mrs. Maggie Waters, ninety-five years old when interviewed, said that Norris delivered all her children—"all eight of them," she emphatically stressed. The first child was born in 1925, the last in 1946. When asked how he could have delivered all eight babies when so often he was out of the county at meetings, she replied that she had no idea. She just remembers that he was there for the births of every one of her children and that he charged seven dollars for each delivery. When asked what she remembered most about his delivering her children, she responded with a chuckle: "I just remember I had a whole lot of pain, that's all."

Compassion and a desire to assure his patients the best care were the driving forces behind his brand of medicine. If a patient was ill and needed care, money was not an issue. Nor was a patient's contagion ever an issue. If necessary, he would bring patients to the upstairs of his little office and minister to them until their health returned. This sometimes caused discord with Theresita, who like any mother, was concerned about contagion and the protection of her small children. While Norris loved his children dearly, he never turned his back on a needy person, regardless of the diagnosis. Once he housed above his office a woman ill with typhoid fever. It was Theresita's lot to prepare meals for the patient and the patient's nurse, and to arrange for the washing of their bed linens. It would be a gross understatement to say that Theresita became extremely upset. She demanded to know "how on earth he could bring someone with such a highly contagious disease with all these small children next door." But Norris did not relent in his obligation to his patient, nor did he skirt his responsibility to his family. He continued to take care of his typhoid-infected patient, and he attempted to vaccinate all of his family. Everyone was vaccinated except Theresita, who refused, and Alice, their oldest daughter, who had a fear of needles. This event had a happy ending. The patient survived, and no one in the Norris family contracted typhoid fever.

From my earliest childhood I observed how he treated his patients, how he would escort them to the door regardless of how full the waiting room was, sometimes even to their cars. I observed how he empathized and commiserated with them. His concern and dedication to the ill was plainly evident, and he spared no effort to assist them.

Medicine, not making money, was his passion. It never mattered what a patient's circumstances were; he would render care and talk about money afterwards. Never once did he ask for advance payment or enter into any type of financial haggling before rendering medical service. Even on Saturday nights, when the young combatants were brought to his office bruised, beaten, cut, and bleeding, he would not demand payment for his services. In fact, he was never paid for many of the sick he treated, the wounds he sutured, and the babies he delivered. There were, of course, many who did pay their way, who were dependable in their financial dealings, and who unfailingly met their obligations. And though some families were short on cash, there was no poverty of spirit. There was no lack of willingness to give something in return for services received. By present day definitions of poverty levels, most of his patients would have been considered poor. One Lancaster County resident put it in perspective when she said, "We were all poor—we just didn't know it."

Patients paid Norris for his medical services in cash or by barter. For a few dollars, or bushel of oysters, or a shad or two, the sufferer would get a consultation, perhaps an injection, an envelope of pills, or a bottle of medicine. Norris never secured a debtor's property against outstanding debt, nor took anyone's land. There was, however, one instance where he did accept land for helping a terminally ill man with no financial resources and apparently no relatives willing to help. The gentleman suffered an extended illness that exhausted all of his money. Somewhere along the way he asked Norris to take care of him and his funeral expenses. In exchange for this commitment, the gentleman willed to Norris a share in fifty-five acres of land on the eastern branch of the Corrotoman River. Norris took care of the gentleman just as promised. Shortly after the burial, a relative from Philadelphia showed up to stake a claim to the property. Norris, without the slightest hesitation, deeded the property to the relative. He even permitted the relative and his mother to stay as guests in our home while the estate was being settled.

Norris cared for his own family as well. He was always patient and understanding with us. Only once did he become vexed with one of his injured children. When Alice, his oldest daughter, at age sixteen lacerated her wrist on a broken jar while washing dishes, she adamantly refused stitches. No cajoling, persuasive talk, or begging would change her mind. Norris gave up in exasperation. Fortunately for her, no tendons or nerves were cut.

His presence and confidence were reassuring. He shared the care of his sick children with Theresita. In the middle of the night, if the chorus of coughing was too loud and prolonged, it was not uncommon for him to get out of bed, go to his office, and return with a morphine tablet, an excellent sedative and equally effective cough suppressant. No morphine addicts were created by this rather unorthodox treatment, but Norris and his little charges benefited from a peaceful night's sleep.

He believed in one standard of care. What was good for his patients was good for his family and vice versa. On one occasion he even gave precedence to a patient over his family. When Theresita was in labor with her ninth child, Norris left her in the care of a mid-wife to attend a patient whose labor he felt demanded his presence. This move slightly bruised Theresita's pride, but years later when she recalled the episode, she seemed more amused than offended.

Norris was as relaxed with his patients as he was with his family. He was always in control and had a remarkable sense of humor. Alice Dameron, one of Norris's patients, recalled with laughter, seventy-odd years later, an experience she had. She was a young woman and had sustained a scald burn to her right thigh when the handle broke on a saucepan of boiling water that she was carrying.

> Blisters came up as big as half dollars. They told me to keep it dry, not to let anything touch it. They put butter on it, flour and cornstarch. It burned; it hurt something badly. We didn't have a telephone so we drove over to Dr. Norris's office. He was a humorous person; he wanted his patients to be happy, to take their minds off of what was wrong. He observed that I had put butter on it, flour on it, and cornstarch, and he said, "If I had a little bit of flavoring, we could soon make a cake."

Mrs. Dameron said that what impressed her most about Norris was his recognition of the need to help people through recreation, education, and church work. "He was involved in anything to make a round person. At the conventions he would tell the people that the church had its place but you need other avenues to broaden people's education. He thought about the whole person, you might say." Norris understood better than most people, including physicians, the importance of balance to one's health—the importance of the interplay of healthful living, education, recreation, and work.

Norris had many white patients. Considering the prevailing Jim Crow practices and the general climate of race relations in Virginia, this was clear evidence of how this man's commitment transcended racial barriers. More than forty years after his death, on my visits to Lancaster County, it is not uncommon for white Lancaster natives to tell me that my father was their family's doctor, or that he attended one of their relatives or that "he delivered me."

Norris was deeply attuned to the spiritual needs of his community. Just as he brought many a child in the world, he was witness to many deaths,

including that of one of his own childre
patients, and often he would give some c
and what the person meant to the commun.
without hesitation. After long services, whe.
testimony might tax the audience's patience, he i.
to say with a paucity of words. This brevity of expre.
failed to get an appreciative nod from the congregation.

My father once wrote to me: "One minute you are up in .
and the next you are in the valley. So I guess that is mostly the w.
You might also say that is mostly the way of medical practice. Probably, .
of the most dispiriting losses he experienced was that of young Raleigh Carter
in the late 1930s. Carter, a teenager in high school at the same time as Norris's
oldest son, Thornton, was undoubtedly one of the most popular youngsters
around. He lived in Brown's Store, a small, insular community in Northumberland County about three miles east of Kilmarnock. Norris was called to
his home to treat him for a severely infected tooth. In addition to local treatment, Norris gave Carter an injection to relieve the pain. About three hours
after receiving the injection, Carter died suddenly. The community was up in
arms. Nearly everyone suspected that Carter's death was in some way tied to
the injection. Three days later the funeral was held, with Rev. J. J. Nickens
officiating. Nickens, a native of the area, was reed thin, somber, and not given
to the histrionics one might expect of a rural Baptist preacher. He was elegant
in appearance and eloquent in speech. He, too, had young sons and could
empathize with the bereaved parents, but he also understood the vagaries of
life. He recognized the distress of the relatives and the community, and he
spoke at the service as friend and counselor to a family benumbed with grief.
The people agreed that he did not so much preach a funeral for Carter that day
as preach about the history of Norris's practice of medicine in the area and
what he had done for the people of the Northern Neck. The sermon was not an
absolution of Norris but one of understanding. It is said that Nickens turned
an embittered and hostile community around.

ave two boys whose remarkable recoveries surely put Norris
ntop. Their gratitude for his skill and competence extends to
thaniel Giddings, now a retired long distance van operator, is a
nt, erect man of seventy-six years with a resonant baritone voice.
rely conceivable that sixty years ago this man was a scrawny, gangly
ger struggling to hold on to life against the dreaded and deadly disease
own as lockjaw, in which the jaws become clenched from uncontrollable
spasms of those powerful muscles that are for biting and chewing. Other
groups of muscles are affected as well. The neck, back, and leg muscles
spasmodically tighten and pull the body into an inverted "C." The muscles
that control breathing and the swallowing of saliva, fluids, and food are all
affected. The medical term for this frightful condition is called tetanus. A
toxic substance to the nerves, elaborated by a bacterium, causes it.

In 1945, tetanus was a preventable disease. A vaccine had existed since
1938, but few people were immunized at the time. There was also an antidote,
the antitoxin. Thanks to the genius of a German scientist, Emil von Behring,
the antitoxin had been discovered in 1882 and was available. While notably
effective, it was not always successful. Tetanus, at the stage that Giddings was
affected when diagnosed, was more often fatal than not.

Giddings has total recall of his illness except for the time "I was in
coma." He remembers stepping on the nail, applying home remedies for
the puncture wound, becoming ill, and his cousin going to "fetch Dr. Norris
because the family did not have a phone." He remembers Norris coming right
away, that Norris summoned a white doctor from Warsaw, and that they put
a thermometer into his mouth. He promptly bit it in two when his jaws went
into spasm. He remembers the doctors working feverishly to recover the
pieces of glass through a fortunate gap in his teeth. Shortly afterwards, Norris
summoned the Calvary Baptist Church minister, Rev. Thomas Davis, who
took Giddings to Saint Philip Hospital in Richmond, the Medical College of
Virginia's teaching hospital for colored patients.

When Giddings arrived in Saint Philip Hospital's Emergency Room, the doctors were waiting for him. He recalls with striking nonchalance: "I was fading real fast." He could breathe, but he could not swallow. He says that shortly after admission, he went into a coma for two weeks. When he emerged from the coma, he had to be kept in a dark, quiet room for five days. The slightest sound would send him into wrenching spasms. A feeding tube was passed through his nose into his stomach, and a catheter was placed in his bladder. He had two wounds, the puncture wound on his foot where the nail had entered and the other on his leg where the skin graft was taken to cover the foot wound. (A pillar of treatment of tetanus is to cut away the devitalized tissue at the puncture site.) Giddings remembers the "terrible stomach cramps" that he had when the feeding tube was removed and he was fed by mouth. When he was discharged from Saint Philip Hospital, he says, "I was a walking skeleton." Norris resumed treating him at that point. He gave him medicine to prevent infection and stimulants for his appetite and dressed his wounds. Giddings had become ill in December and by March was able to return to school. He made a full recovery, was drafted into the United States Army during the Korean War, and was at the front line in Korea when the armistice was signed.

There was one interesting aspect to Norris's management of Giddings's illness. Why would he summon a white doctor in consultation? After all, he would not have had a problem with the diagnosis, having seen the disease in all its myriad forms. There are two reasons: he needed more tetanus antitoxin, and he needed a liaison to the all-white Saint Philip Hospital staff, a liaison that he did not have.

Another notable success involved Lloyd Hill, now sixty-six and a retired Army major who served two tours in Vietnam. But sixty-one years ago, when he was five years old, had not a prompt diagnosis of poliomyelitis—commonly known as polio—been made, the outcome could have been very different. He recalls with clarity the train of events that led to his ending up in a hospital for six months, much of the time spent in an iron lung. He was stricken in 1945, seven years before the Salk vaccine was first tested. He remembers that he was playing outside, fell down, and could not get up. He also developed a swelling in his groin. After some rather unorthodox home remedies over the course of the next few days, he was not getting any better. A call was put in for Norris. He came to Hill's home and upon examining the youngster told his parents that he had to be rushed to the hospital. Norris arranged for him to be taken immediately to Saint Philip Hospital, where he was put in an iron lung on arrival. When Hill was discharged from the hospital, he required home therapy before he could return to school. He was a full year behind when he returned, but he says "I caught up." He did catch up and passed some of his schoolmates in the process. He graduated with his peers, and went from high school to a twenty-year career in the Army, two master's degrees, and finally, a position as athletic director for Alcorn State University in Mississippi.

Poliomyelitis, one of the most feared diseases of the twentieth century, was well known to the medical community and almost as well known to the lay community. Norris was doubtlessly aided in his understanding of the signs and symptoms of the disease through his attendance at the John A. Andrew Clinical Society meetings in Tuskegee. A polio unit for colored polio victims had been established at the John A. Andrew Hospital in 1940.

In the years that had passed since Norris got his M.D. at Howard University's College of Medicine, the transformations in travel, communications, technology, and science were phenomenal. Giddings would not have survived in 1916. Hill would have certainly died, for the iron lung was invented only in 1928, and probably a decade elapsed before one was acquired by the Medical College of Virginia. (An "iron lung" was an external ventilator. It was a large, steel, cylindrical chamber that encircled the patient completely except for the head. An electrical pump was attached that rhythmically altered the pressure inside the chamber and effectively breathed for the patient whose respiratory muscles were paralyzed.) With the coming of the twentieth century, medical science began an unrelenting march forward that spanned Norris's career and beyond. But one constant remained. The essence of the country doctor as caring, compassionate, and dedicated was as vital to the health of his patients in 1916 as it was in the decades after. It is to Norris's credit that he made every attempt to stay abreast of advancements in medicine and he never lost that essence.

CHAPTER 14

Challenges on the Home Front –
Discrimination, Disease, and Illiteracy

In 1917, the United States was waging wars on two fronts. One front was called the Western Front, and it was far away on the European continent with exotic sounding names like Belleau Wood, Château Thierry, Somme, and Saint Mihiel. There were clearly marked demarcation lines no better demonstrated than the zigzagging trenches that cut across the European landscape like gigantic wounds.

The second front was on America soil, and the names were more prosaic like Memphis, Chester, East Saint Louis, and Houston. The demarcation lines were less defined but the enemies—discrimination, disease and illiteracy—were as damaging and deadly as the Kaiser's bombs, bullets, and phosgene gas. World War I ended November 11, 1918, but the war at home raged on and would rage on interminably. The United States government never brought to bear on the foes on its shores the immense resources that it had expended on the war effort abroad. In 1918, no national effort was marshaled against the destructive triad on the home front. Rather, the federal government left it to the states to deal with these matters in a piecemeal and desultory fashion, and that is just what they did when they dealt with them at all. Oddly and ironically, the battles would be fought by the hapless victims who were least equipped to vanquish relentless and intractable foes.

Racial turbulence gripped the country, and it reached into the furthest extension of the Northern Neck. A horrible incident had occurred in Lancaster's adjacent Northumberland County in the summer of 1917 when Norris returned to Lancaster County. William Paige, a young colored man, had been lynched by a white mob in August.

The *Norfolk Journal and Guide* reported in its October 6, 1917, issue that "a colored man named Paige was accused by two white women of attempting criminal assault upon them, and within two hours after the alleged crime was reported, Paige had been lynched by the farmers of the community." Mrs. Alice Dameron, a frail but alert and proud nonagenarian colored resident of Northumberland, recalled the lynching eighty-four years later with startling clarity. (Her recollection was that it was a lone white woman, riding home from the post office in a horse and buggy, and when she turned into a tree-lined lane to go home, she alleged that Paige jumped on the buggy.) The lynching occurred when Dameron was only a child. She and her parents were in their horse and buggy on their way to an August revival at Shiloh Baptist Church. The route from her home to the church passed the grounds of her school where the body hung. "As we passed by the school ground, there was the body of Paige hanging from a tree!" For over eight decades, the emotion that had lain dormant welled up with volcanic fury. She exclaimed in a tremulous voice, "My mother nearly fainted." When asked why no one had cut down the body, she replied, "They [the colored people] were scared to death." (The *Journal and Guide* reported that the whites misinterpreted this fear as disinterest: "Paige had a family, and because they refused to have anything to do with his remains after the mob had finished with them, the whites thought that the colored people had taken the matter entirely without resentment." The whites were in error. The colored people showed their resentment by boycotting the leader of the mob and refusing to work on his farm.) That lynching was the only one that occurred in the Northern Neck.

Northumberland County was just a microcosm of the greater South. Vicious race riots erupted the summer of 1917 in East Saint Louis, Illinois, and Houston, Texas, as a result of the seismic shifts in colored populations, conscription of colored men in a military that was a mirror image of Southern society, and a growing militancy of Negroes. Lynching of Negroes occurred frequently. Thirty-six Negroes were lynched in 1917. (The number spiked to sixty in 1918, seventy-six in 1919, and thereafter declined steadily over the next decades.)

Despite the ugly episode in Northumberland County and the racial tensions throughout the South, the Northern Neck experienced "a relative racial harmony" that Northern Neck historian, James B. Slaughter, attributed to the "lack of economic strife." To some extent this is true. The economic boom did not come to the Northern Neck during Norris's lifetime, as moneyed retirees were just discovering the area, but certainly no one was starving with the abundant fish, oysters, clams, and crabs, and the farm produce that poured forth from the rich soil. But make no mistake about it, parallel societies existed in the Northern Neck just as they did all over the South and much of the North.

Norris had to reckon with another foe, one as intractable and as deadly as discrimination—disease. When he came to Lancaster County, the five leading causes of death among Negroes in the United States were, in order of the mortality rate, tuberculosis, heart disease, influenza, kidney disease, and lobar pneumonia. The leading causes of infant mortality were premature births, pneumonia, bronchitis and influenza, and gastro-intestinal disease. The average Negro male born at that time had a life expectancy of 40.5 years compared to 54.1 for a white male. The Negro female fared just a little better—42.3 years versus 56.4 years for the white female. Virginia's death rate for colored was nearly twice that of whites: 18.9 per 1,000 for Negroes versus 11.6 deaths per 1,000 for whites.

The white physicians in Lancaster County were considered excellent and compassionate, and they readily treated colored patients. Yet alarming numbers of illnesses occurred among the colored people in the area. County health departments had not been developed, and poverty and illiteracy were still the lot of many of the colored residents of Lancaster County. When Norris returned home in 1917, over one-third of the colored population of rural Virginia was illiterate. Among children ages seven to thirteen, one out of four did not attend school. Nearly thirty percent of the Negro population of Lancaster County was still illiterate in the 1930 census!

A long fight lay ahead, and Norris had no illusions otherwise. How best to approach these problems required a strategy, and it is without doubt the general outlines that existed in his mind had been honed during his journey from Yonkers, New York, to Hampton to Lincoln to Howard and finally Tuskegee.

Upon returning to Lancaster County from Tuskegee, the first thing that Norris concentrated upon was introducing sanitation and health education. Norris felt the role of the physician was much more than treating the sick and crippled. He knew that to contain and even eradicate disease that he had to educate as well, and the key was working together. But he knew that he needed venues to reach the people, and what better venues were at his disposal than the colored churches? While at Tuskegee, Norris had written the ministers of the need for conservation for the war effort. Upon returning to Lancaster County, he immediately joined the Northern Neck Baptist Association, an organization of all the Baptist churches in the Northern Neck, and he was the featured speaker on health and education at nearly every annual convention. (The Northern Neck Baptist Association is still in existence.)

Norris could be found in church every Sunday morning, not necessarily his own church, which was Calvary Baptist Church, but churches in both Northumberland and Lancaster Counties. Rev. John Otis Peterson, a native of Northumberland County and pastor of a large church in Alexandria, Virginia, recalled that as a boy he was in awe that at First Baptist Church in Heaths-ville, where Rev. Henry C. Roane was pastor, Norris was one of the rare laymen who were invited to the pulpit. This courtesy was extended to him in the colored churches throughout the Northern Neck. He often found time to attend the evening activities and special programs in addition to the regular Sunday morning service.

Norris possessed an uncanny sense of timing of the services. He never sat through an entire service, but would enter just as the minister was about to start his sermon. After the sermon the minister would issue a call for new converts, a hymn would be sung, and just before benediction, he often would call on Norris to say a few words. (There were no female ministers in the Northern Neck during Norris's lifetime.) Norris would give a brief, thoughtful, extemporaneous talk on either of his favorite topics, health or education.

Baptist churches, by virtue of their organization, are contentious bodies. Because the congregation elects the ministers, the members commonly side with one of the two factions, those who support the minister and those who oppose him. Norris, though an active deacon and a stalwart supporter of his church, never took sides, but his patients were in both cliques. Yet he was remarkable in the adroitness with which he navigated the disputes, never once permitting himself to be pulled into the frays.

He knew the Bible as well as most ministers and would sprinkle his talks and letters with religious quotations. Sometimes he would engage the ministers in discussions about biblical topics. I once witnessed him methodically and soundly demolish a minister's incomplete understanding of a biblical passage, but rather than humiliate the poor fellow he seamlessly segued into another topic. Norris cultivated a special relationship with the clergy until his dying days. He knew if a dent were going to be made against illiteracy, disease, and discrimination it would be through the colored churches.

The Negro Organization Society of Virginia provided another venue that Norris needed to reach the people. In the first half of the twentieth century, the society did more than any other organization to raise the consciousness of Virginia's colored population to the responsibility of improving their living conditions and health. It was the only organization of its kind among Negroes in the entire South, and it had an incalculably favorable effect on the lives of Virginia's colored citizens.

At the turn of the century, the high incidence of illness and premature deaths among blacks in the South was so alarming that Negroes felt that if anything was going to done, they would have to do it themselves. In a much-heralded and thoroughly scientific study, *Health and Physique*, W. E. B.

Du Bois demonstrated that in certain diseases "the Negroes have a much higher rate than whites, especially consumption, pneumonia, and infantile disease." Du Bois pointed out that economics undoubtedly played a role in the disparity, but he pointed out that other factors were as important: "lack of training, polluted water, unskilled labor of men, work of women leading to neglect of their children, unwholesome and improper feeding, ignorance, and improper education." The race was considered to be on the verge of extinction.

My father once told me an interesting, although quite possibly apocryphal, anecdote when we drove up to a running, jumping, rollicking group of colored children. "Son, it is said that when General Ulysses Grant was riding about in the South after the Civil War and he came upon a group of colored children like these, he uttered, 'Poor little things; by the end of the century there won't be one on the face of the earth.' Well, I wish the good general could come back and see how wrong he was." General Grant wasn't alone in his doomsday prediction of the fate of the colored people in the South. Statisticians, educators, politicians, and physicians shared his prediction right into the twentieth century.

When reconstruction ended in 1877 with the federal government's withdrawal from the South, the states were left pretty much on their own regarding care of their citizens. The watchword was self-help, and the mantra was "Pull up yourself by your own bootstraps," but it was pretty hard to pull up yourself by your own bootstraps if you were barefoot. Many colored people did, and miraculously so. They had developed self-help organizations even before the Civil War. After the war, all sorts of lodges, secret orders, Sunday school conventions, and church groups came into existence. The genius of Robert Russo Moton, the entrepreneur Maggie L. Walker, President John Gandy of the Virginia State College for Negroes, and the Slater Fund's W. T. B. Williams was that they were able to forge thirty-one of these disparate groups with overlapping objectives and competing interests into a single organization. The Negro Organization Society was founded in 1911. Dr. Gandy came up with the motto: "Better Homes, Better Farms, Better Schools and Better

Health." The motto was expanded later to include "Better Business" and by 1941 had two more "Betters:" Civic Participation and Jobs. For each of the "Betters," a committee was appointed. The objectives of the organization were reported in the *Southern Workman* in May 1911: "to weld into one unit, for the improvement of the morals, health and education, all the organizations of the race represented in its membership, to unify all the forces for the betterment in any given community."

Robert R. Moton, Norris's friend and mentor, is generally given credit for the founding of the organization, but the idea originated at the annual Hampton Negro Conference, a meeting of leaders of both races begun in 1896 and held at Hampton Institute until 1916. The primary mission of the Hampton Conference was to devise measures to address the dire social and economic conditions facing Southern Negroes.

In 1913, the Negro Organization Society launched a Clean Up Day in Virginia. A booklet entitled *A Health Handbook for Colored People* was published by the Virginia Department of Health in preparation for Clean Up Day. The handbook states that "much of the material used has been prepared by the Negro Organization Society, and many of the suggestions in this bulletin are in the exact language employed by the colored workers most active in the betterment work."

At its annual meetings in 1913 and 1914, the nascent society invited Booker T. Washington to speak. Washington saw in Virginia's Clean Up Day the perfect opportunity to shape his agenda for improving the health of colored Americans. He came up with the idea of a National Negro Health Week. His on-site sociologist at Tuskegee, Monroe Work, had just come up with shocking statistics on the state of Negro health in the South. Forty-five percent of deaths among the colored were preventable. The number of seriously ill colored persons numbered 450,000. Work estimated that the annual cost of sickness of these 450,000 persons was $75 million. The cost of sickness and death of Negroes was estimated to be $100 million. Work came up with an interesting and prescient prediction. He estimated that the consumption by Negroes of pure water, pure air, and pure food could add ten years to their life expectancy.

Ironically, it was Moton's organization that gave Washington the idea of the National Negro Health Week, but Moton, by virtue of replacing Washington at Tuskegee, and persuading the U.S. Public Health Service in 1932 to take over the administrative responsibilities of the event took National Negro Health Week to a new level. Roscoe C. Brown, a colored career staff member at the U.S. Public Health Service, brought aboard Howard University, the National Medical Association, and the National Negro Insurance Association. Brown, a former Richmond dentist, greatly expanded the movement.

Norris, who had been introduced to National Negro Health Week during his internship at Tuskegee, was instrumental in helping shape the focus of the annual event in Lancaster and Northumberland Counties. In 1928, Norris was appointed chairman of the Better Health Committee of the Negro Organization Society, a post that he held for nearly twenty years. The position of chairman of the Better Health Committee gave him a forum from which he could espouse his vision and initiatives for measures to improve the health of the residents of Virginia. It also afforded him contacts with leaders of both races in the state of Virginia. He pushed for better health programs with direct involvement of the citizenry through his association with the Negro Organization Society. Working in tandem with the society, he helped promote the dissemination of health information through posters and talks and encouraged the colored citizens to whitewash their buildings, paint their houses, and clean their yards and homes. Health clubs were formed in Lancaster and Northumberland Counties in the mid 1930s, with ministers and teachers taking a central role in promoting hygienic and preventive health measures.

Norris, along with working with the Negro Organization Society to press for better treatment of Virginia's colored tuberculosis patients (see Chapter 20), pursued another agenda. That was the fight against venereal diseases. Sexually transmitted diseases (euphemistically referred to in the papers at that time as "social diseases") were taking a high toll among Americans, and, just as other diseases, affected Negroes disproportionately. Norris was invited to attend a national Conference on Venereal Disease Control Work held in Washington, D.C., December 28-30, 1936. He was among nine hundred persons from forty-five states, and U.S. territories. The 1937 annual report from the Surgeon General's office reported that the three-day course was attended by "leading clinicians, scientists, private physicians, representatives of volunteer agencies, nurses, social workers, teachers, newspaper reporters, and a great many interested laymen." (An historical note: The conference had a brief report on the study of "Untreated syphilis in the Negro," later to be known as the infamous "Tuskegee experiment.")

An outcome of Norris's attendance at the conference was that on April 13, 1937, he brought to Lancaster County Dr. Otis Anderson of the United States Public Health Service to lecture and present a film on the spread, dangers, and cure of venereal disease. In 1937, Norris could not stage such a presentation in a church and it would have been impolitic to use the school, so he prevailed upon his friend, Negro businessman and entrepreneur Floyd Clark, to hold the session in Clark's Masonic Temple near Kilmarnock. Dr. Elmer R. Moorman, one of the local white physicians, attended. The writer of the "Among the Colored People" column in the *Rappahannock Record* reported that "People crowded into the Masonic Temple ..." to attend the lecture.

Norris's committee chairmanship gave him credibility in dealing with state officials. He gained added leverage through his appointment as a trustee of Hampton Institute and from having been so effectively involved in the education of the youth of Lancaster County. At the society's 1937 annual meeting, he outlined the following objectives:

1. To carry out more fully our Health Program, of vaccination, administration of toxoid and anti-toxin with aid of the State Health and State Board of Education.
2. To wage war, fight and control, as far as possible, venereal disease.
3. Particular effort in the study and prevention of tuberculosis, with an aim toward a sanatorium for tubercular children.

4. Further attempt an effort to establish a home for feebleminded children in the State.
5. A Negro Public Health Nurse in every one of the one hundred counties of Virginia.
6. A larger and broader cooperative effort through all the available forces for a larger Health Program.

The Negro Organization Society was effective for the simple reason that the Negroes of Virginia were determined to make it effective. The members gave fully of their time, energies, and finances. In this, Norris was not unique; he was simply another ant in the ant colony. The officers "not only paid their transportation and living expenses year after year to attend the annual meeting, but have also made significant financial and other personal contributions to see that conditions among Negroes were improved." In 1939, Norris brought the annual meeting of the organization to Lancaster County at White Stone, Virginia.

By the end of the 1940s, Norris had turned over the chairmanship of the Better Health Committee to his colleague, Dr. James B. Blayton, of Williamsburg, Virginia. Norris remained involved with the organization, until the mid-1950s when, depleted and enervated by illness, he was no longer able to serve effectively.

While National Negro Health Week and the health programs of the Negro Organization Society had similar goals, and their programs were interrelated, they were separate. An event took place on February 15, 1951, that had ominous and foreboding repercussions for the Negro Organization Society's health committee. The Federal Security Agency terminated National Negro Health Week. The *Journal of The National Medical Association* reported that the director of the agency, Oscar R. Ewing, stated ending the program was "in keeping with the trend toward integration of all programs for the advancement of the people in the fundamentals of health education and welfare."

The Negro Organization Society soon met a similar fate. With the coming of racial integration in Virginia, the organization lost momentum and direction. It died just about the same time that Norris died, and by the end of the 1970s, it was but a footnote in the annals of Negro history.

CHAPTER 15

Bringing the Specialists to the Patient

D uring the first half of the twentieth century, there were no specialists in Lancaster County, and until 1977, there was no hospital. For those unfortunate people in the lower Northern Neck who required specialty care before 1928, the most accessible facilities were Johns Hopkins Hospital and Provident Hospital in Baltimore. The best hope for the ill was to get to Baltimore via steamboat up the great Chesapeake Bay, just as Norris's own father had done at the turn of the twentieth century. In 1927, a bridge was built across the Rappahannock River at Tappahannock and travel to Richmond was greatly facilitated.

It was difficult and expensive to transport the ill and afflicted to specialists in distant cities, and Richmond was no exception. Few people had automobiles. Emergency medical services did not exist. The closest thing to an ambulance was the undertaker's hearse, and if that were not being used in a funeral then it might be put into service. Norris did the logical thing to help solve this problem: he brought the specialists to the sick. He started his first clinic in 1921, four years after returning to Kilmarnock.

In 1978, Theresita explained how the first clinic was held. It was springtime. Her second child was just four months old. With no prior discussion, Norris told Theresita that his mentor, Dr. John A. Kenney, Sr., was coming for a visit. They had a spare room in the three-room upstairs living quarters, but no bed. Norris went to the local general store and bought a bed for his guest. Kenney arrived on the steamboat as scheduled, and Theresita dutifully prepared dinner for him. Norris was called away to an ill patient during the dinner hour so Theresita was left to dine alone with Kenney.

At one point during the meal Kenney asked Theresita: "Where am I going to keep the patients?"

"What patients?" she asked in astonishment.

Kenney replied: "Didn't Norris tell you I am having a clinic tomorrow? He is having quite a few patients for me to examine, and perhaps I will operate on one or two of them."

"Where?" continued a bewildered Theresita.

Kenney demurred, "I guess in his office."

Theresita continued in utter disbelief, "But we don't have anywhere to keep people."

Kenney begged off offering a solution, replying that he was told to come prepared to perform operations.

The next day, he removed tonsils from three or four patients and examined several ill patients. The post-operative cases were placed for recovery in whatever space could be found—Kenney's new bed, a pallet that had been prepared on top of a cedar chest, and the couch in the dining area. Fortunately, the weather was favorable. Kenney had brought a nurse with him, and Mrs. Sarah Campbell, the local midwife, assisted as well. Theresita told the interviewers with an air of resignation: "Well, we got through that all right. I said to him [Norris] afterwards, 'Before you start any more clinics, I wish you would wait until we get some room.'" Norris told Theresita that they would get the room when they could, but they had to have the clinics. The next specialist to visit was an eye specialist from New York. He stayed for two weeks.

Theresita supported Norris in his clinics, but admits that she was "irked" by the mixing of the medicines near her foods and by having to share her limited quarters and give up her kitchen for the sterilization of the instruments. This arrangement would go on for six more years, until 1927, when Norris built a home "with all modern conveniences" for Theresita and their four children. Four more were still to come!

Norris's first clinics were for eye, ear, nose, and throat cases, although some minor general surgery was performed. By the end of the decade, he had expanded his clinics to include dentistry and the treatment of crippled children and adults with bone diseases and fractures. The specialists were all colored except for one, Dr. Thomas Wheeldon, a Harvard-trained, Richmond orthopedist. The patients were of both races. Although strict segregation was de rigueur in Virginia, once patients set foot on Norris's place, segregation no longer applied. It wasn't that he was above the law, he was only following his dictum: "That which is lawful is not always expedient."

Wheeldon had started a series of regional clinics throughout the state in 1923, and the clinic that he started in December 1929 with Norris became part of his regional network.

In addition to Wheeldon and Kenney, the medical specialists who staffed the clinics were general surgeons Hartford Burwell, M.D., George White, M.D., and Isaiah A. Jackson, Sr., M.D.; an ear, nose, and throat specialist, Ulysses Houston, M.D.; an orthopedic surgeon, Isaiah A. Jackson, Jr., M.D.; and an anesthesiologist, Nathaniel Dillard, M.D. These men were from Washington, D.C., and Richmond. The dentists were Norris's brother-in-law, James A. Chiles, D.M.D., from Richmond; his best friend, Henry A. McAlister, D.M.D., from Hampton; and Grady Poulson, D.M.D., from Middlesex County.

The surgery, orthopedic, and dental clinics were sizeable affairs. Norris's office waiting room and front porch overflowed with patients who spilled into his front and back yards. He purposefully held the surgery clinics in the spring and fall to avoid the stifling heat of the summer and the cutting cold of the winter. The orthopedic and dental clinics were held monthly. Patients and their families began arriving early in the morning, and most did not leave until dark. On approaching the yard surrounding Norris's office during one of the clinics, a passerby might at first sight think that he had stumbled upon a festival because there were so many families with children about. Then, on closer inspection, the subdued atmosphere would tell otherwise. The only criterion for acceptance for treatment was need. Because so many people who required medical attention were poor, payment by the patients was random at best.

The clinics were egalitarian. Norris's family members, as well as leading citizens, were treated. Roberta Russell, whose father was a prominent minister and school principal, poignantly recalls her experience at the clinics seventy-five years later. She was just ten years old at the time.

> I remember going to Dr. Norris's office; the appointment had been made. We knew when Dr. Houston was coming to remove tonsils. … I was, of course, a bit frightened, naturally, as children would be, or anybody else I guess who knew that they were going to be anesthetized. I remember the anesthesia because in those days we had to have ether and that in itself was a frightening process because one whiff and it seems to me you were just out of it, completely. But when I knew anything, the tonsils had been removed, and I was waking up. They took me upstairs, and I lay down and rested. And I probably stayed up there for two or three hours, and I was told that I could have ice cream—I guess it was because of the coldness—but nothing else; you couldn't have anything else to eat. … I got along very, very well. Of course, my throat was sore, naturally. But within a few days, I was almost back to normal. …
>
> … even though we had to undergo an operation, we always liked to go to Dr. Norris's office because to us country children, that was like going to a big city, to a hospital, so it was very exciting. And then, of course, my parents were friends with Dr. and Mrs. Norris, and that made it extra nice.

Roberta also clearly recalls entering the operative theater:

> I can just recall walking in and being rather brave about it. I was never one to fight anything about something that you had to do that was going to be for your own good. I just did it. I didn't cry. Had no problems afterwards whatsoever. …
>
> … Dr. Norris was our doctor, and I can see his face before me so well. He had an upturned mouth, which seemed to be in a perpetual smile. He was always just a loving looking person … and he put you at ease. You weren't afraid when he came around. He had a way of saying, "Well, daughter, let me tell you this. It's going to be alright," and you

believed him even if you were going to be cut up. His very presence reassured you. ... He had such a beautiful smile.

No childhood experience has been with me longer than having been an unwilling candidate for treatment at the ear, nose, throat clinic. And I was not nearly as compliant as Roberta Russell. When I was about five years old, it was decided that I needed to have my tonsils removed. As Dr. Houston and Norris were discussing the necessity for my tonsillectomy, I immediately began plotting how to avoid the snare. (The snare is the name given to the instrument for removal of the tonsils. It is essentially a wire loop passed through a tube connected to a three-holed handle; the loop encircles the tonsil and when the wire is pulled back through the tube, it cleanly amputates the tonsil.) Over and over, I had heard Norris tell the parents of the children who were to have tonsillectomies that they were not to eat or drink anything the morning of surgery. At age five, I did not understand the dangers of a full stomach on anesthesia induction, but I fully understood that if I ate there would be no surgery. Twice, when Houston came for the clinic, I would proudly announce that I had eaten. The third time, my mother awakened before I, and she placed me under her watchful eye until Houston sent for me. I did not go quietly. It was a fight to the operating table and when the ether mask was put on my face I put up a furious struggle, but it was not long before the ether quelled all resistance. I felt as though I were suffocating. Sixty-eight years later, whenever I smell ether, I have total recall of Dr. Nathaniel Dillard, the anesthesiologist, gently tapping on the ether mask and repeating over and over in a dry monotone: "Blow it away, Jimmy."

The tonsillectomy was the most commonly performed surgical procedure at the surgery clinics. Recurrent infections of the tonsils and chronically infected tonsils were the primary indications for removal. After the advent of antibiotics in the 1950s the operation was performed infrequently.

Norris used open-drop ether for general anesthesia over the entire period of his clinics. A gauze mask was put over the face of the patient and ether was dripped onto the mask until the patient was asleep. Ether is now barred from all American hospitals and clinics because of its explosiveness. Yet, for over thirty years, hundreds of patients underwent surgery at Norris's office without a single fatality or a single accident.

Wheeldon's clinic was probably the first integrated clinic in the state of Virginia. Initially, Wheeldon came only to Norris's office. Dr. Jeter Edmonds, a white Kilmarnock physician, saw the wisdom of having a clinic for white patients at his office after observing Norris's clinic. Wheeldon then arranged to the see the white patients at Edmonds's office and the colored patients at Norris's office. Edmonds died on December 13, 1934. Wheeldon then saw all patients at Norris's office. Often, as many white patients had casts and crutches as colored.

Wheeldon's work at the orthopedic clinic, which was held the second Saturday of every month, consisted of consultations, minor orthopedic surgery, and the application, changing, and removal of casts and spicas—the body casts extending from the armpits to the pelvis that are used in treating spinal deformities. In those days, plaster of Paris did not come in the neatly prepared rolls as it now does. The plaster, a fine white powder that looked like flour, came in a tin container about the size of a small drum. It was scooped up and mixed with water in a basin until a gooey mixture was obtained. It was then gently but rapidly kneaded into the muslin wrap that had already been applied to the extremity. By using a circular, smoothing action while working the plaster into the fabric, the doctor would create a marbleized shell. The extremity was held motionless until the plaster set. Fast-setting plaster had not arrived on the scene, so the limb sometimes had to be held steady for as long as ten minutes. The plaster had to be applied in a careful manner to avoid pressure on the skin.

No major orthopedic surgery was performed at the clinics. If surgery were necessary, Wheeldon would arrange for the patient to be admitted to a hospital in Richmond. He would then do the follow-up care at Norris's office.

The clinics were not restricted to Northern Neck residents. Jeanne

Valentine, a resident of Washington, D.C., recalls being brought from her native Washington, D.C., at age seventeen or eighteen (late 1930s) to the clinic for treatment of a heel cord shortening. She said the visit was arranged through her mother's consultation with Norris. Following the initial visit at Norris's clinic, Wheeldon performed the tendon lengthening procedure at Retreat for the Sick Hospital in Richmond. Valentine remembers that the colored patients were all confined to the basement of the hospital that was staffed by only "colored nurses." Nevertheless, she feels she received excellent treatment and said, "Dr. Wheeldon treated me royally." She remembers him as being "kind and compassionate."

Except for Wheeldon, all the surgeons stayed at the Norris home place for several days. These home visits were a boon to Norris, as not only would the surgeons be around should a complication occur, albeit rare, but they gave Norris a chance to interact on a professional level with his surgical colleagues. He would often bring in complicated cases for consultation. The trips to the country had advantages for the surgeon and his spouse as well, for not only did they have the opportunity to get in relaxation and fishing on the Rappahannock River, but they also had a chance to partake of Theresita's legendary culinary talents.

CHAPTER 16

To Build a School: A "Most Difficult Job"

In 1928, when the patrons of the New Kilmarnock School League asked Norris to take over the drive to build a new elementary school, he agreed. At the time he was already juggling too many tasks. He was conducting a full-time medical practice; leading the Northern Neck Progressive Association in staging an annual fair; conducting his surgery and orthopedic clinics; attending continuing medical education programs at Tuskegee, the National Medical Association, and the Old Dominion Medical Society; and chairing the Health Committee of the Negro Organization Society. With these manifold duties, it was neither prudent nor desirable for him to head up the drive for a new school, but as a parent of five children (three more were to arrive), he felt compelled to rise to the challenge. The commitment caused him to exclaim later in a letter to Hampton Institute's president, Arthur Howe, "It was the most difficult job from every angle I ever attempted."

Building the school proved not only difficult but also expensive. The school was nearly completed by mid-1932, but funds had been exhausted. Then Norris even committed some of his personal assets toward the effort. That worried Theresita.

Theresita had every right to be worried. By then she had seven children ranging in age from a few months to thirteen years. It was the height of the depression, and Norris had mortgaged their home for the $2,500 needed to complete the building. To complicate matters, Norris had put up an additional $1,000 of his own money to pay for labor and supplies. The Lancaster County School Board had no money, and there would be no contributions from the Julius Rosenwald Fund, which had pledged to help fund the school. (The Rosenwald Fund had pledged $1,200 to the school, but by 1932, its monies for the school program were depleted. Stock in Rosenwald's company, Sears Roebuck, had fallen from $180 per share to $10 per share in two years.) In desperation, Theresita wrote of their plight to a white acquaintance, Arthur Wright, of the John Slater Fund. Wright had been a principal in the Richmond schools when she was a young teacher. He also had served as [Virginia] state agent for Negro Rural Schools. A letter of support from President Arthur Howe of Hampton Institute to Jackson Davis of John D. Rockefeller's General Education Board helped. Wright responded promptly. He brought to Kilmarnock, Thomas Jesse Jones of the Phelps Stokes Fund, New York; S. L. Smith and Fred McCuistion of the Julius Rosenwald Fund, Nashville; and Walter B. Hill and Jackson Davis, Richmond, Virginia. After consulting with his colleagues, Wright advised Norris that they would provide money to pay off the bank loan, but that they could not do anything about his personal loan. That arrangement was acceptable. (The General Education Board had agreed to fund all the schools to which the Rosenwald Fund had committed—but there was one problem. The new Kilmarnock school was not on the list of schools submitted by the Rosenwald Fund to the Board. But even that hurdle was surmounted. There is considerable correspondence around the contribution to the school in the archives of the General Education Board. Virginia school officials displayed an alarming dereliction in providing the General Education Board with the proper documents so that the $1,200 could be released. The General Education Board almost withdrew the offer. An extension was granted to the state to complete the documents, but only after some rather frantic pleading from Norris.)

With that funding, the school was completed and opened for the 1933-34 school year, ten years after Norris and a colored farmer, Spencer B. Caster, had approached the local school board about building a school. It took four more years and many more rallies before Norris recouped his $1,000.

Had a sociologist wanted to study the utter failure of the "separate but equal" doctrine espoused by the 1896 Supreme Court in its *Plessy v. Ferguson* decision, Lancaster County's school system would have been the perfect laboratory. In the third decade of the twentieth century, the Lancaster County school-age population was tilted toward colored, 1,612 versus 1,325 white. Yet, in the late 1920s and before consolidation of the four four-year and two two-year white high schools in Lancaster County, colored students made do with a single high school. It was called a "training school" at that and would not be approved as a high school until 1931. It was located at the extreme end of the county, while the three white high schools that resulted from consolidation were evenly distributed in the county. White teachers' salaries were nearly double those paid to colored teachers, and expenditures for buildings and equipment were four times as much for whites as for colored.

In Virginia, the education of colored children was simply not a priority of the custodians of public education. While a supposedly free public school system has been in existence since 1870, the state had mandated separate schools for white and Negroes. And until the mid 1930s, if the colored population wanted a school, they had to purchase the land, contribute a major portion of the funds for construction, maintain the schools after they were built, and supplement the teachers' salaries. The school situation for colored citizens in Virginia, as well as the rest of the South, would have been even worse but for the vision of Booker T. Washington and the benevolence of the Jewish philanthropist Julius Rosenwald.

It was against this backdrop of inadequate funding and the dire need for education for colored children that Norris took over the leadership of building an elementary school. The new school would replace a crumbling old two-room schoolhouse located one mile south of the village of Kilmarnock that he had attended as a child and a one-room school in Mars Hill, a colored community just west of Kilmarnock.

The campaign to build a school for the colored children had started in 1925 under the prodding of the venerable and esteemed colored minister and leader, Rev. Daniel Harrison Chamberlayne. The campaign moved forward by fits and starts until the leadership of the New Kilmarnock School League was given to Norris. The *Rappahannock Record* reported at the top of its front page

JULIUS ROSENWALD

Booker T. Washington must be given credit for persuading Julius Rosenwald, the president of the Sears Roebuck Company and the man who more than anyone else brought retail merchandizing into just about every household in America, to devote his energies and considerable wealth toward building primary and secondary schools for Negroes throughout the South. During a period of twenty years, 1912 to 1932, Rosenwald contributed to building 5,357 new schools in 883 counties across fifteen southern states through his fund. In Virginia, Rosenwald schools were built in seventy-nine of the ninety-five counties.

The fund's focus widened in 1928 to include coverage of medical services for poor Americans, assistance to colored students in medical education, and fellowships that benefited many fledgling artists and scholars such

on September 13,1928: "$5000 DRIVE NOW ON FOR COLORED SCHOOL." He summoned the biggest guns he could find for his inaugural push. Dr. Robert R. Moton, principal of Tuskegee Institute, came from Alabama. Virginia State Senator Robert O. Norris of Lancaster County and W. S. Brent, the superintendent of the Lancaster and Northumberland schools, were on the program.

Eleven acres of land were purchased from the estate of W. C. Currell and deeded on March 1, 1930, to the colored trustees of the school: a minister, Hovey R. Young; an undertaker, Robert Campbell; three farmers, Travis Robbins, William J. Wiggins, and Charles Towles; and Norris. Two of the six signatories on the deed signed their names with "Xs." They were illiterate.

Construction of the school began in late summer of 1930, just about two years after the committee had launched the drive for $5,000. The contractor was a local man, John Q. Garrett. The school was built on the "Rosenwald plan"— the architectural plan promulgated by the Julius Rosenwald Fund. The school was built almost entirely by funds raised from the patrons, from contributions from Lancaster County's colored and white residents, and from people in cities and towns in Alabama, Maryland, Missouri, New York, Pennsylvania, and Tennessee.

The creativity that was brought to fundraising would be the envy of any enterprise. The New Kilmarnock School League held quartet performances, dollar rallies, and assorted contests as Marian Anderson, Gordon Parks, and Ralph Ellison. Rosenwald died in 1932, and the stipulations of his will called for the fund to be terminated twenty-five years after his death.

An interesting historical note: Rosenwald, who had the brain of a capitalist but the heart of a socialist, offered to America in the 1930s a paradigm for universal medical care, but he was no match for the muscular opposition of organized medicine.

and carnivals. Chicken rallies were conducted where the patrons would each bring a chicken. When enough chickens were obtained, they would be shipped to the market in Richmond. The league periodically published lists of contributors in the local paper, along with the amount given and how the contributions were spent. No contribution went unacknowledged.

As costs for the project escalated, the school committee had no qualms about admonishing the citizens to give more. In a plea for contributions published in the *Rappahannock Record* June 18, 1931, it lamented:

> To build a school of this type requires sacrifice. Although we have spent over $7,500 on land and building the County Board hasn't as yet assisted us in any way. We are in a strait. If the building is closed in and a subfloor laid we can use it for entertainments to raise money. We can do this if every interested person will contribute to this cause. This is no one man's problem, we must pull together to put this project over.

Norris solicited from whomever he knew, and no one was exempt. Even the Norris children were encouraged to contribute their savings toward the school fund. The Bunkers, for whom Norris had worked, Mrs. Alfred I. duPont, white citizens in Lancaster County, every pharmaceutical company, or, for that matter, any company that he dealt with were all contributors. Nor did

Norris have any reservations about returning to his benefactors for further contributions.

In September 1928, business was humming merrily along on Wall Street, and almost no one had the slightest presentiment or forewarning that economic calamity was one month away! Nor did the New Kilmarnock School League realize that $5,000 would be about one-third the amount required to complete the school. Although Chamberlayne had written in his weekly column that "God helps the people who help themselves and so does the School Board," he had no way of knowing, at that time, that he was fifty percent off the mark. He was right about God, but pathetically wrong about the school board. Little help would come from the board.

During the five years that the patrons struggled to complete the school, Norris headed a group that went before the Lancaster County School Board and literally begged that the board borrow monies from the Literary Fund, a fund established in Virginia from fines and escheats solely for the purpose of financing school construction. Norris's committee came away empty-handed.

After relief finally did come, Norris, in a letter to Howe, gave Howe and Moton credit for persuading the Slater Fund and the General Education Board to come to the rescue; however, without a doubt it was Theresita's letter that had provided the stimulus.

Just before the fall session of 1933, the committee announced that the school was complete except for painting and the installation of amenities such as a water cooler and shades. Notices went out to the patrons of the new school that help was needed to prepare for opening—"women to clean the building and men to clean the grounds." A dedication service was planned for October 22, and the keynote speaker was to be Dr. Sidney B. Hall, superintendent of Public Instruction. Ironically, he had selected as his subject "Equality of Educational Opportunity in Virginia." He failed to appear at the dedication exercises to deliver that speech. We are left to imagine what he planned to say to the colored patrons and the teachers.

The school opened under the stewardship of Rev. George S. Russell, with Miss Julia Anne Beane and Miss Elsie Byrd as the new teachers, all college graduates and all solid instructors. Russell was a Baptist minister and pastor of the Mount Vernon Baptist Church in White Stone, Virginia. The community was fortunate that he had just arrived in the county in 1928 to take over the pastorship of the church. Tall, urbane, with a striking baritone delivery of impeccable cadence, he could not have arrived on the scene at a more propitious time. He led the community of White Stone in helping with the numerous drives to raise money for the new school.

Russell had been trained as a minister at Virginia Union University's School of Theology. Not only did he know how to organize and run a church, which he did exceedingly well, but he also knew how to organize a school and how to teach. His philosophy was that education begins at home, and there were no better examples of exemplary students than those of his own children, who were consistently on the honor rolls, consistently involved in school and church activities, and consistently scoring at the top on intelligence tests. Russell demanded no less from his charges than his own children. He was a strict disciplinarian, not that it was often needed. Miss Byrd, the first and second grade teacher, who later taught grades three through seven also, was even stricter. She gave no quarter. When the little first graders trooped into her class on those crisp October mornings (the colored elementary schools did not start until October 1, fully two weeks behind the white schools) the introduction to learning and decorum that they got was akin to a baptism. (The author had his entire grade school education under Miss Byrd. Seven years!)

The school set a new standard for elementary schools in the county. A Parent-Teachers Association was organized in the spring of 1933. Oratorical contests, spelling bees, debates, children's plays, and pageants became standard fare.

The financial input from the Lancaster County School Board had been minimal, but before the state would certify the school as part of the county educational system, it required the league to deed the land and building to the county. This was done. Nearly eight acres of the eleven acres that had been acquired were deeded to the Lancaster County School Board along with the school building. This stipulation had to be met before teachers would be assigned to the school.

At the dedication of the school, the first brick school for colored children in the Northern Neck, the exterior had been completed, but the interior required painting. Shortly after the dedication ceremony, Norris was told that the contract for the painting had been awarded to the Kilmarnock Planing Mill. The mill was owned and operated by Mrs. Helen Davis and her sons. Norris was present the day Mrs. Davis sent the painters and was astonished to find that she had sent only white painters. He immediately voiced his objection to Mrs. Davis about not having hired any colored painters. She responded that the school board had given her the contract and she was free to hire whomever she wanted. Norris said: "I looked straight into her blue eyes and said, 'Mrs. Davis, when there is a principle involved, I will die for it! We have capable painters in our race, and we built that school with our sweat and I demand that you hire Negro painters!' " Negro painters were hired.

The impact of the stately brick building, high on a hill, with four classrooms and an auditorium—modern in every respect—energized the community. The large auditorium was ideal for political meetings, social meetings, and entertainment such as plays and movies. Just as the building was completed, the Roosevelt Administration embarked on a number of initiatives to provide employment for the citizens. Under the Public Works Administration, a recreation center was established at the school. Programs were initiated for children up to twelve years of age. A preschool and kindergarten were set up for the four- and five-year-olds. Sewing classes were started, and even adult education classes were held in the evenings.

The unveiling of the school name took place December 16, 1934, at an elaborate ceremony. The new name was The Morgan E. Norris Graded School. The Health Clubs of Lancaster County presented a portrait of Norris done by the renowned Negro portraitist and Theresita's friend, Gwendolyn Brown of Brown's Studio of Richmond, Virginia. The portrait now hangs in the Lancaster County Courthouse.

From the first day that any pupil enrolled in the school, the parents of that child would know that the pupil would receive as fine an education as could be had. It set a new paradigm for what a school ought to be through a strong Parent-Teachers Association and programs such as a community library, community recreation center, and a strong athletic program. And when World War II came, and there was a national drive for home gardening, Morgan E. Norris Graded School also had a garden. Randolph Grimes, a farmer and a patron, contributed the fertilizer.

The new school also had a galvanizing effect on the entire community. The colored patrons had built four schools between 1920 and 1923 with supplemental funds from the Rosenwald Fund and the county. After that, no new schools were built for colored children for nearly ten years until The Morgan E. Norris Graded School was completed. Shortly afterwards, in 1934, the whites in Ottoman got a school. By July 1935, the Lancaster County School Board had decided to build the Mount Jean Elementary School for Negroes in Weems, Virginia. This $15,000 brick school building was built with funds from the Literary Fund and the Public Works Administration. The patrons were not completely free of all responsibility, though. They were expected to contribute monies toward paying for desks.

In 1954, the U.S. Supreme Court ruled in *Brown v. Board of Education* that school segregation was unconstitutional. In the ensuing years, Virginia's white leadership mounted a "massive resistance" effort. It was led by Virginia's U.S. Senator Harry Flood Byrd, Sr., and implemented to some extent by Governor Lindsey J. Almond, Jr. Some schools were ordered closed rather than integrate the races, and those in Prince Edward County remained closed for five years! The ill-conceived policy wilted in the face of a concerned and reasoned citizenry and under the relentless onslaught of legal maneuvers led by the brilliant and intrepid attorney, Samuel W. Tucker, husband of Theresita's first cousin, Julia Jeter. The issue of segregated schools in Virginia was laid to rest with the decision of the U.S. Supreme Court in *Green v. New*

Kent. A creative attempt had been made by whites to circumvent *Brown v. Board of Education* in Virginia through the assignment of white and colored pupils to schools by a State Pupil Placement Board. The plan was given the rather incongruous title, "freedom of choice." The test case was in New Kent County. Tucker argued for the petitioners, and in the most momentous ruling on segregation in public schools since the Brown decision, "freedom of choice" was ruled unconstitutional.

In August 1966, the Lancaster County School Board made the decision to close the Morgan E. Norris Graded School, less than three months after Norris had died and 33 years after it was built. On May 14, 1968, the school board passed resolutions to sell the Morgan E. Norris and A. T. Wright Schools (the then closed colored high school) at public auction. Theresita wrote a poignant letter July 9, 1968, to the Lancaster County School Board asking that $5,000 of the proceeds of the sales of the schools be set aside for scholarships for Lancaster County students. Race was not mentioned in the letter. She ended her letter with a moving plea after chronicling details of the struggles that the patrons had endured in building of the school:

> Now we have read that both of the forementioned schools are to be sold in the near future at public auction. We can do nothing about that but as a taxpayer and a citizen who has spent years helping to improve conditions here, I am making this request and I am sure it will be endorsed by many of the older citizens of the County.
>
> The sum of $5000.00 if invested will give at least $250.00 annually and I should like to ask if you will give $5000.00 from the sale of these schools to the Teachers Association to be used to give annual scholarships to children of Lancaster County.

Her request was denied. The building with seven acres of land was sold to Joseph B. Packett, Jr., at public auction December 21, 1968, for the paltry sum of $6,600, less than half the cost of the construction. Today, the building is a Jehovah's Witnesses Kingdom Hall.

CHAPTER 17

Free Bus Transportation for Colored Students

Norris, in his own words, "lurched from one crisis to another." In 1939, he took on the Lancaster County School Board over free bus transportation for the colored children. The problem of who should pay for the transport of the colored public school students—the parents or the school board—was like an old wound that had been festering for a long time.

Although the white and colored student populations of Lancaster County were about equal during the 1930s, even after consolidation of the high schools, a school for white students remained in each of the villages of Lively, Kilmarnock, and White Stone. They were rather evenly located in the county. The single colored school, the A. T. Wright High School, was located at the southeastern end of the county.

Transportation to the white schools was free. Some white students did walk long distances, but those who rode buses did not have to pay. Free bus transportation for whites had started in 1923. For the colored students, there were essentially four ways that they could travel to A. T. Wright High School: by foot, private bus, horse and buggy, or the rare automobile. Our neighbor, Narvel Wiggins, a colored farmer and an insurance agent, started the first private bus for colored children in 1931. Two other colored owners, Herbert Ball and the Smith brothers, later joined him.

Effie Jenkins Stroud, a graduate of A. T. Wright High School's class of 1935, said she walked to school every day—two miles each way—except when it rained. On rainy days her father would take her and her four sisters to school by horse and buggy.

Dorothy Norris Cowling, a resident of Lancaster, Virginia, who also graduated from A. T. Wright in 1935 recalls her perfect attendance record once was in jeopardy because of a snowstorm. There was no transportation so she started walking to school despite her parents' concern. She had resolved not to miss a day of school. On her way to the main highway, a car stopped and offered her a ride. Norris was the driver. He was returning from a house call in her neighborhood. He was so impressed with her determination that he drove her to A. T. Wright. She graduated with her perfect attendance record intact.

Ten years after the whites got free bus transportation, the colored parents asked for free bus transportation. Theodore Williams, a colored resident, presented a petition to the board in April 1933, "requesting the board to furnish transportation to the Negro children of the county to the various schools of the county beginning next session." The board declined to act on the petition.

Four more years elapsed before the parents went before the board again. The minutes of the Lancaster County School Board from April 13, 1937, recorded that a patron had appeared before the board "requesting them to provide transportation for the Negro high school students for sessions 1936-1937. The board took his request under consideration and will give a decision at a later meeting."

The board had already been moved to help the parents cobble together some semblance of a bus system. Rev. D. H. Chamberlayne wrote about this clumsy effort on April 22, 1937, in his column "Among the Colored People" in the *Rappahannock Record*. He was an iron-willed little man, and a perpetual smile on his face masked an implacable resolve. He had an inimitable way of intentionally understating problems to make a point. A person would have to be pretty dense to miss the insinuation in this paragraph that appeared in his column in the *Record*:

> Thirty-five children from the A. T. Wright High school are out of school this week. Until last year children have been transported by private buses and cars. In the fall of 1935 the Board gave a chassis and the P.T.A. [Parent-Teachers' Association] gave a body and operated one

of the buses. The other bus, privately owned, needs a license and tires and the owner is unable to purchase either just now. The parents are meeting the different board members this week to discuss this matter and to suggest plans for improving conditions here for our children.

On May 11, 1937, Wright, the principal of the colored high school, appealed for help before the board. The board "advised him they would not consider transportation until the next meeting. Professor Wright presented bills to the school board for transportation, and the board voted to disburse an amount toward the bills not to exceed $100." This was like putting a Band-Aid on a broken arm.

The little dance around free bus transportation would continue between the school board and parents. Paying twenty-five cents per pupil per day for bus transportation was an onerous burden for most of the parents in Lancaster County and some families had several children of high school age. The Depression was full-blown and unrelenting. A rare student, if any, had a car during those years. Few families had a telephone or indoor toilets, let alone some type of private transportation. In 1937, Norris had three children who were riding the bus to school.

For the next two years, the parents dutifully carried their requests to the school board, but they met with a stolidly resistant attitude. By the summer of 1939, the colored parents had reached a consensus on the issue: they would demand free bus transportation.

The August 8, 1939, minutes of the Lancaster County School Board reported:

A delegation of Negro citizens appeared before the board requesting that the transportation of Negro children be increased equal to that of [w]hite children. The board gave this request very careful consideration and decided to have the bus which was used for transportation last year put in first class repair and to furnish oil and gas for same during the session and keep the bus in good repair with the understanding that the Negroes will employ and pay the driver.

This was not exactly what the "Negro citizens" had in mind, and the school board decision, short of what was expected, was patently unacceptable. The parents called a meeting at Chamberlayne's New Saint John's Baptist Church on a Sunday evening in early September, to plan strategy. Norris gave an impassioned speech before the group and called for a boycott of the schools. He urged the other parents to stand fast with him. At the end of his speech he thundered with climactic resolve: "Before I pay another cent for a child of mine to ride a school bus to school, hell will freeze over!!" In 1939, "hell" was considered profane. No one had ever heard Norris curse, and certainly not in a church. His statement electrified the parents.

The following morning, the yellow buses rumbled along the dusty country roads but found no students to carry to school. One school bus driver came to our home and told Theresita that he would carry the Norris children free of charge if Norris would call off the boycott. Theresita politely declined his offer. It was only a matter of hours before the school board capitulated. Chamberlayne's distinctive column in the *Rappahannock Record*, known for its coverage of important events in the county, carried not one word about the meeting. Nor was there a report in the *Record*. Two sentences in the Lancaster County School Board minutes of September 8, 1939, dryly reflected the capitulation:

> Margaret Kenner was appointed to drive the Negro school bus from Bertram section to the New Negro school and below Queen Ester to the New Negro school at a salary of $15 per month.

> The board upon motion duly made and carried decided to allow Herbert Ball $60 for the transportation of Negro school children.

CHAPTER 18

"We Will Have Our Own Fair"

"**F**or Whites Only." Three words on the 1926 Chesapeake Fair Program jumped off the page and hit Norris with the force of a lightning bolt. He wasted no time in confronting the chairman of the fair at his store and demanding an explanation. "Oh, Doctor, we didn't mean you and your family. Why, y'all would be welcome." Norris was not mollified; he was insulted. His lips tightened, his nostrils flared, his eyes narrowed to slits: "Let me tell you Mister, anywhere I go, my people will go. We don't need your fair. We will have a fair as big and as fine as any you have ever had." He tossed the program into the merchant's face and spun around to exit the store as he fired this volley of words to the stunned merchant: "… and I will never put my foot in this store again as long as I live." He didn't.

This outburst led to the launching of the new Afro-American Fair that opened in the fall of 1927. The fair ran for over thirty years and outlasted the Chesapeake Fair by a quarter of a century. Norris gave a written account of the imbroglio twenty-seven years later in a letter to two of the shareholders of the Afro-American Fair, Mrs. Annie B. Wright and W. H. Dudley:

> Our group was told frankly that the so called Negro fair would be operated by one of their stockholders, and that would be for us and the Chesapeake Fair would be operated for "White Only" and we might be only admitted as servants and certified by some white person. This made some of our blood boil. The men who opposed such a move openly and inwardly were, as I recall, your husband [referring to Mr. Wright], Spencer Caster, John Watkins and Allen Williams. I, of course, opposed the dastardly movement to such an extent when the Manager presented me a book of the Fair, in all good faith and the first words

inside were for "White Only," I, in anger, threw it in his face, told him that it was not for me, walked out of his store and never put foot inside the building or the store as long as he operated for a number of years after. So there is a long history to the "old sore."

Fairs have existed for centuries. There is hardly a culture on the planet that does not have some version of a fair. In the early 1800s, fairs in this country added the display of crafts, culinary arts, farm produce, and farm animals. Fairs were usually held after the fall harvest and commonly ran for several days. Families could enjoy the merry-go-round, which was introduced in the eighteenth century; the Ferris wheel, which was introduced in 1893; games; displays; horse racing; and foot races.

The Chesapeake Fair started in Lancaster County in 1886. And long before the 1927 fair that Norris helped launch, the first Afro-American Fair started in Lancaster County in 1889, when Norris was just six years old. The last description of the fair that could be located appeared in the *Virginia Citizen* in 1911. In 1895, this description of the sixth annual Afro-American Fair was reported in the local newspaper, the *Virginia Citizen*:

> The Afro-Americans of Lancaster County held their sixth annual fall fair on their fairgrounds at Road View, Va., Thursday, Friday, and Saturday, Oct. 24, 25, and 26, 1895, under the management of L. R. Fleming. It was one of the most successful fairs ever held in every respect ... with Miss Minnie, the Houchee-couchee dancer as a center of attraction.

Fairs were much more than hoochie-coochie dancers. This article skewed too far toward frivolity. While entertainment was a feature at most fairs, great emphasis was placed on farmers exhibiting their produce and ladies exhibiting their handicrafts and canned foods. The major role of the fair was summarized by the sociologist John Malcus Ellison in his work on *Negro Organizations and Leadership in Relationship to Rural Life in Virginia*, published in 1933:

The primary purpose of the fair is to bring to the public the advancement of the agricultural and educational program that is being conducted throughout the county. It further attempts to prove to the public that quality as well as quantity is essential in making farm products more profitable.

The emphasis on farm products at the fairs is understandable when one considers that farming was such an integral part of life in the rural South. Organizations were formed to promote the newest farming techniques and to encourage increased productivity and improved quality in farm products. The colored colleges, Hampton Institute and Virginia State College for Negroes, had extensive agricultural training programs. Conferences on farming were encouraged, and organizations for the youth such as the 4-H Clubs and New Farmers of America were formed.

C. Jackson Simmons, in his documentation of life in Lancaster County during the 1890s, described the agricultural fairs, which "were held throughout the decade." His description wasn't as colorful as the *Virginia Citizen*'s coverage of the Afro-American Fair, "with a wide variety of simple entertainment for all ages: bicycle and trotting races, hunting races, tugs-of-war, pig chases, foot races, potato races, shooting matches, balloon ascension and parachute descents." Additionally, mule races apparently attracted a great deal of interest. Merchants' exhibits and exhibits of handiwork, cooking, canning, and preserving were held with awards for the winners in each category.

It is common lore that the decision to bar colored people from the Chesapeake Fair sprung from an unfortunate incident at the fair in 1926. It is alleged that two colored men had gotten into a fight and that one fellow was injured. The reaction of the fair committee was swift! A policy was immediately set thereafter barring colored from the fair. While it was rumored that the altercation was the genesis of the "For Whites Only" policy, the order may have resulted from the Massenberg Act, passed by the General Assembly on March 22, 1926, "requiring the separation of the white and colored persons at … places of public entertainment and public assemblages."

After his explosive tirade at the Chesapeake Fair's president, Norris set about to organize the Northern Neck Progressive Association and to acquire the land for the fair. He gathered a group of eight men and two women to form the Northern Neck Progressive Association. The two women were Mrs. Monroe and Mrs. Bessie Gray, wife of Shedrick Gray. The men were the Lancaster training school principal, A. T. Wright (the state did not certify the school as a high school until 1931); the agriculture teacher, W. H. Dudley; justice of the peace and store owner, Leonard R. Fleming; and Norris. Additionally, Llewellyn L. Montague, Charles Preston Bromley, W. R. Lewis, M. C. Seamon, and J. Allen Williams were brought aboard. The association bought a 33½-acre tract of land on the highway about midway between Kilmarnock and Lancaster and, by the fall of 1927, held its first fair.

Putting together a group and acquiring the land for the fairgrounds proved a lot more difficult than Norris had anticipated. Had not he engaged in some rather persuasive arguments, his vow to the build a fair might have rung as hollow as an echo. Years later he recounted his tribulations in a 1954 letter to Wright's widow:

> When I picked the location, had it approved by Professor Wright and Mr. Allen Williams, paid the down payment and felt we were all set, Mr. Caster said he was highly in favor but he would have to consider at his age. Mr. Watkins had me to come to him three times and said "No." I then turned to my staunch friend Allen Williams who said he thought I better see "Wright" but he was in accord. My last resort was to your dear husband who did not fail me. We had already received notice that there were two cash buyers, so our purchase was not obligatory or practically desired and my fee as a down payment would be returned. I hurried to Prof. Wright with this information and he said, God bless him, "We will buy it." Then if I remember correctly, he brought in strong young men as Dudley, Lewis, Seamon, and Lou Montague. I still was on the bandwagon and secured the aid of Mr. Flemmings [*sic*], Mrs. Gray, also Mrs. Monroe. I have failed to tell you that I thought in my stepmother I had the "last word," but she said, "My boy, I am too old to go into horse racing."

In the fall of 1927 there were three fairs: the Chesapeake Fair for whites, a fair that was sponsored by the whites for the colored people, and the Afro-American Fair. In the article, "Among the Colored People," in the *Rappahannock Record*, the following commentary on the 1927 Afro-American Fair was written:

Last week there were two fairs held in our county for colored people. The one under white managers was a total failure; while the other run by the Northern Neck Progressive Association was attended by tremendous crowds every day. This proves conclusively that the colored people prefer a fair managed by their people. Those who attempted to stage a fair in opposition to their fair do not know our people. Had they consulted us we would have told them that the result would be a "flat tire."

The following year, after the second annual Afro-American Fair, Rev. D. H. Chamberlayne wrote in his weekly column in the *Rappahannock Record* in 1928: "Breaking a vow of twenty or more years we attended the fair last week. We went, we saw, we were conquered. The Northern Neck Progressive Association Fair was a credit to our people. Dr. Morgan E. Norris, President; Professor A. T. Wright, Secretary; and L. R. Fleming, General Manager; deserve praise for the splendid exposition." After the 1927 split, the Chesapeake Fair had a far shorter life than the Afro-American Fair. In September 1932, the *Rappahannock Record* reported on its front page in a bold, large font: "WILL NOT HAVE FAIR THIS YEAR, Stockholders Decide That It Would Not Be Profitable At The Present Time." It would have been the forty-sixth annual fair. The nation was gripped by a severe depression, and a number of fairs throughout the state had been cancelled. The Northern Neck Progressive Association pressed on and held a successful fair. The reason for the success of the Northern Neck Progressive Association's fair may have been that the fair was not run for profit. One year later, the *Record* was to report in a mournful headline: "CHESAPEAKE FAIR TO BE NO MORE, Stockholders In Meeting Here Monday Decided To Abandon Charter of Association." The writer went on to report that "several of the county fairs in the state were not held last year and many of them are not being held again this year." The Chesapeake Fair was never again held in Lancaster County, although horse racing was held at the white fairgrounds in tandem with the races held at the Afro-American Fair.

Norris was a great lover of harness racing and felt that a fair could not be complete without it. Harness racing or trotting racing is a race where the horse pulls a two-wheeled carriage with a driver. The vehicle is called a sulky. The horse is a Standardbred compared to a Thoroughbred, the horse that races with a saddled rider. The Standardbred is a longer, lower horse, heavier legged and more durable than the Thoroughbred. The races are held on oval tracks just as Thoroughbred racing. A half-mile race track was included in the layout of the fairgrounds, and a grandstand was built for viewing the races. Norris visited Warsaw, Suffolk, and as far as Westbury, New York, to engage horse racing groups. The Northern Neck Progressive Association was a member of the U.S. Trotting Association, and it met all the requirements for horse racing under the umbrella of that organization. Once, Norris had Mr. L. L. Trice, vice chairman and director, District 7 of the U. S. Trotting Association, come for a visit "to outline the best setup we might have in the races." He also brought down the president of the Virginia Association of Fairs. No formal betting was done at the races; betting was not legal in Virginia at that time. The men gathered in groups and bet among themselves on their favorite horses. The owners of the horses were paid a set rate for bringing their horses to the fair. The money to pay them was raised by charging an admission fee to the races.

Nearly forty-five years after the last fair, Mrs. Alice Dameron, the former Northumberland County school teacher and a nonagenarian related with nostalgia: "At the fair, homemakers were encouraged to exhibit their canned products and handicrafts. Prizes were awarded for the best displays. That gave the homemaker something to look forward to."

Norris could be ultra-sensitive about his pet projects—such as the fair—and did not like to be challenged about them. Gwendolyn Jones recalls an incident that happened shortly after she had married Thornton, Norris's oldest son, in 1952, and had moved to Kilmarnock. At that time, she was the home demonstration agent for Lancaster County. Norris was making preparations for a big fair at the fairgrounds, busily lining up events and exhibits. Norris had asked that Gwen coordinate the ladies' exhibits of their artwork and crafts, but there was a problem that required immediate attention—the roof to the exhibits area was leaking. Gwen was sitting with Theresita in the kitchen of our home discussing the situation when Norris walked in. Gwen, who was all of five feet and weighed in at 110 pounds, spoke in the rapid-fire cadence of a Northerner. She was startlingly candid. She proceeded to lecture Norris: "Listen, Doctor, if you don't have that roof repaired, I am not going to let my ladies bring their wares, embroidery, and articles and have them ruined by a leaking roof." Norris, shocked by this verbal assault, stormed out of the kitchen slamming the door. Theresita was amused. She told Gwen he was not accustomed to anyone speaking so directly to him. But what did Gwen know; she said she had always freely expressed her opinions. Norris never said another word, but in his characteristically pragmatic approach to problems, he had the roof repaired by opening day.

Earlier, Norris had faced another challenge concerning his fair. He was determined that the fair would be a superb recreational event with rides and games, horse races, and arts and crafts displays, but what was most important to him was the opportunity to advance his main agenda, education. He always included an Education Day in the program. He often invited dignitaries such as Virginia State Senator R.O. Norris and college presidents to speak to the audience.

The year was 1950 and an Education Day was planned. The president of Hampton Institute had been invited to speak, and he had agreed to bring the Hampton Institute Marching Band. There was one gigantic problem: an Education Day would be meaningless if the colored students in the Lancaster and Northumberland County schools could not attend. When told that the superintendent of the schools, R. E. Brann, would not permit the students to attend, Norris was apoplectic. He hurried to the school board office to plead his case with Mr. Brann, a man whom Norris viewed with no particular affection. Brann was unyielding. He contended that the schedule had been made for the year, and the request to have the students attend Education Day came too late for the schedule to be changed. In view of the late request, he could not, and would not, close the colored schools. Norris was furious, but he knew when all avenues were closed. He told Brann: "All right, well dammit, we are having another fair one year from now, and today I am giving you an entire year's notice!"

The fairgrounds were not only used for fairs, but also for athletic events, car racing, mass meetings, and twin-county (Lancaster and Northumberland) May Day school festivities. In the summertime, the grounds became a baseball field. During World War II, the all-colored baseball team from the U. S. Army's Camp Lee in Petersburg even came to Lancaster. Norris, despite having never set foot on an athletic field of any type, was a great lover of sports. And he was a great believer in the redeeming qualities of athletic competition.

World War II caused cancellation of the fairs. In 1942, a fair was not held for the first time in fifteen years. The post-war fairs never gained the momentum of the pre-war fairs, although they ran until 1959.

In 1952, the Lancaster County School Board eyed the fairgrounds as a site for a new colored high school. The superintendent of the Lancaster and Northumberland School Boards sent Norris a letter in February 1952, in which the School Board of Lancaster County asked Norris for sale of the fairgrounds for a "central Negro high school." Norris penned a note to the bottom of the letter and returned it to the superintendent, R. E. Brann: "I regret to advise that the Fair Grounds are not for sale. There is a tract, I understand, owned by the county known as the 'Poor House' tract that might be available and desirable." The school board persisted, and had the school board attorney contact the shareholders of the fairgrounds.

Norris wrote a letter to Lawyer Ammon Dunton, Lancaster County's Attorney: "There has been no agreement to my knowledge about a definite sale. The property was purchased twenty-five years ago for healthy recreation for our people, the only place of its kind in the section. We have looked forward with the hope that this might supply a very much needed place in the life of the people." He did not fail to let Dunton, and by proxy the Lancaster County School Board, know that he was unhappy with the attention given to the Morgan E. Norris Elementary School: "For your information, when we needed an elementary school, we bought a location, built the second brick school in the county and paid an initial sum of $250 for seats. It has been my deep personal regret that so many needed improvements have been neglected in keeping up this very important gift."

Norris knew the fairgrounds could be acquired by eminent domain, but not a single member of that school board, nor its attorney, had any great appetite to tangle with Norris. No sane man would voluntarily step into a hornet's nest, and the school board knew trying to wrest the fairgrounds from Norris would be tantamount to just that. The board backed down on the pursuit of the property. A parcel was acquired in the vicinity of the fairgrounds, and a high school for the colored students was completed in 1959. A. T. Wright High School closed the same year. The students were brought to the new school, the Brookvale High School, but the name A. T. Wright was left behind. There is now a marker at the sight of the A. T. Wright High School.

Following the decision of *Green v. New Kent* in 1968 and the collapse of "massive resistance" to school integration in Virginia, the school board would soon need a site for a high school for the entire county. The county built a high school for all the children of Lancaster County on property it already owned near the Lancaster County Courthouse, just as Norris had suggested.

CHAPTER 19

An Angel: Jessie Ball duPont

I t helps to have an angel, and Norris found one in a most paradoxical person, Jessie Ball duPont. She was a unique lady—a wealthy, complex, opinionated Southern white woman who carried very definite ideas about the place that colored people belonged. Yet she knew no boundaries of color in assisting the ill and afflicted. She gave generously to Norris's patients and his projects for thirty-six years. Over that same period they carried on an energetic correspondence around her charitable efforts.

For much of Norris's career he got little aid from social services. Public welfare did not come to Lancaster County until 1938, and even after that, the responses of social services to the indigent were feeble at best. Virtually no one had health insurance. Medicaid and Medicare did not exist. (The Medicare and Medicaid programs were signed into law by President Lyndon Johnson in 1965.) The definition of "safety-net," a social services backup of last resort for the needy, had not entered the lexicon. There was one individual, however, who would provide services for the people of the lower Northern Neck from the late 1920s on—Jessie Ball duPont. She was a native of the Northern Neck, and wife of Alfred I. duPont of Nemours, Delaware, and more than anyone, contributed financially to the health and welfare of the white and colored citizens of Lancaster and Northumberland Counties.

Jessie Ball was born in 1884 in Balls Neck, Virginia, near the little village of Ditchley in Northumberland County about four miles from Kilmarnock. Though she grew up less than six miles from Norris and was one year younger, it is doubtful that they ever met each other, given the mores of the period. She was white; he was colored. But had he been white, and had he known her as a child, that would have been about as far as the acquaintance would have gone anyhow. She was from an old-line family; he was not. She was a distant relative of George Washington, and her father fought in the Civil War—for the South. Her family had not been wealthy, but they were much involved in the social life of the Northern Neck. Her mother was a founder of the Holly Ball, an annual end-of-the-year ritual of pomp, parade, and promenade that remains, to this day, popular among the white upper crust of the Northern Neck. Norris was of lesser stock. His father was a poor farmer who owned a small plot of land, and even had he been white, he would not have been in the Balls's class.

At age fifteen, Jessie was sent off to school at the State Female Normal School (Longwood College) in Farmville, Virginia. After one year her father sent her to Wytheville Academy located in the little village of Wytheville, Virginia, southwest of Roanoke in the Blue Ridge Mountains and about 275 miles from home. She was able to get a teaching certificate after one year and returned to the Northern Neck to teach school in Lively, Lancaster County. Despairing of the life of "genteel poverty" in the Northern Neck as was so aptly put by her biographer, Richard Greening Hewlett, in 1908 she took her parents to San Diego to join her brother Tom who had moved there four years earlier. Shortly after arriving on the West Coast, she started a job as a substitute teacher and by 1915 had worked her way up to assistant principal of a large school—a major accomplishment for a woman in the early twentieth century. Jessie was busily working on other matters as well. She was helping to support her parents, she had an active social calendar, she had sharpened her business acumen by astute investments, and she carried on a correspondence with Alfred I. duPont whom she had met when was just a young girl of fifteen years old. (duPont, twenty years her senior, had come with two companions to hunt in the isolated area where her family lived in the Northumberland County. He had docked his yacht at Harding's Landing and was staying at the home of Jessie's neighbors, the Hardings.) With the sudden loss of duPont's wife to a heart attack in January 1920, Jessie was well-positioned to move into the breech. In 1921, she married duPont. (One sentence hardly does justice to the cascade of events that led to this union and if the reader would like to read about a storybook love affair, then Hewlett's biography will fill the bill.) Although she never returned to live in the Northern Neck—her homes were in Nemours, Delaware, and Jacksonville, Florida—she acquired a place in Ditchley in 1933 that she occasionally visited, and she never forgot the less fortunate people of Northumberland and Lancaster Counties.

Mrs. duPont assisted Norris by paying for his patients' medical care, hospitalizations, and orthopedic appliances and devices. Her largesse extended to his patients who required hospitalization at Piedmont Tuberculosis Sanatorium, hospitalization in Richmond, and stipends to help defray living expenses of some of the indigent. One of the infirm was Norris's aunt, Mary Tolson. When Tolson became a widow and lost her sight to glaucoma, Norris appealed to Mrs. duPont for assistance. She sent "Aunt Mary" a monthly stipend until she died. After her death, Norris returned the last check that Mrs. duPont had sent to her and got this response:

> Your letter of April seventeenth returning the check made out to my dear old nurse, Mary Jordan Tolson, was received a few days ago. I am deeply distressed to hear of aunt Mary's death—for her I held great affection and esteem, and had hoped to see her again.

It is doubtful that Mrs. duPont was related to Tolson. She was only adhering to a Southern folkway by addressing Tolson as Aunt Mary. In those days, whites didn't address elder colored folk as Mr. or Mrs., but preferred the sterile titles uncle and aunt.

Dr. Jeter Edmonds, a senior white physician in Kilmarnock and Norris's close friend, may have given Norris the impetus to write Mrs. duPont. Edmonds had a warm and friendly relationship with Mrs. duPont, and according to the duPont papers, their correspondence preceded Norris's by a year. Norris's first letter on record to Mrs. duPont was written June 8, 1928. He requested assistance for the widow of a colored physician who had died in Gloucester and left their home encumbered to the amount of $12,000. Mrs.

duPont responded with a check for $100 although she probably knew nothing about this physician. (His home was saved.)

Mrs. duPont's correspondence with Edmonds and Norris was formal, but she never accorded Norris the leeway with funds that she gave Edmonds. It appeared from their letters that she knew Edmonds well, though on several occasions she misspelled Edmonds's first name as Giter instead of Jeter. But there is no question about her commitment to help the ill, regardless of color. She wrote Edmonds in 1927, "Whatever arrangements you make for the colored people will be perfectly satisfactory to me. Any help or boost that we can give an ill person, it is certainly a pleasure to do."

Mrs. duPont also carried on correspondence with one other physician working in the Northern Neck, the white orthopedic surgeon who conducted Norris's bone and joint clinics. Norris had introduced Dr. Thomas Wheeldon to Mrs. duPont by letter after Wheeldon started coming to Kilmarnock.

The correspondence between Wheeldon and Mrs. duPont was cordial but stiff. After every clinic in Kilmarnock, Wheeldon would send a report on the patients he had seen and the conditions of some of them. His letters invariably ended on maudlin notes about how much she had contributed to the people of the Northern Neck. While his comments were true, they were a bit saccharine. Wheeldon made a number of attempts to visit Mrs. duPont in Delaware and Virginia, and he invited her to become a patron of his newly formed Wheeldon Orthopedic Foundation in 1936. Although she declined his overtures, her letters to Wheeldon were always written in a profoundly apologetic manner. She was determined to keep him at arm's length. As far as it can be known, she succeeded, and apparently she never did meet with him. Nevertheless, she sent a monthly check to Wheeldon for his work in Kilmarnock, and then his foundation, for years.

Whenever Norris appealed to Mrs. duPont for assistance in the care of his patients, he always received a prompt and positive response. Not only did Mrs. duPont respond to Norris's appeals, but she often received direct entreaties from individuals. She, in turn, would write Norris and ask for verification of the person's status. In no instance in which Mrs. duPont gave even a minimal amount of money at Norris's behest did he fail to write her a letter of appreciation.

Their correspondence contains several amusing exchanges. Once, Norris appealed to Mrs. duPont on behalf of a patient who had fallen from a cherry tree and sustained a right ankle injury. She had been treated in a major city hospital without much improvement. Norris consulted Wheeldon who felt that the deformity could be corrected, but an x-ray and plaster casting would be required. In view of the expenses involved, Norris asked Mrs. duPont to help defray the costs of treatment. She wrote back, "One would not think that an x-ray picture were necessary. My cousin Minnie J. Edwards broke her arm just a few weeks ago, and Dr. Moorman is taking care of it without the assistance of an x-ray." (Elmer Richard Moorman was a Kilmarnock physician.) Although Mrs. duPont did not deny the payment for the x-ray, she wanted to discuss the matter further with Wheeldon. Norris was at all times deferential to Mrs. duPont and for good reason, but he was not about to let her dictate medical treatment. He replied in a tactfully appreciative vein and then stated:

> I was very interested in your statement, 'one would not think an x-ray picture were necessary.' That is just how I felt in June when I put it up [sic], having put up fractures of that kind before. However, this did not turn out well so I have had to suffer the harsh criticism both home and abroad of making a dreadful mistake. Well, I am very sorry but I suppose most of us make some mistakes.

It was Mrs. duPont's practice to periodically send Norris a sum of money to be used at his discretion in paying for patients' services. Following receipt of such a stipend, he would always write and detail the disbursement of every penny. On one occasion, he sent her a letter with a list of the persons who had been helped. He received in return a rather peculiar request. She wanted to know which of the patients on the list were white and which were colored.

Norris returned the list with a politely written and appreciative letter.

He put an "X" mark by the white patients. There were 32 patients; seven were white. He went on to detail for Mrs. duPont the conditions of a number of the patients who were beneficiaries of her generosity. He added that he had recently installed an x-ray machine in his office, which he felt would be quite helpful in doing chest work, especially in the early diagnosis of diseases in children. He again thanked her for her kind inquiry and expressed to Mrs. duPont "our deepest gratitude for [your] generous help in so many ways at all times."

Norris did not confine his pleas for funds to the ill and to the afflicted. He asked for help in building the elementary school in Kilmarnock on more than one occasion. Once she sent a check for $250, one of the largest single contributions by an individual to the building fund. Over the years, he asked for and received contributions to the United Negro College Fund, Hampton Institute, Virginia Union University's Science Building, and Richmond Community Hospital. The request for Virginia Union University elicited another interesting exchange. Norris wrote, "Doubtless the president of a colored private college has the hardest job of anyone at this time." Mrs. duPont responded with a firm rebuttal to this statement:

He has no harder job than the president of a white college—both have difficult times trying to retain capable members of their faculties, and at the same time keeping the expenses of operating the college to a minimum. I am sure you can understand this.

She sent a check of $500 "as my personal contribution." Norris responded with a typed two-page thank you letter. He agreed with her comments about the difficulties facing college presidents but told her, "because of my close associations with the presidents in the private colleges of Virginia I thought their jobs were a little harder (smiles)." He then spoke about the entire educational system and obliquely referred to the strains from the dual system:

To tell you the truth Mrs. DuPont the whole question of perfecting standards of education from the public school[s] thru the colleges is one of grave consideration. It will take the best minds coupled with cooperation of all the people. It was just this week that I spoke to one of the teachers in the High School and asked how well are we performing our duties. Certainly if we had more Ralph Bunches we would doubt-less accomplish more. In spite of existing conditions, which are not as favorable as we would like, I think more will be accomplished in having a tolerant attitude plus a willingness to render individual service and a cooperative effort to work for a better society.

Over the thirty-six-year period of their correspondence, Mrs. duPont refused Norris's requests only four times, and none of the refusals had to do with helping his indigent patients: when he asked for her portrait to hang in the new elementary school they had built and toward which she had unstint-ingly donated; a curiously uncharacteristic request by Norris for assistance for his oldest daughter in college; a request to fund a permanent scholarship for students at Hampton Institute; and a request to permit him to nominate her to serve on the Board of Trustees of Hampton Institute.

Norris was persistent in his effort to get Mrs. duPont involved at Hampton beginning in 1935 and continuing through 1958. She did respond to Norris's solicitations for Hampton, but she never visited Hampton Insti-tute although she promised that she would. Nor would she receive Dr. Arthur Howe, the president of Hampton, at her home in Nemours, Delaware. Norris had been trying for some years to arrange a face-to-face meeting of Howe and Mrs. duPont. Norris even took Howe on one occasion to visit Mrs. duPont at her home in Ditchley, but for an inexplicable reason, he did not get out of the car and enter her home.

Her denials to Norris's requests to set up the scholarship fund at Hampton and to serve on the board of trustees may have been a reflection of Mrs. duPont's rather constricted view toward the higher education of colored students. She did support two trade schools in Mississippi and gave individual support to some students. While she was generous in helping the colored stu-dents obtain industrial training, it appears that her benevolence extended less enthusiastically to their higher education.

Mrs. duPont made it clear in a letter June 6, 1944, to Wheeldon her position on Negroes. Wheeldon had written her May 26, 1944, that he had "gotten to know Dr. Norris very well and through him have gotten to know the colored physicians over the state but the question has arisen in Virginia lately as to giving the colored physicians more opportunity to work in their own group." He expressed his support for the initiative that Norris was pressing to get colored staffing at Piedmont Tuberculosis Sanatorium. He added that he hoped to be of "help in some small way in working out this problem and if I do undoubtedly, no small part of it would be the direct outgrowth of an opportunity made possible by you." In her response, she thanked him for his efforts on behalf of the crippled people, particular children of the Northern Neck, and then expounded on the issue of race:

The negro doctor Norris had done good work, I believe. I firmly believe in the colored physicians working amongst their own and in their own group, letting them staff the negro hospitals. I assume high-class Anglo-Saxon doctors will have to keep an eye on them, so to speak, to guide them. Most of the negroes I have known refuse to go to the negro hospitals, nevertheless it is my opinion that they should. I believe in them having their own stores, their own hotels, restaurants, etc., letting them have equal opportunity, in fact, I consider that they have had a little more than equal opportunity—they have taken advantage of it, until the last several years, when one becomes very fearful of what the end may be. There can be no social equality in any part of the United States. The northerner does not wish it any more than the southerner actually—he can do some talking along that line. Of course, the politicians do it for one sole purpose, that of votes.

Nine years later, Mrs. duPont commended James F. Byrnes, the governor of South Carolina and a former U.S. Supreme Court justice, for his segregationist stand at the Democratic National Convention in 1953. She was unalterably opposed to the Supreme Court decision in *Brown v. Board of Education*. If Norris knew of her sentiments in this direction, he never mentioned it.

There was no let up in his requests for funds to help with his patients as well as the many projects with which he was involved. He wrote to her on February 1, 1954, soliciting funds for a purse for President John M. Ellison who was retiring from Virginia Union University: "Mrs. duPont, as you know I am always seeking aid for worthy persons, causes and institutions." How well did she know! For nearly three decades Norris had persisted in supplications to Mrs. duPont. Yet she nearly always responded with alacrity. Regardless of what one feels about her racial attitudes that had been shaped by the times and the events through which she lived, one cannot impugn her generosity when it came to causes for the less fortunate, especially the crippled, the afflicted, and the ill.

Their correspondence continued until July 2, 1964. Mrs. duPont had begun to fail noticeably by then, and much of her correspondence had been taken over by her longtime secretary in Delaware, Mary G. Shaw. The letter below was probably written by Ms. Shaw in response to one that Norris had written in June of that year:

Your letter of June sixteenth was greatly appreciated. I am indeed sorry to learn that you have been in the hospital, and as a result you have closed your office in Kilmarnock. I congratulate you on having practiced medicine for forty-seven years. I think it is time for you to retire, though for one so active as you have been through the years, I can imagine that the readjustment is difficult to make. I send you my deepest sympathy in the loss of your friends

Regarding a contribution to the Richmond County [sic] Hospital, I regret that all available funds have been allocated for the current year. I think you know that I am the sole support of the Alfred I. duPont Institute of The Nemours Foundations, a hospital for little crippled children, created under the terms of Mr. duPont's will. Hospitals are expensive to operate to-day, I can assure you.

Hoping that you will have a quick recovery, and with good wishes,
Very Sincerely yours,
(MRS. ALFRED I. DUPONT)

MGS.

There is no record that Norris responded to this letter even though he customarily responded even when denied a request. It was unusual for Mrs. duPont to deny a contribution to any of Norris's projects such as Richmond Community Hospital, and it is likely the decision was made by Ms. Shaw. Mrs. duPont died September 26, 1970, a little more than four years after Norris.

Through her will she established the Jessie Ball duPont Religious, Charitable and Education Fund, which began giving grants in 1977. Today, more than 325 institutions, many in the Northern Neck, are direct beneficiaries of her vision and her generosity.

Dr. Wheeldon Holds Clinic.

Dr. Thos. Wheeldon of Richmond held an Orthopedic Clinic at the office of Dr. M. E. Norris December 4th. There was a large number of persons attended from various parts of the Northern Neck.

About twenty patients were examined. Plans are being made as rapidly as possible to give a large number of these suffering treatment. It is hoped that by the means of a series of clinics all the cripple children and those suffering from other deformities may be helped. Dr. Wheeldon expressed his deep appreciation for the hospitality shown him while he was at Kilmarnock, and the splendid cooperation given him by local physicians and Miss Ott, county nurse of Northumberland.

A group of ladies mostly from White Stone served a very dilicious lunch to all who attended. Hot cocoa was much in demand as the weather man held the temperature between freezing point and zero all the day. Mrs. Annie Jefferson was kind enough to see that no one went home hungr

Newspaper Reports on Norris's Clinics (courtesy of The Rappahannock Record). Article on left is dated November 29, 1928; article below is dated November 6, 1930. Note that the white physicians cooperated with Norris in the conduct of the clinics.

THROAT CLINIC CONDUCTED FOR COLORED CHILDREN

Dr. U. L. Houston of the Freedman's Hospital of Washington conducted a throat clinic for colored children in the office of Dr. M. E. Norris on Monday. Seven operations for the removal of tonsils were performed. All of the patients remained in the office of Dr. Norris for a day or more following the operation.

The local doctors and the county nurse of Northumberland County cooperated in getting out the patients for the clinic and in the work at the clinic. RR 11/06/30

***Morgan E. Norris
Elementary School, 1953***
(photo courtesy of the New
Journal and Guide, *Norfolk,
Virginia).*

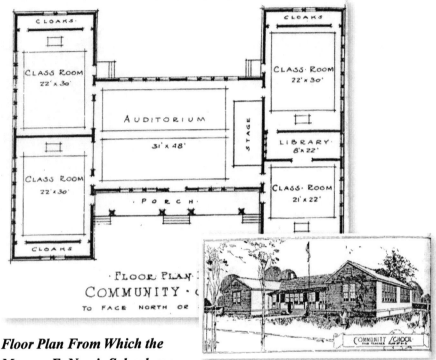

*Floor Plan From Which the
Morgan E. Norris School was
Built (published with permission
from the Fisk University Franklin Library Special Collections). These plans
were taken from a pamphlet entitled Community School Plans (revised in
1931), issued by the Rosenwald Fund, Southern Office, Nashville, Tennessee,
by Samuel L. Smith. The pamphlet described the recommended orientation of
the building for maximum sunlight exposure, site location, minimum acreage,
specifications for landscaping, and building of toilets. (Note there are no
indoor restrooms in this plan.) Professors in architecture at Tuskegee Institute
initially drew the architectural plans for the Rosenwald schools, but in 1920
the administration of the building fund was transferred to Nashville under the
direction of Samuel L. Smith who refined and elaborated on the designs.*

Rev. George S. Russell, First Principal of Morgan E. Norris School (photo courtesy of Queen Street Baptist Church, Hampton, Virginia). Rev. Russell, though in Lancaster County for only six years, had a lasting impact on the religious and educational institutions of the Northern Neck.

Mrs. Elsie Byrd Coleman (photo provided by Morgan E. Norris III). Mrs. Coleman, aka "Miss Byrd" (on left) was among the first teachers at the Morgan E. Norris School. She is shown being honored at the author's fiftieth A. T. Wright High School reunion in 1999. In the center is Julian Allen "Skully" Ball, our neighbor and an outstanding Lancaster County teacher, political worker, and historian. Author is on the right. Mrs. Coleman was a teacher's teacher. She received her bachelor's degree from Virginia State College and did advanced study at Boston University. She started her career at Morgan E. Norris School when it opened and taught there for over twenty years. Her grandfather, Spencer Pinn, was Norris's first teacher.

Mars Hill School (courtesy of the superintendent's office, Lancaster County Schools). The one-room school was located a quarter mile west of Kilmarnock in Black Stump and was one of the three schools of this type that Morgan E. Norris Graded School replaced. Spencer and Hannah Pinn, grandparents of Mrs. Elsie B. Coleman, gave the land for the school.

MEDICAL SOCIETY — The Rappahannock Medical Society met at the home of Dr. J. B. Blayton of Williamsburg, Va., on March 26 to study the proposal to place an all-Negro staff at Piedmont Sanatorium, Burkeville, Va. Those present included, left to right, Dr. N. F. McNorton of Yorktown, Va., Dr. Charles Franklin Sr., of Ruthville, Va., Dr. Tony, Dr. M. E. Norris of Kilmarnock, Va., Dr. F. R. Trigg, president of the Old Dominion Medical Society, Dr. J. B. Blayton, Dr. G. Hamilton Francis, and Dr. E.' D. Burke.

Group of Physicians Meeting to Plan Strategy to Place Negro Staff at Piedmont (courtesy of the New Journal and Guide, *Norfolk, Virginia.) See newspaper caption. Photo appeared in the* Journal and Guide, *April 14, 1944.*

Ad for Chesapeake Fair, 1927 (printed with permission of The Rappahannock Record*). Note advertisement for a Klan meeting adjacent to fair ad.*

Ad for the first Afro-American Fair, 1927 (printed with permission of The Rappahannock Record*).*

The Fair Promoters, circa 1927, (picture from Memorial Bulletin on Morgan E. Norris, 1971). From left are Albert T. Wright, founder and principal of the A. T. Wright High School; Norris; and an unidentified fair promoter, probably Mr. L. R. Fleming. Mr. Fleming for many years conducted a fair that he also called the Afro-American Fair. The relationship of his fair to the white fair was never quite clear—newspapers are unavailable from 1918 to 1924—but Mr. Fleming's group did not own the land.

The Reviewing Stand at the First Annual Fair

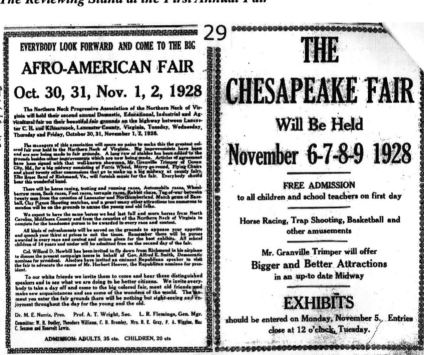

*Ad for Afro-American Fair, October 25, 1928 (printed with permission of
the* Rappahannock Record). *This ad (left) was published adjacent to the ad
for the white Chesapeake Fair (right).*

Miss Ethel B. Pollard, *First Prize in Auto Parade*

**Mrs. Ethel Pollard,
Winner of the Car,
(Top). One of the
Trotters, (Bottom).
(Pictures from
Memorial Bulletin
on Morgan E.
Norris, 1971.) At
first annual fair. Note
grandstand in rear of
photograph of trotter.**

Whitby and Pink O'neal
First Place at 1st Annual Fair

**Record of Races,
1951 (courtesy of
Archives, United
States Trotting
Association).**

U. S. T. A. YEAR BOOK

Esler, Baltimore, Md. Driver, Samuel Conway.
* Placed 5th for pacing.

8. Trot, Class 23. $225.
Powder, b g, 14, by Calumet Crusader.............. 1 1
Gratty's Maid, 2-2; Senator Woollen. 3-3.--2.29½,
2. 37½.
   Owner--William B. Morgan, Jr., Lincoln, De'... -
ver, Clifford Harris.

9. Pace, Free-For-All. $325.
Nosdivad, b g, 9, by Siskiyou................... 1 2
Profilist, b g, 6, by Protector................... 2 1
   Sabra Miss, 3-4; Tiger Man, 5-3; Henry Grattan, 4-5;
Chief Alcar, 6-dr.--2.18, 2.19.
   Owner--(Nosdivad) Nolan B. Pilchard, Girdletree, Md.
Driver, Walter West; Owner--(Profilist) R. A. Benthall,
Rich Square, N. C. Driver, Phillip A. Tabb.

1189   Brookvale, Va.

1. NOVEMBER 1--Trot and Pace, Classified. No
Purse.
Sabre Miss, p, ch m, 5, by His Honor...........1 1 2
Lady Boldwood, p, b m, 8, by Boldwood Jr......2 2 1
   Josedale Play Boy, 3-3-4; Slipping Around, 4-4-3;
Miss Apirl Star, 5-5-5.--2.36, 2.32, 2.39.
   Owner & Driver--(Sabre Miss) Wallace W. Robinson,
Shackleford, Va.; Owner & Driver--(Lady Boldwood)
Chauncey Robinson, Plain View, Va.

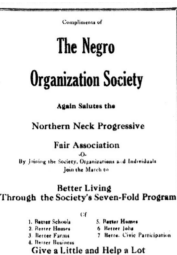

Compliments of

The Negro
Organization Society

Again Salutes the

Northern Neck Progressive

Fair Association
-O-
By Joining the Society, Organizations and Individuals
Join the March to

Better Living
Through the Society's Seven-Fold Program

Of
1. Better Schools   5. Better Homes
2. Better Homes   6. Better Jobs
3. Better Farms   7. Betre. Civic Participation
4. Better Business
Give a Little and Help a Lot
Annual membership Fees:
Individual $1.00; Organization $5 · $10
Contributions in any amount will be appreciated and used wisely
to support the work. For full information, write:

L. C. White, Director
Hampton, Va.

1957
FALL FESTIVAL
AND RACES

Brook Vale Fair Ground
Kilmarnock, Va.

Oct. 31, Nov. 1 - 2, 1957

● Educational
● Industrial
● Recreational

Prizes - Exhibits - Entertainment

Northern Neck Progressive Association

Program for the 1957 Fair (from Norris family collection). There is no record that any fair was held after 1959, thus ending thirty-two years of fairs.

Senator Robert Opie Norris, Jr., circa 1940 (Foster Studio, Richmond, VA; courtesy of Nancy Norris Foster). A Lancaster County native, Senator Norris was a reliable and longtime supporter of Norris in his projects. He assisted him in gaining a loan to complete the school and often spoke on Educational Day at the fairs. A skilled politician, he was esteemed for his oratorical skills. He served for forty-three years in the General Assembly of Virginia—in the House from 1912 to 1928 and in the Senate from 1928 to 1955. The senator was a founder of the Northern Neck of Virginia Historical Society.

Alma's Graduation Class, Syracuse University School of Medicine, 1926 (courtesy of the Department of Historical Collections, Health Sciences Library, State University of New York, Upstate Medical University).

Left: Alma Thornton with her Mother, Mamie Thornton, Norris's Sister, circa 1910, (Norris family photo).

Below: Syracuse University's Alumni Bulletin Report on Alma's Bequest to Syracuse University, Summer 1984 (courtesy of the Upstate Medical University Alumni News Bulletin).

Eva Thornton '26 Bequeathes $300,000 for Student Loan Program

The College of Medicine recently received the largest single bequest ever received at the College. The bequest specified that in excess of $300,000 be used for the Student Loan Program.

In announcing the gift to the Alumni Board of Directors, Dr. Richard Schmidt stated, "Although the funds will come to the Faculty Student Association, undoubtedly the activities of the Alumni Association/Foundation played an important role in Dr. Thornton's gener-osity to the College."

Dr. Thornton began her professional career as a Gynecologist, after much difficulty in obtaining an internship because of the fact that she was a woman. Dr. Thornton resided in Scranton, PA, and retired from the Veterans Administration at the age of 79.

The Alumni Office is currently researching more information on Dr. Thornton for an article in an upcoming issue of the Alumni Journal.

The Board of Trustees, Hampton Institute, 1939 (Norris family photo used with permission of Archives, Hampton University). Norris is second from the right, Howe is second from the left, and Moton is fourth from the left.

Attendees at the Doctors' Helpers Institute with Faculty (Norris family photo used with permission of Archives, Hampton University). Probably Hampton Institute Campus. Morgan E. Norris, top row left. The Virginia State Department of Health organized the Doctors' Helpers program in 1933. The program, though not a direct precursor to the present day Physician's Assistant programs, embodied many of the concepts of the Physician's Assistant program curriculum. Norris lectured at the institutes and encouraged Northern Neck ladies to attend. The institutes were terminated at the beginning of World War II and did not resume afterwards.

ASK CONTRACTION OF TOWN LIMITS

Petition Presented To Circuit Court For Striking 46.5 Acres From Town

Morgan E. Norris and other petitioners have filed a petition with the Circuit Court of Lancaster County for the contraction of the corporate limits of the town of Kilmarnock.

An advertisement appearing in the Record defines the boundary of the territory proposed to be stricken of, the area of which is 46.5 acres, located in the southeastern portion of the town limits, wholly in White Stone Magisterial District.

The petitioners ask that the charter of the town be amended so as to exclude from the corporate limits of the town the territory described and they ask the court to fix a day on which the said petition shall be heard.

The petition requests that no debts or obligations of the town of Kilmarnock be chargeable against the area in question or Lancaster County. The petitioners state that residents of the area which wish to withdraw from the town received no benefits from any improvements for which the debts of the town were incurred.

The petition also states that no corporate property of the town is located within the area in question; that the general good of the community will not be materially affected thereby, and that it will be to the interest of a majority of the people of the territory.

Signers of the petition are Morgan E. Norris, Narvel R. Wiggins, Reuben Moody, Dennis Lee, James Ball, Willie Grimes, Jack Ball, L. H. Lee, Simon Conquest and Rebecca Smith, all colored.

Left: Article on Contraction of Kilmarnock's Town Limits (Printed with permission of the The Rappahannock Record). November 20, 1941.

Below: The Service Station 1953 (Courtesy of the New Journal and Guide, Norfolk, Virginia).

*The Rappahannock Medical Society Annual Clinic at Richmond
Community Hospital with Dr. Charles Drew, circa 1948, (Norris family
photo). Dr. Drew is to the left and behind Dr. Ulysses Houston, who is in the
first row, third from the left. Norris is in the last row, far right.*

*Rappahannock Medical Society at Richmond Community Hospital with
Dr. John A. Kenney, circa 1946, (Norris family photo). Kenney is in the first
row, third from left, and Norris is in the last row, second from left. Matthew
Walker, surgeon, of Meharry Medical College is in the first row, center.*

The Rappahannock Medical Society (Norris family photo). One of the society's monthly meetings, circa 1949. Front row, from left: Eldric Stewart, Silas O. Binns, Ernest J. McCampbell, Unidentified, James B. Blayton, and C. Waldo Scott. Back row, from left: I.A. Jackson, Sr., Morgan E. Norris, George B.D. Stephens, Middleton H. Lambright, Jr., Charles Franklin, G. Hamilton Frances, William A. Franklin, Jaehn Charlton, and Marcus E. Toney. Dr. Lambright was a prominent general surgeon from Cleveland, Ohio, and probably guest lecturer.

CHAPTER 20

No Colored Doctors for Piedmont

It was a simple request. In the early 1930s, the colored physicians in Virginia asked the state to appoint some of their members to the staff of the state institution, the Piedmont Tuberculosis Sanatorium for Negroes. A number of reports had confirmed the need for more trained colored personnel in tuberculosis. It was a logical request, given the devastating toll that tuberculosis was taking on the colored population. The request was denied, twice!

Mycobacterium tuberculosis, the germ that causes tuberculosis, is an equal opportunity bacterium. It does not discriminate between coloreds and whites. Nor does it make a distinction between adults and children, men and women, rich and poor, or saints and sinners. The disease is highly contagious, can affect just about any organ in the body, has profoundly debilitating effects, and is sometimes lethal. The economic toll of the illness is enormous. The human toll is incalculable. At the beginning of the twentieth century, the disease was the leading cause of death among all young people and one of the leading causes of death among all ages of colored residents. Yet Norris and his colleagues would wage a determined but futile battle to get colored staffing at Piedmont. (The Piedmont Sanatorium housed only colored patients.) They twice ran into a wall of opposition—actually three times if the first inquiry in 1914 is counted. Virginia's racial climate in the first half of the twentieth century was hardly conducive to the kind of cross-cultural cooperation so necessary to achieve a bi-racial accord on such a vital issue. No Negro physicians were on the staffs of white hospitals, the Medical Society of Virginia had a "for white physicians only" clause firmly ensconced in its constitution (it was not struck from the constitution until 1954), and segregation of the races was mandated across the board by Virginia state law.

204 James E.C. Norris, M.D.

The response of the Virginia State Board of Health to representatives of a large segment of the state's population that wanted to fight a common foe is utterly confounding. The recklessly indifferent attitude of the Virginia State Board of Health—the very people charged with protecting the welfare of all citizens—remains, to this day, scandalous. After all, many colored people worked in white homes and worked in businesses where tuberculosis could be easily spread. And it appears that the Board of Health gave short shrift to the economic consequences of the disease as well.

A brief review of Virginia's experience with treating its tubercular citizens shows an appalling dereliction of the board's responsibility and obligation to all Virginians.

The first public sanatorium treatment of tuberculosis in Virginia was undertaken in 1904 at a mental hospital for colored, the Central State Hospital in Petersburg, Virginia, under the superintendent, Dr. William F. Drewry. In 1908, the General Assembly appropriated funds for Catawba Sanatorium for whites. Tuberculosis treatment for colored still was relegated to the prisons and insane asylums, as the races were strictly segregated at all levels. As Roy K. Flanagan, a health officer in Virginia, told the Southern Medical Association in 1916:

> The penitentiary and the lunatic asylums of the state were the only places where any tuberculous Negro could get adequate treatment; he had to commit a felony, steal a horse or break into a house, before he had any chance to get well of consumption. The law-abiding darky with consumption could only die, which he soon did after infecting unnumbered other folks.

The Negro Organization Society and Agnes Dillon Randolph, a nurse, political activist, and great-granddaughter of Thomas Jefferson, deserve credit for prodding a reluctant state government to build a sanatorium for its colored citizens. Shortly after its founding in 1911, the society focused on the problem of tuberculosis. It held a "tag day" sale with the goal of raising $3,000 toward purchase of the site for a sanatorium. On April 30, 1915, in a letter from Robert R. Moton of the Negro Organization Society to Randolph, head of the Tuberculosis Bureau of the Virginia State Board of Health, Moton seemed confident that with receipts from the "tag day" sale he could come up with the $3,000 toward the sanatorium.

When this effort was brought to the attention of state officials, they had no choice but to respond. It was not until 1916, however, that the General Assembly appropriated funds for a sanatorium for colored tubercular patients. Randolph, who organized the Tuberculosis Bureau of the Virginia Department of Health and who was executive secretary of the Virginia Anti-Tuberculosis Association, pushed the phlegmatic Assembly into acting. Indeed, the minutes of the Negro Organization Society reported that they "thanked Miss Randolph, secretary of the Anti-Tuberculosis League who spoke so forcefully upon the needs of the colored people for a sanatorium." They urged the adoption of her suggestions for establishment of the tuberculosis farm. While it may be true that Randolph may have been the prime mover behind the Virginia Legislature, the Negro Organization Society through its lobbying efforts and fund-raising, without doubt, provided the necessary leverage. No person would be more knowledgeable about the transaction than Flanagan, the Virginia health officer. He had this to say at the meeting of the Southern Medical Association about the Negro Organization Society of Virginia:

> They set to work and raised a fund. Their appeals went broadcast and the little societies everywhere sent in contributions, many of them in pennies and small amounts. This Society then came before the Legislature and said: "Gentlemen, we have $3000 with which to buy the farm or to help construct a sanatorium for our people," and what could a legislature do under the circumstances? They had to come across, and so an appropriation of $20,000 a year for two years was made available for this purpose.

The State officials had great difficulty locating the site for the facility because of whites' opposition. "Not in my region" was the drumbeat. Finally, a site was selected in Burkeville, Nottaway County, roughly fifty miles southwest of Richmond. The flatlands of that area of Virginia were less than optimal for the placement of a tuberculosis sanatorium. The consensus of physicians treating tubercular patients was that sanatoria should be placed at sites with high altitudes and cool environments. Catawba, the sanatorium for whites, was built in the Allegheny Mountains just west of Roanoke, and the Blue Ridge Sanatorium, also for whites, built just two years after Piedmont, was located near the University of Virginia in Charlottesville. Not only was the Piedmont site subpar, but when the buildings were completed, they too were not up to the level of those at Catawba.

From the moment planning for a state-run sanatorium began, the Negro Organization Society expressed concern about the role of colored professionals. At a meeting of the executive committee of the Negro Organization Society in 1914 at Ebenezer Baptist Church in Richmond, Mrs. Maggie Walker moved for the appointment of a committee to confer with Miss Randolph of the State Board of Health. The society wanted to know her attitude and that of officials in the Board of Health regarding the practice of colored physicians in the sanatorium. The motion carried, and Mrs. Walker, Moton, and A. A. Graham were appointed. There is no record of a response to the committee from the State Board of Health on the role of Negro physicians. The forty-bed sanatorium opened in June 1918, with an all-white staff and a nursing school supervised by whites.

The sanatorium opened just one year after Norris returned to Kilmarnock to practice. That year, 1918, tuberculosis was listed as one of the leading causes of deaths in the colored race. It was also the year of the great influenza epidemic, which, though destructive, was short-lived. Tuberculosis, as lethal as the flu, remained the leading cause of death, particularly in the 15-45 age group, for four more decades.

Norris resumed his interest in combating the disease soon after he started practice. He started a biannual tuberculosis clinic and a biannual malnutrition clinic. He spoke eloquently on prevention to whatever audience he could find. His motto was "Stay well rather than have to get well."

Piedmont had a long waiting list for admission. The sick patient, while waiting to be admitted, was coughing and spreading the deadly bacteria. Norris supervised the building of a little portable airy cabin that could be transported from home to home by truck to assist his patients while they waited for admission. It served two purposes. Isolation was accomplished, and it was constructed to provide ample fresh air and rest to the ill.

When a patient finally did get admitted to Piedmont, it is generally conceded that the treatment was adequate and compassionate. If major surgery were required such as a thoracoplasty (the deforming and radical operation where seven to eight ribs would be removed on one side of the chest to collapse the chest wall against the tuberculous cavity in the lung), the patients were transferred to the Blue Ridge Sanatorium at Charlottesville, and the operation was performed at the University of Virginia's hospital.

In 1932, the Negro Organization Society, under Norris's chairmanship of the Better Health Committee, revived the issue of colored personnel at Piedmont. The sanatorium, after fourteen years, still had no colored members of the administration or the medical staff. This was a matter of grave concern to Virginia's colored professional class. When Norris and President John Gandy of the Virginia State College for Negroes led a group to pressure the state to hire Negro physicians at the sanatorium and the insane asylum, the committee was firmly rebuffed, given the lame excuse that white and Negro professionals would clash. Norris implored Dr. Arthur Howe, President of Hampton Institute, to write the state on their behalf, pointing out that Hampton Institute successfully employed a mixed staff. Norris had hoped a positive statement from Howe would give the Negro Organization Society the needed leverage to gain appointment of colored physicians at both the mental hospital and the tuberculosis sanatorium.

On December 18, 1933, he wrote Dr. Howe:

I have been asked to serve on a committee to consult the heads of some of our state institutions in regard to placing some of our colored physicians in those institutions caring for our people. It occurred to me that you are head of an institution that has both colored and white working together and a line from one who is experienced and qualified might help a good deal.

Howe responded immediately. He wasn't sure what he needed to say and how he should say it. Norris wrote back to Howe on Christmas Day, 1933. He gave Howe the background of their complaints. He pointed out to him the difficulties that colored interns and residents had in gaining appointments to hospitals and felt that it was only fair that physicians should be serving on the staffs of hospitals where the patients were all colored.

> There is a feeling with some of the heads of state institutions that the two groups could not get on together. In order that these gentlemen might be intelligently advised or informed on this matter I thought it would be a good idea to have a statement from the head of some institutions that were working with mixed helpers or workers.

> My plan to use the information from your letter is to state, if such statement is necessary, that Dr. Howe has advised me that white and colored teachers get on very well at Hampton and the institution has grown and developed by their cooperative spirit. ... Our plan is to deal with this matter in a wholesome and constructive attitude, and certainly if possible not defeat our own end.

Howe's response was prompt and just what Norris needed to take to the committee:

> Our experience at Hampton Institute where the staff has been both white and Negro for many years has made me confident of the continued success of having both races work together for the good of other peoples. Such association gives members of both races much more confidence in each other and ultimately will be the solution of some of the racial difficulties our country suffers from today.

Despite the entreaties to the state by Gandy's committee and their irrefutable arguments for the benefits that would accrue to the citizens and the colored physicians by staffing the sanatorium with Negro physicians, the State Board of Health responded with callous indifference.

A decade passed before the issue surfaced again. Colgate Darden, a progressive and visionary governor of Virginia, proposed that Negro physicians staff the Piedmont Sanatorium. A committee was drafted from the Old Dominion Medical Society and the Negro Organization Society to meet with Darden. Norris was on the committee, and he sent a letter of support to Darden:

> This is to thank you for the very fine opinion you expressed in your article that was published in the Sunday's *Time Dispatch* regarding placing Piedmont Sanatorium under Negro personnel. It has been a feeling with some of us for some time that since tuberculosis plays such a large role in the high death rate of our people that a closer linking up with the institutions which are doing so much to combat it would be an advance move and certainly Piedmont ranks first among those. ...
>
> We feel as you that certainly a large up to date staff at an institution as Piedmont should do much, both in treating and educating the people for better health and particularly the prevention and cure of tuberculosis. This should be true under a large mixed staff or a whole Negro personnel.

Governor Darden responded with a letter on July 2, 1943, in which he acknowledged receipt of Norris's letter. He stated that he was "glad that you think well of the plan, and I hope that it can be worked out satisfactorily." On July 30, 1943, a joint committee representing the Negro Organization Society of Virginia and the Old Dominion Medical Society met with the governor. At that meeting, which involved some of the leading colored physicians, lawyers, and educators in Virginia, the group expressed their support for Governor Darden. Norris took to the meeting a list of six leading colored physicians in the tuberculosis field that had been sent to him by Dr. John A. Kenney of Tuskegee Institute. Not one was from Virginia, and that proved to be a point of contention as the State Board of Health had insisted that any appointment must be of local talent. There was no local talent because no colored physician was trained in tuberculosis in Virginia at that time for two reasons: there was nowhere in Virginia for a colored doctor to train in tuberculosis, and if trained there was no place for him to practice. The state health officials knew that better than anyone.

Norris could report that the meeting went well. He wrote the governor the day after the meeting: "It seems to me that your position is very clear and definite as to Negro personnel in colored institutions. We are hoping that the State Board of Health and other agencies may see the matter as you do." But by the end of August 1943, the State Board of Health did not see the matter as Darden did, and rejected it out of hand. Norris wrote to Darden on August 20, 1943:

> We regret that the Virginia State Board of Health will not endorse having Negro personnel at Piedmont. I was afraid of my past experience with them that they would not. It is evident that the gentlemen forming the Board know a very little about our men. ... Hoping that the temporary setback will not defeat the brave purpose which you have so nobly set forth. With every good wish for your future success and the success of this Commonwealth ...

Darden did not give up. He went before the Virginia State General Assembly again in 1944. On February 2, 1944, Norris wrote to the governor:

> This is just a letter to try expressing my thanks and appreciation for the wonderful proposal you've offered to the General Assembly. It shows a gallant and progressive spirit on your part and will tend to bring on closer and more harmonious relations not only among the citizens of our state but will aid in settling one of our national problems. Such suggestions cannot help but provoke thought seriously toward better understanding.

Darden wrote Norris on February 4, 1944, thanking him for his letter of February 2nd and expressing "hope that my recommendations as to Piedmont will receive favorable consideration by the Assembly." He pledged to "continue [his] efforts along this line."

Darden's recommendations did receive favorable consideration by both the House committee and the Senate committee with passage of the Baldwin resolution that called for "all Negro staffs at the Piedmont Sanatorium at Burkeville and at the Petersburg colony." The resolution was essentially gutted, however, by an amendment that the authority to make the change would rest with "controlling boards," implying, primarily, the Virginia State Board of Health. The fox would be in charge of the chicken coop.

A number of major white newspapers in the state of Virginia, including both leading Richmond papers, gave strong editorial support to Darden's initiative, pointing out that while Georgia, Maryland, and Kentucky had all-Negro staffs, in Virginia "there is not a single Negro doctor on the staff of a single state hospital for tubercular or mental patients." Opposition came from delegations where Piedmont was located "principally on the grounds that white patients visit the Piedmont Sanatorium for outpatient treatment."

Despite all these efforts over the years, Piedmont Sanatorium remained without any colored physicians throughout its existence. In 1965, with the passage of the Civil Rights Act, the colored patients were transferred to the white sanatoria, and Piedmont was closed. On July 1, 1967, the sanatorium was given to the State Department of Mental Hygiene as a hospital for mental patients. Dr. J. Belmont Woodson, the superintendent and medical director had resigned, and his successor, Dr. Charles W. Scott, remained with Piedmont even after it was converted to a mental hospital.

Deaths From Tuberculosis per 100,000 Population by Color - Virginia 1940-1951
From a Study of Tuberculosis in Virginia—1952, prepared by the survey staff of the Virginia State Department of Health.

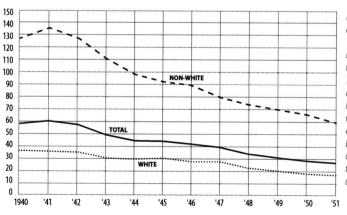

Note the steady decline in the death rate of both races from 1940 to 1951, a trend that began with the first records of tuberculosis deaths in 1910. The steady fall in death rates can be attributed to better hygiene, better nutrition, a vigorous anti-tuberculosis effort by the Virginia State Department of Health, community agencies such as the Negro Organization Society of Virginia, and education.

℞

The concept of sanatoria for the treatment of tuberculosis was developed in Europe in the mid-nineteenth century. It was the basis for treatment for both Negroes and whites in Virginia from 1904 to 1965, and therefore merits further explanation.

Dr. Edward Livingston Trudeau, an American physician and himself a victim of tuberculosis, founded the first sanatorium in America in 1884 at Saranac Lake, New York. The pillars of sanatorium treatment were an invigorating climate, open air, rest, regulation of daily habits, an abundant supply of nutritious foods, and occupational therapy.

But diagnosis and treatment of tuberculosis in the United States remained unsophisticated into the twentieth century. The founding of the National Association for the Study and Prevention of Tuberculosis in 1904 would soon change that. The Association spurred a more focused and a more scientific approach to eradication of the disease. (The organization changed its name to the National Tuberculosis Association in 1918, and with the decline in the incidence of tuberculosis infections, it became the American Lung Association in 1973.) Virginia was not far behind. The Virginia State Department of Health was founded in 1908, and the Virginia Tuberculosis Association was founded in 1909. These organizations speeded the development of sanitoria in the state. The first private sanatorium in the state solely for the treatment of tuberculosis, The Virginia Sanatorium for Consumptives in Ironville, had been chartered in 1905. By 1919, 471 sanatorium beds were available in state, municipal, and private institutions. Three hundred forty-two were for whites and 129 for colored. Although the Negro population accounted for nearly thirty percent of Virginia's total population, the distribution of beds was inequitable because there was a much higher tuberculosis death rate among Negroes as shown on page 211. Accommodations for Negroes lagged far behind those for whites for the first half of the twentieth century.

The prevalence and severity of the disease among Negroes, the paucity of sanatorium beds, and the lack of training opportunities impelled the Negro physicians' desire to seek a voice in tuberculosis management. They recognized another important role of the sanatoria—the removal of infected cases from the families of the ill and the general populace. Yet, the state never accorded Negro physicians a role in tuberculosis care.

In 1917, the year that Norris started practice, the death rate for all forms of tuberculosis in Virginia was 109.2 per 100,000 for whites and a whopping 307.6 per 100,000 for Negroes. The accompanying graph shows the death rate of whites versus Negroes from 1940 to 1951. *(See graph, page 211).*

Despite this higher mortality rate for Negroes, Virginia's response to the management of tuberculosis was woefully inadequate.

In a speech over WMBG, an NBC-affiliated AM radio station in Richmond, on April 7, 1942, Norris delivered the "National Negro Health Week Message." He made an impassioned call for a greater national and state effort in the fight against tuberculosis:

> We are now waging total war. Let's wage it against the enemy within as without, against foes microbic and as deadly as foes military. It is poor strategy to disregard the enemy that kills 60,000 of our citizens annually, most often in life's prime, and puts 180,000 others out of the national effort.

Nearly two years later on February 18, 1944, Norris, in a letter to the Governor of Virginia, Colgate Darden, laid out the dismal situation with profound poignancy:

> Dr M. E. Toney, President of the Rappahannock Medical Society, and myself visited a home just yesterday where there are two inmates [residents], both bright and intelligent young people, who would mean much to society, but who are dreadfully afflicted with that malady of tuberculosis. … One of them has had an application of over three months, but there seems to be no care available. Their parents are willing, but poor; the picture is both pathetic and pitiful. … Since it is a disease that should be treated early, and the most effective treatment is classed as Sanatorium, I wonder if the problem is being approached in its better and fullest light.

The *Journal and Guide* reported April 15, 1944, that three people had died waiting for admission to Piedmont and that a Dr. R. E. Anderson's wife was refused admission in December 1943 at Piedmont despite vacancies at Piedmont being present. She was admitted after Dr. Anderson threatened to take her to Catawba (the white sanatorium), but died five days later.

In the early 1950s, the state embarked on an ambitious program to expand facilities for all tuberculosis patients. Piedmont Tuberculosis Sanatorium for Negroes was to be expanded by fifty beds and a 300-bed facility for Negroes was planned at the Medical College of Virginia. (By 1957, the Ennion G. Williams Hospital was completed and had 242 sanatorium beds for Negro patients.) This rush to address the disparities in beds was surely in response to the mounting sentiment among Virginia officials to stave off integration by meeting the provisions of the *Plessy* decision—"separate but equal."

It was too late in the game. The discovery of streptomycin, isoniazid, and other anti-microbials would shortly consign the tuberculosis sanatoria to a lesser role in management of the disease. With the passage of civil rights legislation in the 1960s, there would be no need for separate sanatoria.

CHAPTER 21

The Loss of a Niece

Norris took life as it came; he rolled with the punches. There was one jab, however, that floored him. His thirty-two-year-old niece, an attractive, fair-skinned young woman with Caucasian features and coal-black, straight hair, told him that she no longer wanted to have anything to do with the family. She was going to "cross over," vernacular for passing for white. Her decision to break cleanly from the family was made in the early thirties—a time when racial divisions in the United States were deepest, the eugenics movement was at its apogee, and the concept of racial purity was finding its most receptive adherent in Nazi Germany's Adolph Hitler. Norris went to Philadelphia in an attempt to dissuade her. He returned home despondent and defeated, and never spoke of her again.

Eva Alma Thornton was the only child of his sister, Mary Jane, whom he affectionately called Mamie. Mamie had left Lancaster at an early age, married Augustus A. Thornton, a handsome bachelor from The Plains, a small village in Fauquier County, Northern Virginia. The couple settled in Yonkers, New York. Mamie was a talented seamstress, and Thornton, who first worked for the federal government, became an undertaker when he retired from government service. Alma was born about 1900 and grew up in Yonkers. While Norris worked for the Bunkers, he saw his niece and her family often but little after he left for Hampton Institute in 1904. He sometimes visited on his trips to the north when he worked summers in New Hampshire.

After her mother's death in 1919, Alma's relationship with Norris cooled. We have just one letter that Alma wrote Norris (circa 1928) and it was a rather perfunctory one at that. It concerned the transfer to Norris of her late mother's share of the property left by Benjamin Norris who died without a will. Thornton, for whom Norris named his first son, had a more cordial relationship with Norris. The tone of his letter (circa 1924) was far different from that of Alma's in its salutation, "My dear Dr. Norris, brother and friend and dear old boy," and ending, "Your family is very dear to me, we are unfortunately far apart. I am sending you all a little something that might please the children. Hoping they are all well and happy. Take good care of John Thornton, the only Thornton down there."

The careers of Alma and Norris were similar in many ways, yet they were so dissimilar. She, too, attended an outstanding undergraduate school, Hunter College. She attended medical school at Syracuse University, became a physician, and just as Norris had become a loyal alumnus of Hampton Institute, she became a loyal alumna of her alma mater. She lost her parents early in life, just as her uncle had, but not as early—first her mother and then her father. She had to fight prejudice, just like her uncle, but of a different kind— that directed toward her sex rather than her race, because to her peers, she was considered white. She never married, and because she severed ties with all her relatives, she chose a life of virtual solitude. She was a private person and frugal. Her father once said, "She holds to a dollar until she has to let it go." It is not surprising that she died a recluse, albeit a relatively well-to-do one. Norris died relatively impoverished in money, but rich with friends and loved ones.

Alma was a popular thespian from the description in her Hunter College yearbook in 1922. She was one of only three women among thirty-eight classmates in her Syracuse University School of Medicine class photo. She interned at Albany Hospital in Albany, New York. After the internship, she taught at Women's Medical College in Philadelphia for five years in the Department of Obstetrics. She was listed as an instructor in obstetrics during the 1928-1929 session, and from 1932 to 1935 was an assistant in clinical obstetrics. Alma gave up obstetrics and gynecology to enter psychiatric training at Philadelphia State Hospital. She then became a psychiatrist at Clark Summit State Hospital in Clark Summit, Pennsylvania. In the early 1940s, she settled in Scranton, Pennsylvania, then the state's fourth largest city in the world's greatest anthracite coal region. Scranton, at that time a major textile, household appliance, and shoe-manufacturing center, is nestled in the Lackawanna River valley bordered by ridges of the Allegheny Mountains. Whether by coincidence or intention, the geography was a perfect fit for someone seeking isolation.

In 1948, Alma joined the Veterans Administration system, now known as the Department of Veteran Affairs, and achieved the highest rank available at the Regional Hospital in Wilkes Barre, Pennsylvania. She was a charter member of the Modern Founders Club of the American Psychiatric Association. In 1967, the governor of Pennsylvania proclaimed "Women in Medicine Week," and Dr. Thornton was among five women from her area who were honored. She was a general member of the American Psychiatric Association from 1952, and was listed in the 1977 directory of the association. Alma died on November 12, 1983. She bequeathed over $300,000 to the Syracuse School of Medicine for student aid.

Alma was a talented musician and brilliant student, but because of her fair complexion and straight hair, she lived in that psychologically wrenching divide in our culture, where among colored she was not considered colored, and among whites she was not considered white. Her attorney says he thought she might have been part American Indian, as she had straight black hair and she expressed an interest in Indians. Charles Harney, a medical book salesman who knew her, said that he remembered her well but had no idea that she was not Caucasian. Having lost her mother at age twenty and her father at age thirty-four, she did what she felt best for her at the time and crossed over.

Passing was a practice that was well-known among colored people. If one had the misfortune of having one foot in the colored world and one foot in the white world, yet belonging to neither, it made sense, if only for practical reasons, to make the hard choice of taking the path of least resistance. This path would often demand that one forsake relatives and heritage and establish a new identity. Many colored people in the North did just that, but only during the day, returning to the security of their colored families at the end of the workday. We had relatives whose hair texture, cream complexions, and aquiline noses made them appear no different from residents of Tuscany, so by day they easily found work in the restaurants and fashion houses of New York City. Norris's first cousin and Alma's closest friend, Coletha Tolson Johnson, was a seamstress with Oscar de la Renta. The fashion designer probably did not know her background, and it is doubtful that it would have mattered if he had, but without knowing her lineage, one would be hard put to consider her anything other than Caucasian. Coletha and Alma had become friends when Coletha, at age fourteen, went to live with the Thorntons in Yonkers. She learned the craft of sewing and dressmaking from Alma's mother. Coletha never once gave the thought of completely crossing over as she was too close to her family. Despite Alma and Coletha being as close as sisters, when Alma made the decision to "go over," she told Coletha that she did not want to see her again.

Unlike Coletha, Alma forsook *all* vestiges of her background, adopted a new persona, and became white. Was her life any different from the escaped prisoner whose existence is no longer bound by prison walls, but finds freedom every bit as constricting as those gray concrete blocks? That she elected to work in rather remote areas and never married bespeaks of attempts to keep her identity hidden. While the thought is purely conjectural, is it possible that she sought refuge in psychiatry to help her deal with the imagined demons? Or was she a contented spinster totally immersed in her work? Theresita made several contacts with Alma after she began passing. They were arranged through a white lawyer who knew of her decision. The communications centered on clearing up her mother's share of the homeplace in Virginia. The last contacts the family had with her were in 1942, when she signed the deed to transfer her mother's share of the homeplace to Norris. When Norris died in 1966, Theresita made an attempt to contact her, but got no response. Alma's will tells how she felt toward the Norris family.

It is my desire and intention to leave my estate to the following named charities because my beloved parents and brother have predeceased me and I have had no contact with my cousins for upwards of forty years. I do not know of their whereabouts nor do I feel that I have any obligation to or from them.

Her will is puzzling in that the family is not aware that Mamie or Thornton had another child. The charities she named were the Lackawanna Branch of the Society for the Prevention of Cruelty to Animals $500; Scranton Chapter of the Salvation Army, $5,000; and Mercy Hospital in Scranton, $20,000. The remainder went to the Medical Scholarship Fund of the Syracuse University School of Medicine. The bequest was in excess of $300,000. The will was made in 1971.

The isolation and loneliness took its toll. She died alone in cluttered squalor, amid the stench of a broken toilet. Old newspapers, magazines, and journals were stacked so densely in her home that there was hardly space for one to navigate. She had adamantly refused to have anyone except her attorney come into her home, and she spurned any offers for assistance. It is estimated that she had been dead for two days when her body was found. Her only friend was an elderly Jewish attorney who visited her almost daily. Whether there was a romantic relationship, it is not known. What is known is that they both were eccentric characters.

Her remains were handled by the local funeral home in Wilkes Barre, Pennsylvania. Cremation was carried out at her request. There was no directive as to what should be done with the ashes. No one in our family even knew about her death at the time.

Her home, which was across the street from Mercy Hospital, was sold to the hospital. The house was demolished and the site was paved over. It is now the hospital's parking lot.

Under "Race" on Alma's death certificate, the coroner listed her as "White."

CHAPTER 22

The Country Doctor Becomes a College Trustee

Norris's appointment to the Hampton Institute Board of Trustees was a curious one. It was just so improbable that a country doctor would be selected over an array of fine candidates to become the second colored trustee of one of the South's most famous schools. He met only two of the six criteria for the selection of three new trustees that the board had set, his youth and his location in the South. The other criteria were a woman, someone in finance, a person from a new locality such as Chicago, Cincinnati, or Cleveland, and a nationally known person. The list of potential candidates included such luminaries and household names as a Rockefeller, a Ford, and a Firestone. Theodore Roosevelt, Jr., several college presidents, and Virginians such as Senator and former Governor Harry Flood Byrd, James Dillard, and Beverly Munford were also on the list. All were white.

Two outstanding white men were selected. One was Dr. Frank Porter Graham, president of the University of North Carolina and a member of the North Carolina Commission on Interracial Cooperation. The other was Robert Abbe Gardner of Chicago, a Yale graduate, amateur golf champion, and captain of the U.S. Walker Cup Team for four years. Gardner was already a trustee of Northwestern University and treasurer of the United Charities of Chicago.

Norris was appointed almost as an afterthought. The Trustee Board minutes of the sixty-fifth annual meeting held April 26, 1934, recorded that after further discussion of Mr. Willis Wood and Mr. Everett Bacon it was decided advisable to elect a colored man to fill the last vacancy on the board, that of the twentieth trustee. The Negro men vetted, in addition to Norris, were either of considerable reputation or substantial means. Dr. William Taylor Burwell Williams was a field director for the Slater Fund (a fund established by industrialist John F. Slater of Norwich, Connecticut, to promote industrial education of Southern Negroes); Professor Benjamin Griffith Brawley was on the Hampton Institute faculty; Charles Clinton Spaulding was founder of the North Carolina Mutual Insurance Company; and Dr. Barnett M. Rhetta was an outstanding physician who practiced in Texas. The board voted that "Dr. Morgan E. Norris, a Hampton graduate living in Kilmarnock, Virginia, be elected a trustee of Hampton Institute." He was fifty-one years old.

There was considerable flak over appointing a country doctor to the Board of Trustees of so venerable an institution. Some critics were quite vocal in their protests. They felt that a more prominent and substantial alumnus than this country bumpkin could better serve the interests of Hampton Institute. Norris's talents, intellect, and sheer energy were grossly underestimated. If the Trustee Board relished in having brought aboard a man they thought would be a groveling sycophant, they would soon discover their naïve miscalculation. Obsequiousness was as distasteful to Norris as biting into an unripe persimmon.

In an editorial in the *Afro-American* newspaper, May 19, 1934, under the head "Great Joy at Hampton," the editor took note of the appointment of Norris. With a mixture of sarcasm and acerbity he wrote:

> In sixty-six years Hampton Institute found only one alumnus worthy of sitting on its trustee board. He was R.R. Moton. Recently it looked around and discovered another, Dr. Morgan E. Norris of Kilmarnock, Va., a graduate of the class of 1908. Strange how the old slaves psychology persists in some schools. Seventy-five percent of the trustees at Cornell and Amherst are alumni.
>
> At Hampton, Trustees are selected because they have the money or can put their hands on people with money. Students are expected to take the education handed out to them, be grateful, and get out without ever having any ambition to share in the administration of their own college.

Norris served Hampton well for twenty-one years. He resigned from the Board in 1955 when illness hampered his ability to serve fully and effectively. He did not have money, but he had friends who had money, and he was dogged in his efforts to get his friends and even some who were not his friends to contribute to Hampton. Moreover, he unquestionably helped shape the administration of the college, possibly to the chagrin of some administrators.

During Norris's tenure on the Board of Trustees he served during four administrations—Arthur Howe, Sr., Malcolm S. MacLean, Ralph Bridgman, and Alonzo Morón, and one acting president, Ralph O'Hara Lanier. The numerous letters he wrote to the presidents of Hampton Institute are testament to his deep involvement in the affairs of the college. He used his influence and his pen to nudge his fellow trustees and the administration toward bringing in more colored administrators and faculty. It would be no mistake to say that he was a gentle gadfly. An inveterate letter writer, his tact in approaching even the most sensitive topic in writing was artful. Most of his letters to the presidents were two typewritten pages in length. He himself typed these letters, as he did not have the luxury of a secretary. Generally the first page would be devoted to fairly mundane matters of school business and would be unfailingly complimentary toward the president's efforts. The second page was the page of substance in which he would get to the issue at hand.

Norris was not the type of person who would confine himself to perfunctory attendance at the annual trustee meeting. He was actively involved in nearly every aspect of the institute's internal affairs—helping to quell student rebellions; becoming a vocal advocate of more colored administrators at Hampton; interacting with the alumni on a national level; fund-raising; engineering appointments to the Board of Trustees; and perhaps even getting the first colored president appointed to the institute.

In alumni relations, his activity was not only limited to the Northern Neck of Virginia but extended to the national level. He frequently visited alumni groups in major cities. In a letter dated November 4, 1946, to Dr. Ralph Bridgman, the president of Hampton Institute, Norris wrote of his meetings with alumni groups:

> I have been doing a little running around since I saw you in N.Y.
> Of course I stopped by Baltimore and Washington returning home. We
> were able to get to the Warrenton meeting of the N.O.S. [Negro Orga-
> nization Society.] Then the next day I took a little hop by the way of
> Richmond to Cincinnati, Saint Louis, Chicago, Indianapolis and the
> surrounding territory seeing all the people I could and spreading as
> much good will for Hampton as I could. I saw many Hampton gradu-
> ates, but Mr. Phillips in Saint Louis, Brokenburr in Indianapolis and
> the boys at the Chicago Defender deserve special mention not omitting
> Clyde Reynolds at Provident Hospital in Chicago.

By virtue of Kilmarnock's geographical proximity to Hampton, he made
frequent trips to Hampton Institute during the 1930s and 1940s to give talks
to groups such as the New Farmers of America and the Doctors' Helpers Institute. At times he was asked to represent the Trustee Board at commencement.

Travel over the two-lane, serpentine paved roads between Kilmarnock
and Hampton could be treacherous. The distance was only sixty-five miles
but two rivers, the Rappahannock and the York, had to be crossed by ferries.
Bridges would not be built over the York until 1951 and the Rappahannock
until 1957. A ferry had to be taken to cross the Rappahannock River at Grey's
Point in White Stone to Topping in Middlesex County. To cross the York
River, the ferry ran from Gloucester Point to Yorktown. The ferries ran only
until 10 or 11 p.m. When returning from Hampton, if a ferry were missed
at Topping, it meant going back to Hampton or driving nearly eighty miles
through Tappahannock. Filling stations or garages were few, and if the car
broke down, the driver had to wait until a passerby would come and help.
On those country roads after dark, it might be a long wait. The riskiest time
to travel was during wintertime when the days were short and cold. Weather
prediction at the time was unsophisticated. Norris was caught in an expected
snowstorm on more than one occasion. Another great hazard was fog. The
corridor from Kilmarnock to Hampton lies entirely in lowlands along the

coast and the changes in temperature sometimes result in fog so dense that it is aptly described as "pea soup."

The presidents and the fellow trustees of Hampton Institute did not intimidate Norris. He was not one to assume a subservient role. He had his disagreements with members but in all his letters that involved contentious matters, he always sought the middle ground. Conciliation to him was not a sign of weakness but the realistic approach to most situations. If pushed too far, and it made no difference who was doing the pushing, he would push back. He once had such a heated argument with one of the trustees that the poor fellow collapsed in the meeting and died of a heart attack. Norris told me about the episode with a rueful tone in his voice, "Son, I have killed only one man, and that was Frank Darling during a Trustee Board meeting at Hampton." Apparently the argument was about Dixie Hospital, which was on the campus of Hampton Institute, yet was strictly segregated and had no colored physicians on its staff. It was the only hospital for the students, and there had been some concern among the alumni about accommodations for the colored female students. The minutes of that Trustees Board meeting, written as insipidly as the small print on an insurance policy, did not give the slightest description of the debate. The secretary recorded that President MacLean intoned about what a fine hospital it was—"one of the best small hospitals connected with any college or institution in the country"—and how by working together the differences could be resolved. The secretary then wrote, "After some further discussion, the meeting ended abruptly because of the sudden death, by heart failure, of Mr. Frank W. Darling." In another reference to this incident, Norris wrote to me in October 1959: "It takes an ole veteran like Dad to set those boys at Hampton straight. He is not long doing it. The slogan is remember Captain Darling and Doctor Norris when Darling fought to the last, but it was simply a matter of David and Goliath."

Norris had a warm and cordial relationship with Arthur Howe, the first president with whom he worked. Howe had married Margaret Armstrong, the daughter of Hampton's founder, General Armstrong and Mary Alice

Armstrong. That fact alone contributed toward his amicable accord with Norris. Howe was a decent and dedicated man—taciturn, deliberate, and all business. He was a 1912 Yale University graduate and a direct descendant of John Howe, an Englishman who had come to America before 1640. A graduate of Union Theological Seminary and an ordained Presbyterian minister, Howe was appointed president of the college in 1930, succeeding Dr. George P. Phenix who had died suddenly. Norris and Howe had struck up a lively correspondence well before Norris became a trustee, and their correspondence reflects a mutual affection as well as mutual respect. Norris twice elicited help from Howe before he became trustee, when he was building the elementary school and when he tried to have black professionals assigned to the Piedmont Sanatorium.

Howe guided Hampton Institute through a most financially challenging period of its existence, the Great Depression. He was caught off guard, however, when the students rebelled in 1939. The uproar had to do with the firing of a popular colored professor, James Waldo Ivey, by his white department head, George Adrian Kuyper. Norris and a fellow trustee, Dr. Henry Wilder Foote, were given the charge of sorting out the imbroglio and assuaging both sides.

Foote was a clergyman in the Unitarian Church and pastor of the First Church of New Orleans. He had served on the Trustee Board of Hampton Institute since 1918. The committee of two conducted a thorough investigation. They met with the president of Hampton; a committee of alumni; the two faculty representatives of the Virginia Peninsula Teachers' Union, Local 607; twice with students' representatives; several other members of the staff; and Ivey. Kuyper, though not on campus, gave the committee a detailed statement. A full report was sent to the Trustee Board. The committee recommended, "the Trustees take no action in the matter of the students petition." They noted that the "vehemence (of the petition) though poor in taste, however, does serve to indicate the depth of feeling among the students." The situation was considered so inflammatory that the committee recommended that should Kuyper offer to resign, his resignation be accepted and, if not, then he be given a year's leave of absence to complete work on his doctorate. Ivey received one year's salary and assistance in finding a position at another institution. It appeared Ivey was mollified by this arrangement.

In its report, the committee also addressed the inequities in hiring at Hampton. The report noted that most of the positions held by Negroes were subordinate positions. For example, it was pointed out that of the thirty-four members on the Educational Board, only eight were Negroes and of the ten members of the Administrative Board, only two were Negroes. The committee called for greater balance in the staff and recommended the hiring of a Negro Dean of Women, a Negro Director of Education, and an increase in the number of Negro heads of departments.

Norris's agitation for the appointment of a Negro Dean of Women finally paid off. In 1940, Flemmie P. Kittrell was appointed Dean of Women. Kittrell, a 1928 Hampton graduate, was an extraordinarily distinguished woman, particularly for the 1930s. She had obtained her doctorate in nutrition from Cornell University in 1936. She came to Hampton Institute after having served as Dean of Women and director of the Department of Home Economics at Bennett College, an all female, colored college in Greensboro, North Carolina. Kittrell, a slender woman and small in stature, gained a reputation among the female Hampton students as being gentle but tough. She addressed her students as "little dears," but she was a strong disciplinarian. It must have been a challenge for this feisty woman as the first colored Dean of Women at Hampton, but a greater challenge would lie ahead. She had taken her new position just before the United States entered World War II. Hampton Institute contributed significantly toward the war effort. The campus became a virtual military base, but there were no shenanigans between the students and the military personnel, as Kittrell kept firm control of her charges.

Howe had resigned from his position as president in 1940 and did not participate in Kittrell's growth. That was left to his successor, Malcolm S. MacLean.

MacLean, born, educated, and employed in the Midwest, came to Hampton in 1941. He was a former newspaper editor, holder of a doctorate in English, and an innovator in education. His father was a prominent Denver lawyer and he was grandson of John MacLean, a Congregational minister who had come to Pennsylvania before the Civil War.

MacLean had his own ideas about how an institution ought to be run. It was not long before Norris's relationship with the new president became quarrelsome. First, MacLean was not enamored of Kittrell's performance and began making her life uncomfortable as Dean of Women. Norris, upon hearing of the schism between the president and Kittrell and of her threat to resign as Dean of Women, was beyond angry and had this to say in a civil, but acid letter to MacLean:

> Now Dr. MacLean, Hampton needs you very much; probably more than any one else, it needs Dr. Kittrell. My last word of kindly gesture coming from one who has both of your interests close to heart is "Let there be no strife between me and thee" but that every thing may work in unity for the building of a greater Hampton.

MacLean's February 6, 1942, reply to Norris was swift, unequivocal, and condescending to Kittrell. It did little to placate the angry trustee. MacLean said she was "miscast as a Dean of Women."

In a patronizing note on Kittrell, he assured Norris that she would have no problem as long as she

> ... acts sensibly. We shall move with caution. We shall take every precaution to preserve her reputation intact. And, further, you may be sure that so long as I am here I would under no circumstances select or appoint other than a colored woman for the deanship. Hence, there can be no question of raising the racial issue. It is simply a matter of finding the way, when the time comes, to place Miss Kittrell in the job which she can perform with greatest service to the race, to herself, and to education.

The year of 1942 would bring further strains between Norris and the president. Norris intervened in a disgruntled professor's complaint that he was being sacked by MacLean, and Norris responded directly to a student who had written to him about conditions at the school. MacLean was thoroughly chafed by the tone of Norris's response to the student and wasted no time in letting him know just how he felt. On December 3, 1942, he sent Norris a two-page, typewritten, single-spaced response and ended the letter with a stinging rebuke:

> I think it is necessary and right that the trustees should answer this letter [referring to the letter from the student]. Only I think it might have been well had you expressed a general confidence in the administration here if you feel you have such confidence. Dean Lanier, Mr. Davis, Mr. Reynolds and I and others have put everything we had and have into giving students at Hampton Institute better living conditions, better teachers, better food, better health service and a better educational program. If that is not enough, then it is only necessary for you to decide as trustees that it is not enough and to change administrations.

It did not take long for MacLean to come to the conclusion that running Hampton Institute was not for him. He resigned, and for a brief period Dr. Raphael O'Hara Lanier, a forty-three-year-old Lincoln alumnus, was acting president and the first colored man to be at the helm. Lanier had studied and gained high marks at New York and Harvard Universities. He would have been an outstanding president of the college, but Hampton's Board of Trustees and, astonishingly, some of the Hampton alumni (Norris was not among the group), were not ready for a colored president. Lanier left after one year to become U.S. Minister to Liberia. In 1948, he was appointed president of Texas Southern University. The Hampton board selected, instead, Ralph Parkhurst Bridgman as president. Norris was in favor of Lanier becoming president and let his fellow trustees know that. They responded by letting Lanier go and hiring Bridgman, a Bostonian, a Phi Beta Kappa graduate of Harvard College, and a magna cum laude graduate of Union Theological Seminary. He came to Hampton Institute as its fourth president and seventh head. (The first three leaders of Hampton were called principals.) After attending the Trustee Board meeting where Bridgman was selected as president, Norris wrote to Mr. J. Henry Scattergood, a fellow Hampton Trustee, on September 14, 1943:

It was a very great pleasure to attend the meeting and see the very fine spirit expressed on the part of all concerned to see Hampton go forward. I plan to write Dr. Bridgman shortly expressing my intention to do what I can to help him. I am very grateful that I have had the opportunity over a period of many years to know and be associated with many of the very fine white people who have in every way done so much for Hampton and the Negro race. However, as well as I love Hampton, its traditions, and those very fine saintly white people who have served our group so efficiently and effectively in the past, I do feel with Mr. P. B. Young [editor and publisher of the *Norfolk Journal and Guide*, a respected colored newspaper] that with the changing times, the outside pressure, particularly the Negro press, and the trend of the Negro youth that the day will not be far distant when the only alternative will be a Negro head. I say this in the kindest and best spirit.

Norris's relationship with Bridgman never reached the level of contentiousness that he had had with MacLean, but neither did it approach the congenial and mutually supportive relationship he had cultivated with Howe. Bridgman's reign was about as uneventful as a college president's could be. It was not long before he realized that he was out of his element at Hampton, and he moved on in 1948. At an Executive Committee meeting of the Trustee Board February 16, 1948, an "interim Administrative Committee" composed of Hampton Institute administrators was appointed to run the college. The chairman of this committee was Hampton Institute's Business Manager, Alonzo Graseano Morón. As chairman, Morón had access to the files in the president's office and had available to him the clerical services of that office. Morón was de facto president of Hampton Institute. In 1949 he was appointed the first colored president of Hampton Institute.

Morón was a native of Saint Thomas, Virgin Islands. He was tall, handsome, urbane, and reserved, his demeanor more befitting a banker than a college president. He seemed to be a man far more comfortable with numerical figures than human figures. Gregariousness was definitely not his forte.

Norris soon developed a warm relationship with Morón, an affinity helped by Morón being promoted to his post at Norris's instigation and not hurt by Morón's marriage to Leola Churchill whose family resided in Sharps, Richmond County, Virginia—a county contiguous with Lancaster County. She was from a family that Norris served as its physician.

One of Morón's first major acts in reorganizing the curriculum at Hampton Institute was to eliminate the trade schools. Hampton had traditionally been strong in technical training—an area of education that Morón was convinced did not belong under the purview of a four-year college. When Morón took the helm at Hampton Institute, one-eighth of the student body was enrolled in trade programs. Instruction was provided in twelve trades that included cabinet making, carpentry, electricity, forging and welding, machine shop technique, painting, plumbing and heating, and printing. Morón felt that Hampton should further strengthen its science and liberal arts education programs. In Morón's estimation, trades could be taught in high schools or at technical schools but they had no place in the Hampton Institute curriculum. Norris never challenged Morón on this issue, although he was confident that there was a place for technical education in the training of Negro youth, and that Hampton Institute should continue to provide some level of instruction in industrial or vocational education. Nevertheless, he accepted Morón's arguments and was entirely supportive of Morón throughout his administration.

Morón was not immune to the turbulence that engulfs the president of any college or university. After ten years as head of Hampton Institute, it became doubtful that he could stem the tide of dissent against him. Norris voiced his support for the beleaguered president, but he was no longer a trustee and there was little he could do except write his friends:

Too, in view of the fact there has been a little stir about Dr. Morón, I hope we shall bend backwards to show our support. In my judgment it would be nigh tragic to have him resign at this time. He is young, wise, competent, an administrator of note and he has made Hampton well known to many, many agents.

When Morón was forced out in July 1959, Norris wrote to a friend: "Doubtless you have heard that Dr. Morón is not with us at Hampton anymore. Many, many of us are greatly grieved."

I visited Morón eight years later when he was in Puerto Rico. He did not seem bitter about having been shepherded out of Hampton. If he were bitter, he was too self-assured and reserved to display acrimony. He did express his dismay that the white trustees of Hampton Institute felt that there was a glass ceiling for colored. As a former business manager, he was critical of the manner in which the endowment had been managed. He felt that the trustees had not been creative nor aggressive enough with the investments and that instead of diversifying they had, for too long, kept the major portion of Hampton Institute's portfolio in railroad stock. In discussing the situation with one who was knowledgeable about the trustees' side, a different picture emerged from the one Morón had painted. Morón had proved difficult and uncompromising in his relations with the board.

It was during Morón's administration that Norris's tenure as a trustee ended. Norris knew the end of his service was nearing, but he was determined to place one person of substance on the board. Four months before he submitted his resignation, he nominated Ellsworth Bunker to the Trustee Board. The board unanimously accepted the nomination. Norris was intensely proud that his friend had agreed to serve on the Board of Trustees at Hampton. Bunker had adequate reasons to beg off on this new responsibility. He had already served as ambassador to Argentina, and at the time of his nomination was president of the American Red Cross. His plate was full. And his portfolio would grow with assignments by U.S. presidents to trouble spots around the world. But he knew the depth of Norris's love and concern for Hampton, and he would not let ambassadorial demands interfere with coming through for his friend.

It is sobering to review the posts held by this tall, ramrod straight, patrician Easterner. He served as ambassador to Nepal from 1956 to 1958, then India from 1958 to 1961. In 1962, President John F. Kennedy sent him to the settle the dispute between the Netherlands and Indonesia over what is now Irian Java and then to Yemen to settle a dispute between Saudi Arabia and Egypt. He was off to Panama at the request of President Lyndon B. Johnson when the students rioted over the canal, and was subsequently made representative to the Organization of American States. He received a presidential Medal of Freedom for his work in negotiating a resolution to the Dominican Republic crisis in 1964. Additionally, he was appointed ambassador at large. At age 73 he was named ambassador to South Vietnam for six years and served under both Johnson and President Richard M. Nixon. Bunker returned from Vietnam in 1973, and at the request of President Jimmy Carter, worked from 1974 to 1977 negotiating the Panama Canal treaties.

But Bunker did not let these manifold duties interfere with his service to Hampton Institute. He served for eighteen years as trustee and then six years as an honorary trustee.

Norris's resignation from the Board of Trustees was by no means the end of his association with Hampton Institute. He made a startling comeback from his illness of 1955 and although his usual high-octane drive was blunted by age and infirmity, he was a vigorous campaigner for Hampton until the year he died. Not a single one of his acquaintances or friends or even family was spared his requests for a donation for Hampton. His letters were warm and friendly, but unfailingly persistent. In a letter to me, he wrote: "Thanks for the assurance that the extra fifty dollars would be sent into the institute. Hampton has meant much to me and to our race, so I feel that we should try to carry what little of the load we can." He was not reticent about letting Arthur Bunker, Ellsworth's younger brother, know that there was no place for parsimony in his contributions to Hampton Institute. Norris wrote Morón, October 5, 1957, that while he was visiting Bunker in New Hampshire, "without my bringing up the subject, he said that I had prodded him a good

234   James E.C. Norris, M.D.

deal about doing something for Hampton and that he thought he would give me then a thousand dollars which I promptly turned down." Norris went on to tell Morón that he told Bunker that he expected at least $5,000 or more appropriately, $10,000.

Not only did Norris personally raise nearly $5,000 as his Golden Anniversary Gift to the school in 1958, but he was also the director of a $50,000 fund-raising event for Hampton Institute.

In 1959, he wrote fellow alumnus Steven McDew about his service on the board and in characteristic understatement said, "my experience was very, very challenging and interesting." Once, in an indirect reference to the whims of university administration and trustee board machinations, he said to me when I was but a teenager: "Son, I don't know what you plan to do in life, but whatever you do, as long as it is above board, I will support you. But there is one thing that I ask you not to do, and that is, work for a university."

CHAPTER 23

Pushing Back on Kilmarnock

Too often, politicians either don't know history or they choose to ignore it. The practice of taxation without representation or just compensation is as old as government, and it has backfired just as long, particularly when the politicians underestimate the resolve of their constituents. Kilmarnock, a small town in Lancaster County, made just that mistake after incorporating in the 1930s.

Kilmarnock was no different from the myriad of other Southern towns where whites were clearly separated from colored. Parallel steel rails that sliced through the terrain divided most towns. But in the Northern Neck, there were no railroads, so the dividing line was where the streetlights ended, the sidewalks stopped, and the water and sewer lines were capped. The racial mixture of Southern towns varied. Many towns were lily-white; a few were all colored. Rarely, there might be a town such as Tappahannock, Virginia, where housing was thoroughly integrated, but by and large, the residents of the villages, towns, and cities were segregated by race.

The little village of Kilmarnock, named by the local merchants of Scottish descent for Kilmarnock, Scotland, incorporated in 1931. A tight line encircling the whites was drawn around the village, except for a little bulge to the south where it enclosed a good part of our colored neighborhood. Though no advantages accrued to the colored residents within the corporate limits, there was an advantage to the town. The colored residents paid taxes.

This arrangement apparently caused no great problem until the town made one misstep. It sent Morgan E. Norris, M.D., a bill, a license fee of $10, which was levied on all physicians who had offices within the corporate limits.

Now, $10 in today's currency might be a pittance, but in the 1930s, it was a significant tax. Coupled with the levy was the indignity of getting nothing.

Norris went before the Kilmarnock Town Council on July 17, 1939, to protest this assessment. He asked to be relieved of paying the fee because he received no benefits from the town. He negotiated with the town officials for almost a year. Norris realized he wasn't getting through. He then engaged a young white attorney, Charles H. Ryland, of neighboring Warsaw, Virginia, to appear with him before the Town Council. Norris and Ryland met with the council, but neither was able to convince the council of the unfairness of the tax. The town leaders remained resolute and would not abate the tax. Norris then surprised the council with a Solomonic proposition: "I will pay the thirty dollars for the three years that I owe but I am asking that the limits be moved to exclude me from residency in the town."

On August 31, 1940, Norris wrote a letter to Ryland recounting his individual meetings with Kilmarnock merchants and the postmaster. Norris wrote, "To my mind the thing that will probably settle the matter is to draw in the area of the town as you and Senator Norris have suggested. [Robert Opie Norris, Jr., was a Virginia state senator and the Town Counsel.] If a petition is needed, we can have it with plenty of signers."

Norris also sought support from the Virginia Commission on Interracial Cooperation. In October of 1940, he wrote to Mr. L. R. Reynolds, the white chairman of the commission: "I wish I could feel that we could get along here together. Mr. Reynolds, it is very embarrassing to me to be in a stew all the while, but what shall we do?"

No progress was made with the town. More than a year later, Norris and his neighbors petitioned the Board of Supervisors of Lancaster County to contract the town's corporate limits. The majority of the tax-paying residents of the neighborhood south of Kilmarnock, all colored, united behind Norris in signing a petition to redraw the boundaries. Norris was able to get nine petitioners. The advertisement in the *Rappahannock Record* ran for four weeks, from November 13 to December 4, 1941. It defined the boundary of the area to be stricken (a total of 46.5 acres of land) and made clear that:

the court should make no order as to the payment of any debts or obligations of the said town as between the county and the inhabitants of the said town, because the area proposed to be stricken off has received, during the ten or more years since the incorporation of the said town, no benefits of any improvements for which the debts of said town were incurred.

On February 2, 1942, Judge E. Hugh Smith of the Circuit Court of Lancaster County granted the petition for contraction of the corporate limits of the town of Kilmarnock, but the court decision was not the end of the saga.

The town did not give up its attempts to collect the protested taxes (from the 1941 tax year) from the excluded residents. The town policeman, Sgt. William E. Bussells, was told to collect the taxes from the residents who lived in the stricken area. Norris, with his neighbors Willie Grimes and Narvel Wiggins, went before the Town Council in October 1942 with a plea to have the taxes abrogated. The council members agreed to have the town's attorney and Norris's attorney determine "whether or not such taxes can be legally relinquished."

As late as January 1944, the town published in the *Rappahannock Record* a "List of Uncollected 1941 Town Taxes." All the petitioners owed taxes. Norris and Simon Conquest, the owner of the beer garden and restaurant across the road from Norris, owed the largest amounts. No records show whether the town of Kilmarnock ever collected. The boundary remained in place until 2007, although over the last 65 years the town has expanded east, west and north.

Sixty-three years later, I had an opportunity to interview Mr. Ryland. He still resides in Warsaw, Virginia. In 1940, he was a 27-year-old attorney when he took the case. He said Norris engaged him because

he couldn't find anyone else. ... He found that I was a young lawyer just starting out here in Warsaw and, of course, I was looking for things to do, and I suppose the main reason he was coming to me [was] because of my father's interest in colored education. My father was a professor at the University of Richmond. He was a trustee of Virginia Union.

Ryland said he first talked to the mayor of the town of Kilmarnock, Dr. Lowe, but didn't get very far with him. He then talked to Senator Norris. "He said: 'Well Charlie, you have to bring a suit.' I brought a suit." Even Norris was not convinced of the wisdom of Ryland taking on the senator, and told him, "You've lost your mind. You're going to lose that case." Ryland retorted: "No, I am not."

Ryland continued with an unmistakable relish in his voice, not in the least diminished by the passage of six decades:

There was a special statute that was passed by the legislature many years ago that said if the town is in two counties, then certain rules apply to it that don't apply to other towns and I brought the suit under that statute. And we got into court and it surprised Senator Norris, he didn't know it. The judge, [Hugh] Smith, ruled in my favor and sort of laughed because they [he and Senator Norris] were of the same generation and Senator Norris was not accustomed to losing cases. He lost that one, and I enjoyed it very much.

Ryland has total recall of his client. His comments describe a man who was fearless, defiant, and always striving to make changes. "He loved to tell people what to do. I had to learn to make him be quiet and listen to me," Ryland said. Ryland gave a candid view of Norris from the perspective of the white citizens of Kilmarnock. He said the white officials in Kilmarnock "thought he was a troublemaker. Part of it was his attitude. He lectured them. … He was too aggressive … then he'd lose his temper. So that's just the way he was." Ryland added finally: "Your father was a pushy fellow. I had to slow him down a little."

CHAPTER 24

From a Cow Barn to an Auto Repair Garage

"No" was not a word that most people in Lancaster County would say to Norris. When it came from a white garage owner at whose business he had been a loyal customer, he was stung. And when he was stung, he fought back, but not by raving and ranting and hurling threats and expletives. Rather, he withdrew to own resources and took the attitude, "Fine, I won't bother you anymore; I will build my own garage."

Having a place where colored people could take their cars for repairs and not have to endure slights fit in nicely with his penchant for self-sufficiency. When he built the garage, no colored person in Lancaster County had a combined auto repair garage and service station. Some colored businesses had a single gasoline pump, and a few mechanics did auto repairs in their backyards. They would jack up the cars on wooden blocks and use a block and tackle swung over a tree limb to lift out the engines; but no one had a garage with auto stalls, a grease pit, a lift, and a service island (where the gasoline pumps are located.)

The Second World War had just ended. No new cars had come out of Detroit since 1942 because the manufacturing capacity of General Motors, Ford, Chrysler, and Studebaker Motors had retooled to produce jeeps, tanks, armored cars, and planes for the war effort. Norris's Ford, which he affectionately called "Tin Lizzie," had traveled thousands of country road miles and was in constant need of repair. Only the ingenuity of the mechanics kept his little Ford running. He could not be without the car a single day, as he had to make house calls in three counties.

This particular morning in 1945 had begun, like so many of his mornings, with an urgent call to visit a sick patient. When he started the engine to his Ford, a disturbing clanking replaced the gentle hum of the dependable V-8 motor. He visited his patient and then stopped by the auto repair shop in Kilmarnock. When he arrived at the garage, he was abruptly told to wait. The patience of the mechanics had been stretched as thin as their customers. There was not a car in the county less than three years old, and the battering they had taken from coursing over rough country roads had left the springs, shock absorbers, and motors perilously worn. Few mechanics were around because all the young and not-so-young, able-bodied men either had been drafted for the war or had moved to cities to work in the defense industries. The combination of too many beat-up cars and too few mechanics could easily lead to frustration with the inevitable fracturing of relationships. Norris was on the receiving end of a nasty tirade from an irate owner. He returned home and resolved never again to depend on his mechanic in Kilmarnock.

In a matter of days, he went to Hampton Institute to meet with his long-time friend and Dean of Men, Major Walter Brown. He let Brown know that he did not want just an auto mechanic; he wanted the best graduate Hampton had. And he got him. Jack Taylor, a student from South Carolina, agreed to come to Lancaster County to run the business. There was, however, a bit of a problem. He now had an auto mechanic, but he had no garage. For Norris, this was in no way insurmountable. He went no farther than his barnyard to locate a garage. The barn was a solid two-story wood frame structure conveniently situated by the road. He proceeded to renovate the barn where, for years, he had kept his cows. What had been cow stalls became auto repair stalls. Understanding how much Norris loved his cows, this was the clearest gauge of the depth of his indignation.

Other problems had to be solved. He needed lodging for Taylor and Taylor's new wife. That problem, too, was surmounted. He renovated the upstairs of the little medical office where he usually housed his patients, and Taylor and his family were given living quarters there. Taylor brought not only his wife but also his two brothers to work in the station. Getting the garage going was tantamount to running an obstacle course. Norris had his mechanic, had solved the problem of the garage and lodging for the mechanic and his family, but he had not considered that they had to eat. A kitchen had to be put in as well. A kitchen had not been in place since 1927 when my parents moved to their new house. While Taylor and his family were waiting for the kitchen to be set up, to Theresita's profound consternation, they boarded in our home. Theresita was unhappy about this hasty arrangement, but she never would torpedo any of Norris's projects.

In short order, Norris had a service station and a car repair service that ran for three decades. When Taylor and his family left after several years, Norris found the best talent available to take his place. Morgan Ward, a young man from Whitestone, named for Norris and son of Mrs. Sadie Ward (see pp. 78-79), and Ellis Jones, from Remo, Northumberland County, took over management. Nellery Morris, also a Northumberland County resident and a master mechanic, was brought in. Morris was known throughout the lower Northern Neck for superb workmanship. Norris's venture soon became one of the most popular auto repair garages in the county.

On September 12, 1950, a fire completely destroyed the garage, an automobile belonging to a customer, and all the equipment. A watch repair shop housed in the station and operated by Ward was also destroyed. Undaunted, Norris immediately had plans drawn up for a new service station. He looked to Coleman Treakle, his white friend and the Texaco representative for the area, for help. Treakle, a ruddy-faced, corpulent, avuncular man and the quintessential Southern gentleman, let Norris have a Texaco franchise. By the time the new station was built, Norris had enticed his oldest son, Thornton, to return home. Thornton, who had studied barbering, opened a barbershop in the new building and managed the station and garage. In 1956, my parents deeded the station to Thornton.

Norris was justifiably proud of his enterprise. He liked the idea that the colored people had their own businesses. He was not a racist, but a realist. In a society where so much was defined by the color of a man's skin, he felt that in addition to receiving service with dignity, colored people needed their own places to learn and to grow. No person demonstrates better what Norris had in mind than one of the young men who got his start at the station. That young man, Wendell Beale, now a successful real estate broker, insurance agent, and owner of two retirement homes in New Jersey, unabashedly attributes his business success to having started out in the station. He began work in 1957 when he was in his early teens. He was not paid a salary, but in exchange for pumping gas, he was allowed to keep all the income he made from washing cars and fixing flats. He found no disfavor with this arrangement. At the age of fifteen, he had the ideal outlet for his entrepreneurial instincts. He attracted a set of car-wash customers whose names, forty-five years later, tumble forth like a roll call of Lancaster County residents. Norris delighted in having such an ambitious and eager youngster around. That Beale was an early riser endeared him to Norris. Norris taught him the importance of laying out his day early in the morning. Simple but essential tasks, such as sorting the empty soda bottles for pickup, and setting up the service island in preparation for the day's work, left an indelible mark on an impressionable young mind. He took advantage of the auto repair section to learn about cars, and soon he was breaking down engines so that the mechanic could repair and reassemble them.

An impish grin flits across Beale's face as he tells how Norris would let him drive on the narrow county roads. Norris was not one to tarry in his Tin Lizzies, and he treated Beale no differently from the other fellows who drove for him. As Beale was negotiating the curves, hills, and valleys of those back roads, Norris would tap gently on the dashboard and say: "Let's push along little man." (He called Beale "little man" because at age fifteen he was reed-thin.) Beale was amazed that Norris would let him take the wheel, as he was too young to qualify for a driver's license. In wide-eyed amazement he exclaimed: "I thought: This man is a deacon in the church, and here he is letting me break the law!" At age fifteen, Beale would not have known that the man who was tutoring him knew every crook and bend in those country roads, and that he had reared three of his own sons and had assisted in rearing numerous other men's sons. He knew well when to and when not to "break the law."

Beale's training at the station stood him in good stead when he entered military service. His military occupational specialty was "Guided Missile Installation Mechanic." It was his responsibility to keep the generators going at the guided missile sites.

Thornton, tiring of country life and chafing under the constant meddling of Norris, sold the station in 1965 and moved to Richmond. Probably the thing that vexed Thornton more than anything was Norris opening the station early in the morning (Norris was awake at four o'clock in the morning; Thornton was not) and letting the customers have gas on credit. Thornton was justifiably concerned that he very well might never get paid. Norris, who had an abiding faith in the fairness of his fellowman, wasn't driven so much by profit but by his strong belief in the need for people to have somewhere they could have their cars serviced.

Thornton sold the station to Treakle's protégé, a tall, angular young man named Johnny Christopher, who proved to be every bit as shrewd a businessman as his mentor. He paid Thornton $10,000 for the station and a half acre of land. The entire Norris clan was shocked by Thornton's summary decision to sell part of the homeplace. Though Norris was never one to stand in the way of something his children wanted to do, he was devastated by the sale. One of Norris's daughters, Alma, bought the station from Christopher to "bring it back into the family." The cost to Alma five years later was $20,000, a tidy 100 percent profit for Christopher.

The building remains in the family, but it is no longer a service station. The place is leased for a hugely successful yard monument business run by a gentleman named Joseph Curry whom Norris mentored.

CHAPTER 25

County Medical Examiner: Appointment Denied

Norris did not believe in entitlements. He often said, "In life, nothing is guaranteed." But he felt he deserved to be reappointed to the position of medical examiner in Lancaster County in 1952, an office that he had held since 1948—the first colored physician in the state of Virginia to do so. His appointment came shortly after the emergence of the medical examiner system in the state. The denial of his reappointment occurred after the medical examiner system was placed under the Department of Health and appointments came through the local medical societies. He vainly sought to have his appointment restored.

Until 1946, in Virginia, it was not difficult for a man, or woman for that matter, to get away with murder, and it is entirely possible that some people did. The county coroner's offices that were supposed to investigate unexplained and suspicious deaths were so incompetent that Alan R. Moritz, M.D., the brilliant and blunt Harvard professor of legal medicine and the foremost forensic pathologist in America at that time, labeled the system "hopelessly ineffective." Moritz rendered this grim assessment in an editorial in the official publication of the Medical Society of Virginia in 1943. In a searing indictment of the system, he exhorted the medical society to "exert their powerful influence on the legislature to remedy the sad state of affairs."

The state medical society did act, and swiftly. Within three years, it got Virginia's General Assembly to pass legislation that propelled the state to the forefront of the country's medical examiner systems. It was such an advanced system that the state, in addition to Massachusetts and Maryland, was exempt from a study of the status of coroners in the United States in 1953.

The title of coroner originated in England in the twelfth century. The word is derived from the Latin term "corona" meaning crown. The duties of the coroner were to ensure that taxes owed by a suddenly deceased person were paid to the king. Over the centuries, the duties of the coroner evolved into the investigation of violent or sudden deaths.

The coroner system in Virginia, patterned after England's, had remained unchanged for about two hundred years. The usual practice was that the circuit court of the county would send the names of two candidates to the governor, who then would appoint one of the nominees as coroner. A candidate did not have to be a physician.

A constitutional convention in 1901-1902 made changes in the entire legal code of Virginia. The governor, upon the recommendation of the circuit court of a county, would appoint the coroner. A justice of the peace could serve as coroner, and the coroner could act as sheriff in some cases. Every county in the commonwealth was required to have at least one person appointed coroner. The coroner would hold an inquest in the case of any person suspected of having died an unnatural or violent death. A jury of six persons conducted the inquest, and if it rendered a verdict of murder or assault, the coroner would issue a warrant for the arrest of the person who had committed the crime.

A brief, almost perfunctory account of a coroner's case appeared in the *Virginia Citizen*, a Lancaster County weekly, under "Afro-American Notes" on February 15, 1907. L. R. Fleming, a colored storeowner in Lancaster County, Virginia, was the justice of the peace and acted as coroner. The report, almost a caricature of what an inquest should be though surely it was not intended as such, was just over a hundred words. It preceded Moritz's prickly critique of Virginia's coroner system by thirty-six years!

Stephen Miller, a resident of Mollusk was found dead in his bed Monday night. . . . stiff frozen with pants and vest on, lying in bed just as if he had laid down to rest. Justice L. R. Flemings [*sic*] was notified and he summoned a jury of six and held an inquest at the house over the dead body. The jury gave in the following verdict: "That Stephen Miller, came to his death Saturday night, February 2nd, 1907, from natural causes." The Justice then turned the body over to the True Reformers, of which order he was a faithful member.

This crude process of handling unnatural deaths continued until 1946, when the General Assembly abolished the coroner system and appointed a Commission on Port Mortem Examinations. The commission was given the function of appointing a chief medical examiner for the state. The appointment was for a term of three years. The "quasi-judicial and quasi-investigative features" were placed under the Commonwealth attorney's offices and law enforcement officials. The medical aspects became the "exclusive responsibility" of the medical examiners. In 1950, the medical examiner's office was then placed under the Virginia State Department of Health.

The first chief medical examiner appointed was Thomas Breyfogle, a thirty-six-year-old pathologist from Dayton, Ohio. Breyfogle resigned October 1, 1949, to study law and was succeeded by Geoffrey T. Mann, his assistant.

In 1947, the *Virginia Medical Monthly*, the official publication of the Medical Society of Virginia, listed all the medical examiners in the State. A. Broaddus Gravatt, Jr., M.D., was the medical examiner for Lancaster County. Gravatt had been appointed coroner in 1946 to succeed Maryus Curtis Oldham, who had died on February 27, 1946. Gravatt's appointment took place before the Commission on Post Mortem Examinations became effective (October 1, 1946).

In 1948, a revised list of medical examiners was published by the state medical society and Norris's name had been added to the list. Lancaster County then had two medical examiners. Norris was apparently appointed through his contacts with Dr. Henry B. Mulholland, assistant dean of the University of Virginia School of Medicine, and Dr. William T. Sanger, president of the Medical College of Virginia, as they all served on the executive committee of the Virginia Council on Health and Medical Care. Sanger also served with Norris on the Hampton Institute Trustee Board. Lonsdale J. Roper, who had served as Health Commissioner since 1946, was supportive of Norris's appointment.

However, when Norris came up for reappointment in the early 1950s, he was not reappointed. Changes had been made in the procedure by which medical examiners were appointed. In a statute enacted by the General Assembly and approved March 11, 1952, the State Health Commissioner was given the power to appoint medical examiners. One of the stipulations of the act was that a physician must be a member of the local medical society. Norris was not a member of the Northern Neck Medical Association, the white local medical society, or the Medical Society of Virginia, as its constitution also limited membership to whites. The local medical societies in Virginia patterned their constitutions on the constitution of the Medical Society of Virginia.

Norris was not helped by the loss of his friend and supporter, Dr. Roper, who died in 1951. Mack I. Shanholtz, M.D., had replaced Roper and was not in the least sympathetic toward Norris.

Having been the senior physician in Lancaster County and having served the citizens of his county so faithfully, Norris was rankled when he was passed over for reappointment. During the years that he was in practice, the frequent causes of accidental death were drowning and auto accidents. Altercations between colored men also accounted for a disproportionate share of violent deaths in the county. It was not uncommon for the mortally wounded to be brought to Norris's office and, on several occasions, to die there. Once, the body of a shooting victim was brought to his office porch by several young men and dumped as though it were a sack of grain before they vanished. Norris had to wait until the white coroner decided to show up to investigate the death. Invariably, when Norris was called to a death scene, he had to wait for the coroner to arrive for the inquest. When two teenagers were electrocuted in 1934 by a fallen high voltage line, although he was the first physician on the scene, the inquest was turned over to Dr. Hubbard of White Stone. Hubbard had been in Lancaster long before Norris. But when Norris became senior physician in the county he felt, and with a measure of justification, that he was entitled to the appointment.

Norris made a valiant attempt to have his appointment restored, but

Shanholtz and Mann refused to reappoint him. Norris wrote to Senator Harry F. Byrd to enlist his support. He got a tepid response from the senator, who forwarded Norris's letter to Mann with an accompanying equally tepid and non-committal missive.

In a July 1959 letter to Waldo Scott, an eminent colored general surgeon in Newport News and a fellow member of the Old Dominion Medical Society, Norris wrote:

> As you know I am engaged at this time in a fight with the Commissioner of Health and Dr. Mann, Chief Medical Examiner, for their attitude toward Negro medical examiners. . . . since Dr. Mann states and I have witnesses to prove it by two other physicians . . . that he was not interested in the matter of Negro examiners as his office was well staffed. Too, he stated frankly that he would not appoint a Negro where there was disapproval by his white examiner. To you, Dr. Scott, if our men swallow that stuff, damnable far be it from me. I hope that you are not one who will submit to such unscrupulous rulings.

Shanholtz and Mann stubbornly refused to budge. But neither was Norris giving up. Norris attended a Rappahannock Medical Society meeting in December 1961 and observed:

> They [the Rappahannock Medical Society] brought up having a committee meet with the State Board of Health again. I warned them to put on some real men who had guts, intestinal stamina plus I further warned them that the days of Uncle Tommie, handkerchief heads, and stool pigeons were outdated. Go cussing and fussing and not give a D____. Well, I am not quite religious as I should be to be a deacon in the church.

Norris never regained his appointment. He suffered a series of illnesses beginning in 1960 that sapped his vitality and left him with little energy and time to continue the fight. The chief medical examiner's office prevailed by default. In an interview with Gravatt in 2007, he did not recall that Norris had ever served as medical examiner.

CHAPTER 26

Integration of Virginia's Medical Societies: "A Delay in Accomplishment"

A 1937 survey of two thousand Black physicians nationwide found that only 40 percent had engaged in any form of postgraduate education during the previous decade.

THOMAS J. WARD[1]

In the first half of the twentieth century, it was no simple matter for a colored physician to obtain postgraduate education. His white Southern colleagues effectively excluded him from any opportunity to participate in local continuing medical education programs. He was denied membership in the Southern state and county medical societies, and in the North, he was at best tolerated. Unless he had the good fortune to be located in a metropolis where there were enough colored physicians who could organize their own medical society, he was relegated to attending only one or two meetings a year, the annual colored state medical society meeting and the annual National Medical Association (NMA) meeting, both counterparts to the white organizations.

Travel was especially difficult for rural physicians of any color. Many were located in places far away from cities. The roads were poorly developed, and hotel accommodations were often non-existent. Physicians also found it difficult to find another physician willing to cover during their absences. Sometimes the white physicians would not treat colored patients. Norris once

---

1 *Black Physicians in the Jim Crow South,* The University of Arkansas Press, Fayetteville, Arkansas, 2003, p. 86.

had to abort a trip to the NMA meeting in New York City to return to an ill patient precisely because of a problem in coverage.

Acceptance of Negro physicians into mainstream medicine has a long and tortuous history, and the depiction of Norris's experience with medical societies illustrates too well what so many of his southern Negro colleagues experienced.

The exclusion of Negroes from medical societies began on the national level with the American Medical Association (AMA), an organization founded in 1847 with the purported object of representing the interests of all physicians practicing medicine in the United States, improvement of their "knowledge" and "usefulness," and the promulgation of a *Code of Medical Ethics*. In 1870, when faced with the prospect of admitting three Negro physicians to membership, the AMA waffled and by 1874 had developed a coherent policy to address the issue of admitting Negro physicians. It did not admit the three doctors and set a policy that only members of constituent societies could become members, knowing full well that none of its constituent societies in the South and many in the North did not accept Negroes as members. The AMA never had a written policy on discrimination, but by refusing to rein in the local and state medical societies that openly discriminated against Negro physicians, the effect was de facto discrimination. Negro physicians denied membership in the local and state medical societies and the AMA were adversely affected because of the circumscription of educational opportunities. They were hit in the pocket book as well because membership in the medical societies and the AMA was often a prerequisite for appointment to hospital staffs, obtaining malpractice insurance, and gaining local and state government and private industry appointments.

Faced with the prospect of nearly complete exclusion from organized medicine at a national level, Negro physicians formed their own association—the NMA. The NMA was founded in 1895 in Atlanta, Georgia, at the suggestion of I. Garland Penn during the Cotton States and International Exposition held in that city. (Penn was not a physician, but a journalist and high official in the Methodist Episcopal Church.) This was the exposition where Booker T. Washington delivered the speech that would cause him to be forever labeled an accommodationist. It is ironic that publication of the *Journal of the National Medical Association,* the official publication of the association, was initiated in 1908 under John A. Kenney, M.D, at Tuskegee Institute with a good deal of help from none other than Washington who made available to Kenney the full resources of Tuskegee Institute including its publishing capabilities.

The journal's masthead stated its raison d'être in elegant and diplomatic prose:

> Conceived in no spirit of racial exclusiveness, fostering no ethnic antagonism, but born of the exigencies of the American environment, the National Medical Association has for its object the banding together for mutual cooperation and helpfulness the men and women of African descent who are legally and honorably engaged in the practice of the profession of medicine.
>
> - C. V. Roman, M.D. (1908)

The phrase, "born of the exigencies of the American environment," was sheer artful tact. The American environment to which the masthead referred was one of blatantly oppressive discriminatory practices that, if not already, would soon be codified in every Southern state. The NMA was founded the year before the United States Supreme Court ruled in *Plessy vs. Ferguson,* the decision that laid the foundation for the separate but equal doctrine that would influence race relations in this country for the next seven decades.

∽

Norris already knew where he stood in American medicine before he left Tuskegee. That he could not belong to the white local and state medical societies and by extension the AMA would not put a dent in his determination to stay abreast of medical developments. After he returned home in the summer of 1917, he journeyed to Philadelphia to attend the annual meeting of the NMA. He was a member of the organization for the remaining forty-nine years of his life. He missed very few meetings, and he never sought elective office, but he did serve as assistant secretary for a period. He had no interest in being at the epicenter of the organization preferring, instead, to help shape events from the sidelines. He was instrumental in arranging for his friend, Ellsworth Bunker, then president of the American Red Cross, to speak to the fifty-ninth Annual Convention of the NMA in Washington, D.C., in 1954.

Norris wrote to me July 10, 1959, about his plans to attend the NMA meeting in Detroit. He penned a comment about the association that, though simple, was profound for its understatement: "I enjoy the National [Medical Association] a great deal and it has meant much to me." John T. Givens, M.D., his colleague and secretary of the organization, paid a fine tribute to him upon his death:

> On behalf of the National Medical Association and on behalf of myself, I am sending this [telegram] as a token of our great loss in Dr. Norris. He was a most valued and faithful member of the National Medical Association and his place will be hard to fill. He stood high on the council of that organization and was highly respected and loved by the entire national membership.

It would be a mistake, however, to assume that the colored physicians had accepted the status quo and were not challenging the policies of the AMA and, by extension, the white state medical societies and white local medical groups. Negro physicians made numerous attempts to break down the barriers to AMA membership. The AMA leaders met every attempt by their Negro colleagues to gain membership with callous indifference. Not until the end of the fourth decade of the twentieth century did Negro physicians, buttressed by support from Northern white associations, make a serious and sustained challenge to the AMA's policy of racial exclusion. At the AMA's House of Delegates meeting in 1948, the New York State Medical Society introduced a constitutional amendment: "No component society of the AMA shall exclude any qualified physician from its membership by reason of race, creed or color." The amendment was referred to an AMA committee for review and action. The committee reported the following decision to the main body:

It is the recommendation of your reference committee that the component medical society is the sole judge as to whom it elects to membership, provided the applicant shall meet the medical requirements for membership, and so recommended.

Bigotry had triumphed again! In 1949, the editor of the journal of the NMA excoriated the AMA for failing to adopt the constitutional amendment. He wrote a strong rebuttal to the association and ended by stating:

Progress cannot be forever stayed and someday right will prevail. That day must not be indefinitely thwarted and postponed. Our unremitting efforts will be joined with other fair-minded people until the American Medical Association redeems itself in the eyes of a critical world.

During the next twenty years (1948 to 1968) there was sporadic acceptance of colored physicians into state and local medical societies, but many societies, particularly in the South, continued to exclude colored doctors. The AMA would not "bar medical societies that refused to accept black physicians as members." At the 1963 meeting of the AMA, a group of physicians led by John Holloman, a colored internist of New York City and a friend of Norris's, "shocked the medical establishment by picketing the AMA meetings." It took many more protests over the five years after this episode before the AMA finally amended its constitution in 1968 to forbid any discrimination in membership. Norris had been dead two years.

ɢᴚ

The picture at the state level was not very different from that of the national scene. Colored physicians found it necessary to form their own medical societies on the state level as well. Shortly after returning home to practice in 1917, Norris joined the colored physicians' state medical association in Virginia, the Old Dominion Medical Society. The society had been founded in 1905 for the same reason that the NMA had been founded—Virginia's colored physicians were excluded from the Virginia state medical society. In 1902, a group of colored doctors had made an unsuccessful attempt to join the all white Medical Society of Virginia—the same year the society revised its constitution. In keeping with the tenor of the racial animus that was gaining currency throughout the South, some members of the Medical Society of Virginia attempted to insert "white" in the revised constitution as a condition for membership. More tolerant heads prevailed and the matter was tabled, but in 1905 "white" mysteriously appeared in the printed constitution. It would take nearly fifty years for "white" to be expunged from the document.

Racial relations in America took a decided turn for improvement following World War II. American armies had just led the allies in defeating Nazi Germany, modern society's foremost proponent of white supremacy and fascism. We were locked in a Cold War with Russia, a major critic of our dual society and communism's major advocate. The U.S. Supreme Court had declared segregation on interstate carriers unconstitutional (1946). Major league baseball was integrated—voluntarily (1947). President Harry S. Truman issued the executive order desegregating the United States armed forces (1948). Medical schools (Arkansas, 1948) and Southern medical societies (Florida, 1950) began lowering their barriers to integration. It was in this climate that the Medical Society of Virginia in 1948 began exploring gingerly the question of inviting "colored physicians to their scientific sessions and exhibits." The matter was submitted to the society's House of Delegates' fall session for action. The matter was discussed in great detail at the meeting by an *ad hoc* committee that consisted of about fifteen officers of the society and Dr. L. J. Roper, state health commissioner. The major concerns were whether colored physicians would be accepted at the white hotels and where they would be seated in the conference halls. One member of the Norfolk County Medical Society told the gathering that their society had "invited *them* [Negro physicians] and set aside a portion of their meeting hall for *them*. Thus far none of *them* has ever attended a meeting." (All italics added by author.) It was finally decided that a delegation would "be appointed to confer with a committee from the Old Dominion Medical Society to see if there was some way this could be ironed out to the satisfaction of both organizations."

The matter of Virginia medicine becoming more inclusive toward its colored physicians had been driven into the consciousness of thinking whites by Zenobia Gilpin's address to the Monday Club, a civic organization in Richmond composed of case supervisors and executives of health, educational, and welfare agencies. On March 31, 1947, Gilpin, a female colored physician, spoke eloquently and compellingly about the health of her fellow colored citizens. She pointed out the appallingly high incidence of diseases among Virginia's colored population and the lack of adequate educational facilities and staff positions open to Virginia's colored doctors. Her full address was published in no less than the Medical Society of Virginia's monthly journal. But the issue of admitting colored physicians smoldered in the turgid discussions at the society's annual meetings.

It took four years and a courageous statement by its president, C. Lydon Harrell, in his presidential address in October 1951 to jolt the society out of its Southern comfort:

If we wish to preserve our democracy we must be tolerant of our brother practitioners, regardless of race, color or creed, tolerant of those among us if they can prove their worth, who are qualified and willing to do the right thing. There is a phrase in the constitution of The Medical Society of Virginia, which states that only members of the *white* race may become members of this Society. This means that no member of the Japanese, Chinese, Philippine, Indian or Negro race, no matter how well qualified could become a member of this Society. This means that because of his color Noguchi, a Japanese scientist, who gave us our present knowledge of neuro-syphilis; Hinton, an American Negro, who developed the well known serological tests for syphilis, known by his name; Dr. Khanolkhar, a noted pathologist of India, who has contributed much to our knowledge of tumors, could not join our Society. Fellow members, we should delete the word "white."

It is not fair. It is not just. It is not democratic. It does not manifest the Christian spirit to limit membership in this Society to white people only. If we wish to preserve our freedom and our American way of life, we must think on these things.

But the jolt fell short. The next year when a vote was taken to delete the word "white" from the Medical Society's constitution, the resolution failed for lack of a two-thirds majority. In 1954, the motion to delete "white" from the constitution was put to vote again; this time it passed.

The matter of race, however, was not yet laid to rest. Membership in the state society had to come through membership in the component or county societies, and unless the local societies would admit colored doctors, the barrier was ever present. Many local societies elected to remain lily–white. The recalcitrance of some of the local societies provoked a sharp rebuke in 1955 from the state society's president, Dr. Carrington Williams:

> It seems to me that the best interests of all would be served by the local societies following the lead of the State Society and accepting this new order. . . . It seems to me not wise and not fair to accept them [colored physicians] for membership in some localities and deny them membership in other places.

The refusal by the local Virginia societies to open their membership to Negro physicians prompted C. Waldo Scott, a University of Michigan medical school graduate and a virtuoso surgeon, to say in his presidential address to the Old Dominion Medical Society meeting in June 1956:

> It might be expected that men in medicine, with their broader scientific training and cognizance of their noble calling, would be less intolerant and harbor fewer prejudices than their fellow man. It is reassuring that this is proving so, for even in such a reactionary State as Mississippi, Negro physicians have been admitted to white medical societies. Though we normally like to think of Virginia as progressive, there are still many constituent local societies of the Medical Society of Virginia who have not seen fit to follow the State Society pattern and admit Negroes. It is hoped that by next year the number of such societies will

be in the vast minority in the State.

Norris was not totally pessimistic about the prospects of Negro physicians being accepted into mainstream medicine. In June 1961, Norris attended
the Old Dominion Medical Society meeting. He wrote to me:
> The Old Dominion Medical Association had a two days meet at
> Hampton Inst. We enjoyed the association of the fellows so much.
> Youth was a little evident in its folly, but the intermediates and ole boys
> were very constructive in their approach for a better-integrated society.
> The days of Uncle Tommies and handkerchief heads are rapidly being
> obliterated. Indeed I wonder if we are not becoming too militant. The
> slogan is "No more black medicine." The O.D.M. Association is asking
> for a completely integrated state in all of its ramifications. It came as a
> shock to me. First, they want to clear their skirts by becoming a compo-
> nent part of the Medical Society of Virginia. Then they are asking for
> professional courtesies in all state institutions and hospitals both for the
> Doctors and Nurses. It is the most sweeping movement I have seen in
> Virginia since 1954.
>
> Well, son, I am happy to know that I am alive to see such drastic and
> radical efforts, even if there is delay in accomplishment.

Unfortunately, Norris did not live long enough to witness integration
of Virginia's local medical societies. The Northern Neck Medical Association
never extended Norris an invitation to join, and there is no record that he ever
applied for membership.

The practices at the white regional and county medical societies reflected
the pattern that existed at the state and national level. But Norris and other rural
Negro physicians in the upper tidewater area of Virginia had not waited for
the regional society to provide them with continuing medical education. They
did it on their own. In 1943, Norris along with James B. Blayton, a prominent
family physician in Williamsburg, and Marcus Toney, a general practitioner of
Middlesex County, founded the Rappahannock Medical Society, an organization that included physicians from the Northern Neck, Middle Peninsula, and

The National Medical Association did not always walk lockstep with the American Medical Association. Many Negro physicians, and white physicians too, were in the thick of the fight against venereal diseases during the first half of the twentieth century. In the 1930s, a push was made at the national level to do something about the appallingly high rate of venereal disease infections among Americans. Surgeon General Thomas Parran stated in his book *Shadow on the Land: Syphilis*: "The first national organization to vote cooperation with syphilis control of the Public Health Service was the National Medical Association composed of Negro physicians." He went on to say in his book that "the whole nation owes the Negro doctors a debt of gratitude … I hope that the rest of us may measure up as well to our share of the responsibility."

Lower Peninsula. Norris was fortunate to have a younger and energetic colleague in Blayton. Blayton was a lean fellow with the physique of a long distance runner. And he was as unflappable as he was lean. He was the kind of person who talked softly and coolly but wasted little time in setting priorities and getting things done. In 1951, he built his own hospital—fourteen beds and seven bassinets—for colored patients in Williamsburg. The other founder, Toney, was the only colored physician in Middlesex County. A short, serious, taciturn man, he did much to promote the health and welfare of the people of his county. The reasons for forming a local medical society were the desire of the physicians to meet more frequently, restrictions on travel during the war, and proposed termination in 1941 of the annual clinic funded by Rockefeller's General Education Board that had been held at the colored Saint Philip Hospital at the Medical College of Virginia in Richmond since 1931. (The funding of the clinics was taken over by the state of Virginia in 1940. The clinics continued to be held until the mid 1940s.) Norris first attended the clinic in 1932, but the clinic only met annually and provided postgraduate education to a limited number of physicians. The course was two weeks long and from the attendance records in the General Education Board's archives it appeared that few rural physicians attended regularly.

In 1944, one year after the founding, the Rappahannock Medical Society held its first annual clinic at the Richmond Community Hospital, a colored-owned, non-profit, non-stock hospital in Richmond that had opened in 1934. The clinics included lectures by invited professors, demonstrations of clinical material, and the treatment of patients.

While the monthly Rappahannock Medical Society meetings were primarily geared to the exchange of medical information, the physicians took advantage of the time to include their families. Martha Norris Gilbert, Norris's youngest child, and Barbara Blayton Richardson, the daughter of Dr. and Mrs. Blayton, poignantly recalled their memories of the Rappahannock Medical Society gatherings. They were five years old when the first meeting was held, and they attended most of the meetings until they went away to boarding school. Martha said that the sessions in today's parlance would be called professional development seminars. They were held on the first Sunday of every month and approximately ten to twelve doctors attended. She recalled that the physicians shared a collegial relationship and were all male. No attempt was made to exclude female physicians; there just weren't any practicing medicine in the rural counties. Case studies and specialists' presentations dominated the programs. Martha remembers:

After the "medical meeting" there was always a time for together-ness (all the doctors and their families). Papa prided himself on having plenty of good "grub" for his guests. Mama prepared platters of fried chicken, bowls of corn pudding and candied sweet potatoes, two or three green vegetables, hot rolls, jellied salad, ice cream and cake, and gallons of iced tea. Papa coaxed his guests to "eat up." These dinners were lively exchanges of information, family news, and jokes. When Papa and Mama hosted, he [Papa] augmented the post-meeting agenda with unconventional additions like a gospel concert or a political speaker. Consistent with his all-embracing response to others, he was not averse to the idea of including one or two extras in the dinner count if he/she happened by on the day of a meeting, nor did he hesitate to invite a bachelor cousin to ride along with us to a meeting out of town. While these impromptu invitations galled Mama, Papa was not perturbed in the least. Never mind that the extra person, cousin, or neighbor had no intrinsic interest in the business at hand.

Barbara remembers that Norris:
    was a wonderfully warm man who always checked in on the children during the meetings. I especially remember that he called us "daughter" and I loved that. He was very serious and committed to making certain that we were doing our best and that we had the best.

Thus, through the John Andrew Clinical Society, the NMA, the Old Dominion Medical Society, and the Rappahannock Medical Society, Norris was able to keep abreast of medical advances.

ભ

An Historical Footnote: On July 10, 2008, the AMA issued an apology to Negro physicians "for its past history of racial inequality toward African-American physicians, and shares its current efforts to increase the ranks of minority physicians and their participation in the AMA."

VIRGINIA COUNCIL ON HEALTH AND MEDICAL CARE

Jim Crow Virginia was filled with paradoxes. Norris could not belong to any of the white medical associations in the state and, by extension, the American Medical Association, yet he served with distinction on the Virginia Council on Health and Medical Care. The council, a private non-profit organization, was founded in 1946 by Dr. Henry B. Mulholland, president of the University of Virginia School of Medicine, and Dr. W. E. Garnett, a rural sociologist of the Virginia Polytechnic Institute. The goal of the council, which served as an umbrella organization of thirty-seven health and health-related organizations, was to address the "acute need in health care in the state" with "emphasis on the approaching crisis in the physician shortage in rural communities."

Norris was appointed to the council shortly after its organization and served on the Executive Committee. His appointment may have come through his acquaintance with council member Dr. William T. Sanger, president of the Medical College of Virginia, whom he had met at the annual clinics sponsored by the General Education Board. Norris also served on the Hampton Institute Trustee Board with Sanger (1945 to 1953). (Sanger was president when the first Negro student [Jean Harris] was admitted to the Medical College of Virginia in 1951.)

Norris surely had a hand in the bulletin below that appeared in the *Journal of the National Medical Association*, July 1951:

> The Virginia Council. . . made a special plea, at their annual meeting in Richmond in January, in behalf of the Roanoke Medical College [*sic*] and the Norfolk Community Hospital urging that the white medical colleges in Virginia help these two hospitals to raise their standards to meet the American Medical Association requirements.
>
> The Council noted that at present there is no hospital in Virginia in which a colored medical student may serve his internship.

Norris served on the council until he became ill in 1955. Edgar J. Fisher, the charismatic director of the council wrote to Theresita upon Norris's death in 1966 that he "attended meetings faithfully and supported our organization, both morally and financially."

CHAPTER 27

Coda

The end of the journey will come. There is no dispute about that. How and in what manner the soul exits this flesh is the unknown in the equation of life. The end can come with the cataclysmic swiftness of a bolt of lightning; it can come in slow, almost methodical decrements as a furtive thief creeping in the night; or it can come in spasms of pain and agony, as one moves inexorably to the last breath.

For Norris, it began with a loss of vitality in 1954 when he was seventy-one years old. A recognition that he could no longer be effective as a trustee at Hampton Institute was among the first signals that things were not well. In the spring of 1955, he sought medical advice for continued loss of energy and strength. He was told that his condition was due to the aging process. He knew better than that, so he sought a second opinion, and colon cancer was diagnosed. In December 1955, he underwent removal of the cancerous section of his colon at Freedmen's Hospital—the same hospital where, nearly forty years earlier, he had started his medical career. His surgeon was the eminent Burke "Mickey" Syphax, a debonair man endowed with extraordinary intellect, unique ability, and virtuoso dexterity. Syphax had been a surgical resident at Howard University under the renowned Dr. Charles Drew, and was one of the first Negro surgeons to be certified by the American Board of Surgery.

Despite a rocky post-operative course, Norris bounced back. When told that he had a liver metastasis and should return for partial removal of his liver, he declined to go back under the knife. (Effective chemotherapy was not available for colon cancer in 1955.) He was recovering slowly but steadily, and he wanted nothing more than to get back to work. Furthermore, I was a junior in medical school and he was literally counting the days until I would join his practice in Kilmarnock. He struggled to hold on. After a prolonged convalescence he did return to practice and even planned a fair in 1957. He gave no further thought to his illness, at least overtly. In those pre-chemotherapy days, it was no use to dwell on a diagnosis of malignancy anyhow. He either was going to live or not live, and he had decided he was going to live.

His letter writing returned to its pre-illness fervor. He wrote Charlie Williams, his Hampton Institute classmate and friend, who had introduced him to his future wife on that summer day in 1917: "I am waiting for my Baby Boy to come and take over (for a rest period for me)." He resumed delivering babies, seeing patients, and making house calls, as it would be not long before "my son will join me in practice."

The big day arrived July 1, 1958, when I returned to set up practice with him. There was a noticeable uptick in his spirits. With unabashed pride, he introduced me as his new partner. He was anxious to turn over the reins to me, but the elation would prove to be short-lived. I had enormous difficulties adjusting to my return home as a physician. Many of the older patients did not consider the young man they had known as "Jimmy" to be a physician. The last time most of the residents of Lancaster County had seen me was when I was a gangly high school student. Now I was no longer "Jimmy," but Doctor Norris, and a lot of people were not impressed. When they came to see "Dr. Norris" and I answered the door, there was nearly a constant refrain: "I don't mean you Jimmy, but your father." I did have some patients, but it did not take a discerning mind to fathom that the people much preferred Dr. Morgan E. to Dr. Jimmy.

After a month together, Norris felt secure enough about his neophyte partner to leave me with the practice while he attended the National Medical Association meeting. Hardly had Norris gotten to Richmond, a two-hour drive from our home, before I received a telephone call late in the evening that one of his patients had gone into labor. I arrived to find my father's patient in hard labor with her first child. I meticulously set up for the delivery, laying out the sterile towels and instruments. My sixth sense gave me a foreboding that this delivery was not going to be an easy one. As the woman's uterine contractions became increasingly protracted and painful, the patient screamed at the top of her voice: "Somebody, get Dr. Norris!" Despite her mother-in-law's exhortations, "Hush your mouth, child; the doctor is here," the expectant mother was not to be soothed. "I want Dr. Norris!" she yelled with all her lung power.

I was suffering nearly as badly as the patient. Enormous beads of perspiration cascaded down my face, and my legs turned to virtual rubber. I held on to any object that could be grasped to conceal the embarrassing tremor of my hands and made a valiant effort to give an aura of confidence with every move and every utterance. But with each new contraction, my patient gave an eardrum-shattering shriek. I struggled to maintain my composure. When she had a contraction, I urged her to "take a deep breath and push."

"Push my eye!" she screamed. "Somebody, somebody, please, please get Dr. Norris," she pleaded through sobs. My exasperation caused me once to utter almost audibly, "When the hell is this little rascal going to come out?" Finally, to my relief, a healthy baby girl was born. The ordeal for the expectant mother and this young physician lasted only two to three hours, but to me, and probably to her as well, it seemed like an eternity. It had to be the longest night I had ever experienced. Events like this put a damper on my staying power.

Neither was my father's antiquated payment schedule a compelling incentive for me to stay in Lancaster County. Too many bills for house calls and office visits went uncollected or were carried on the books. My medical school classmate, Maxie Maultsby, had located to Cocoa, Florida. A steady influx of new workers were making their way to the new space center, Cape Canaveral—now Cape Kennedy—and Maultsby assured me if I came to Florida that I could prosper and "serve the people as well." With the prospect of establishing myself as the other Doctor Norris becoming increasingly remote, I confided to my mother and my oldest brother, Thornton, that I wanted to go Florida to look over the possibility of relocating. I was not ready to approach my father until I was certain of my decision.

My hand was forced sooner than I had planned. It was a Sunday evening, and as I was watching the Ed Sullivan television show, my father joined me. He rarely, if ever, watched television. Immediately, I was gripped with an uneasiness that something just wasn't right. Then he dropped the bomb: "Son, I understand you are thinking about moving to Florida." I felt as if I had been delivered a blow to my solar plexus. All I could muster in response was a timid, "Well, I was thinking about it." In a flash of anger, he shot back: "Well dammit, if that is what you want to do, then you can leave tonight!" I was astounded. Of course, I could not have left that night, even if I had wanted. (To this day, I am not sure who informed my father of my plans.)

The next day, when the atmosphere was less charged, I explained my predicament to my father and got him to understand that it would be difficult for me to continue in Kilmarnock. Always the pragmatist, he suggested that we travel to Florida together and look over the situation. After a trip together to Cocoa and Melbourne we saw that there was the possibility of my having a thriving practice there. He acquiesced in my decision to move to Florida, but with a stern admonition: "Son, I am not going to tell you what to do or how you should run your practice, but there are two things I ask you not to do; do not get involved in [illicit] drugs and do not do abortions." His "ask you not to do" was tantamount to an order and one that I would never defy.

Within seven months from the date of my arrival in Lancaster County, flushed with hope and promise, I was leaving. During the brief period that I worked with my father, I learned much from him about the art and science of medicine. I learned about compassion. Once, my father and I were making a house call together on an elderly gentleman. We entered the small, spare room where our terminally ill patient lay next to an open window to catch what breezes might pass through on a hot, humid summer day. His gaunt frame resembled more the cadaver that I had dissected in medical school than a mortal being. He was too weak to fan the flies that were crawling around his nose, his mouth, his ears, and even his eyes. Norris gently examined the old fellow, gave him an injection, and left a bottle of medicine with his feeble but attentive wife. Then he opened his wallet and gave her several dollar bills. As we were about to exit, he turned to me and said, "Son, I want you to go the hardware store, get some screens, and put them in the windows."

I learned about physical diagnosis. I shall never forget the young man whom I was treating for what I thought was a severe strep throat. He had a high fever, he could not swallow, and he was drooling profusely. His infection was not responding to the penicillin injections. I told Norris of the patient's condition and he said: "Let's go down and take a look. You go in to see him and while you are examining him, I'll just come in and glance over your shoulder and see what is going on." I entered the house and shortly afterwards Norris came in, and as always, he was relaxed and totally confident. He peered over my shoulder as I was examining the patient's throat. He then gently nudged me to the side with the explanation, "Son, let me have a better look." As he held the depressor on the patient's tongue, he said to me, "Son, pass me that bistoury." I did not have the vaguest idea why he wanted a bistoury (a long narrow surgical knife), but this was not the time to ask questions. With lightning swiftness, he deftly placed the bistoury where it needed to be, right in the center of an abscess of his tonsil. Pus spurted from the man's mouth. Then, with the first words that the patient had spoken since our arrival, he said to Norris, "Thank you, doctor!!"

I learned about decisiveness. Norris had given me the responsibility of taking over some of his obstetrical patients. The first deliveries were relatively uneventful, but once I was called early in the morning to a lady who was in labor. I arrived to find that her membranes had ruptured and her cervix dilated. I waited all morning, but there was no progress of the labor. It seemed as though the contractions were just not strong enough to propel the infant into his new world. After about six hours, with both the mother and myself tiring, I summoned help from Norris. He came immediately to the patient's home. He entered, exchanged greetings with the nervous father and exhausted mother, washed his hands as was his routine practice, and proceeded to examine the patient. He deftly examined the abdomen, listened to the fetal heartbeat, and assessed the contractions, and then did an internal examination. Each step was carried out with an expertness and confidence that mirrored his over forty years of delivering babies. Then he said to me, "Son, give her an injection of Pitocin." Pitocin is a drug that stimulates uterine contractions. It is used by physicians to induce labor at term, contract the uterus after delivery of the placenta, and treat uterine inertia—ineffective and weak contractions during labor. Uterine inertia is the condition my patient was suffering. Within a half hour we had a healthy crying baby, an intact placenta, a relieved mother, an enervated neophyte, and a satisfied mentor who said, "Son, you can't spend a whole day waiting on these events."

And I learned about technique. On this delivery and several others he taught me a technique of "ironing out the perineum." This is a procedure where the physician takes advantage of the natural elasticity of the tissues of the pregnant woman. By gently manually massaging the outer rim of the birth canal, the tissues can be stretched out to promote passage of the newborn. He did this to avoid doing episiotomies. An episiotomy, the controlled incision that the physician makes at the entrance to the birth canal to prevent tearing of the tissues during delivery of the infant, was a procedure that he rarely performed in his practice, and he felt that it was not indicated if one carefully ironed out the perineum and guided the head through the vaginal canal. We had been taught in medical school and during internship that episiotomy was a pretty standard procedure. It was almost routinely done, particularly in a woman who was delivering her first-born child. Norris's dictum has now come full circle. Episiotomies are now not done nearly as frequently as they were done fifty years ago when I was trained.

With my father having taught me so much and with so much more to learn, there would a wrenching separation. The separation was even more difficult because it was the abrupt ending to my father's fondest wish—that one of his children would succeed him in Lancaster County. In February 1959 as I was packing my medical instruments, books, and supplies, I turned to see my father standing in the middle of the room, crying like a child. I steeled myself and continued packing, but I would have my turn at crying, too. When I drove across the Virginia-North Carolina border and saw the sign, "North Carolina," I stopped the car and began to cry. I gave serious thought to turning back, but reality took over, and I continued south. After a night's rest in Charleston, South Carolina, I awoke at sunrise and continued the drive on U.S. Route 17 to Florida.

I drove nonstop through Georgia, scrupulously adhering to the Georgia state speed limit—for the last thing I wanted to do was end up in a Georgia jail. Monroe, Georgia, was far to the west—180 miles—but the memory of reading about the two colored couples lynched there in 1946, though thirteen years past, was still near in my mind. On that early February morning, I saw in the distance a sign that read: "Welcome to Florida." As I passed the sign, I gave a deep sigh and said to myself: "I must go on." I had crossed the Rubicon.

My father would try to hold on, but he was deeply disappointed that I had left. The next year, in the spring of 1960, he became profoundly depressed. I returned home for a visit in May of that year to find a lethargic, frail man. He was not eating and was rapidly becoming emaciated. He refused to go to a hospital. After a mix of pleading and persuasion by the family, he consented to return to Freedmen's Hospital. There he was placed under the care of an attending physician at Freedmen's who was known for his brilliance, but was as arrogant as he was smart. He had an imperious demeanor and felt that he was above being questioned. He showed little patience and even less compassion toward his ill colleague. What the doctor did not realize was that he was missing the diagnosis, or if he had made the diagnosis, he certainly went about treating it in the most obtuse manner. His patient was suffering from depression and his physical condition was deteriorating. After a month, frustrated by Norris's poor response to treatment, the physician felt that there was nothing further he could do. He sent Norris home. To die.

The National Hampton Alumni Association had planned to present Norris with an Alumni Merit Award June 5, 1960, but he was too ill to make the trip. He was honored along with four other alumni including the noted

soprano, Dorothy Maynor. Laura Taylor, a friend and Hampton alumna, Class of 1910, stood as proxy. His fellow alumni paid him a fine tribute. No words could have better captured the essence of his fidelity to Hampton Institute:
> Your loyalty to Hampton and its alumni has been the first order of the day with you year in and year out. You have been generous in your support both morally and financially. During the past two years you have given of your own funds and solicited gifts of nearly five thousand dollars for Hampton Institute.
>
> For courage, initiative and resourcefulness, health service to your community, on the improvement of public schools, and your many years of loyal support to Hampton and its alumni, the national body desires to present to you this, its 1960 Merit Award.

That he was so debilitated he could not make it to Hampton Institute to receive this award portended an ominous progression of his illness. He was anorexic, listless, and weak. A funereal pall had gripped the Norris home. The family, however, was not ready to accept the inevitability of death, at least not at that time. Norris was taken to Community Hospital in Richmond, Virginia, a modest facility where many of his family members and patients had been treated. He was placed under the care of a compassionate and astute Haitian-born physician, André Numa, who made a quick, but thorough assessment of his patient and initiated an intensive therapeutic program. Numa began to wonder if he were fighting a losing battle. A chest X-ray examination showed findings consistent with tumors in his lungs that had spread from the colon cancer. Numa's patient was moribund, but Numa was not ready to give up.

With ingenuity and persistence, he pulled Norris from the abyss. The x-ray film had been misread—the patient did not have tumors in his lungs, but rather, pneumonia, an inflammation of the lungs. The summer of 1960 would be long, but by September 9, 1960, Norris was able to scrawl in downhill sentences a letter to me: "About two weeks ago, the cure seemed sensational, but there has been a setback and it has caused me to progress rather slowly." He continued to strengthen, and I knew he was getting better by the steadiness of his handwriting. By late fall, he was able to write a detailed letter, and for the first time, he was candid about how he felt about his medical treatment. He was appreciative of his care at Richmond Community Hospital but in one of his rare expressions of negativity about anyone he wrote:

I think the Doctors at Richmond did a good job. While the fee was large, they worked hard and constructive. So I was willing to pay it. I am afraid that the boys up at DC [referring to Freedmen's Hospital] are so filled with ego that I feel too much time is spent in reference. I think, one of my disposition would have a hard time with that deceitful bunch. Of course, all this is confidential. I wish you could have seen the overall picture and you could then evaluate the standard. With my appetite gone and no elimination they would send up the largest pieces of corn bread and chuck beef. Some of the members of the staff would come around and ask why I did not eat, saying all the rest were eating. Although some of them were nasty I did not lose my temper. Only one day I told [my physician] I consider his statements both inaccurate and unnecessary. Well so much for that. That is all past history as I am now eating and drinking to my heart's delight.

Norris was not one to harbor bitterness, but the experience in the spring of 1960 at Freedmen's Hospital left him with an unmitigated antipathy toward the doctor who had treated him. He once said to me: "Son, I am sorry to say this to you, but there is one thing I will not give you very much credit for, and that is sending me up to Freedmen's Hospital in 1960."

Recovery was slow but steady, and by Christmastime he could pose cheerfully with the family for a photograph. Norris returned to some activity but at a considerably diminished pace. He had virtually no investment income, no pension, and no Social Security. Social Security was not given to the self-employed, and Medicare did not exist. He was embarrassed by the need to be dependent upon us children, but was appreciative of our largesse. He once wrote to me: "Dear Son: Thank you so much for your good letter and your enclosed check to Mother. We are sorry that we have become such parasites, but I guess such is life."

In 1961, Norris was strong enough to travel to Florida to visit me. He was heartened by my robust practice and my stature in the community. For the first time he admitted to me that the move to Florida had been a sound idea. When he was introduced to a Melbourne resident, the gentleman exclaimed: "What a pleasure to meet the great Dr. Norris!" to which he responded: "My good friend, you are just seeing a shadow of that man." And, indeed, no truer statement could have been made. He had returned to medical practice, but his work was limited to a few elderly people who had refused to give up on him. Despite the ravages of illness and old age, he kept abreast of medical developments. In August 1961, he attended the National Medical Association meeting in New York City.

The years of 1962 and 1963 were rather good ones for Norris, marked by the return of much energy and strength, but he was ill much of 1964—"a rather dark year," he said. In December 1964, he did something totally out of character. He wrote to his friend, Ellsworth Bunker:

> Ellsworth, I am asking a great big favor if possible. If the Arthur Bunker Foundation is still active if I could be considered for a monthly stipend, as I am sure I shall never be able to work again? Organizations and people have been very good including you and dear Katharine [Ellsworth Bunker's sister]. However, you are quite aware that in my home there is a need that is not too easily supplied. Don't let this tax you other than is convenient.

The request was uncharacteristic because Norris disdained any type of personal solicitation. Somehow, one of the children learned about the letter. We were mortified! There was simply no need for our father to ask for outside help. Bunker did not want to refuse his friend, but we were adamant that Bunker not give his money. My sister Alma and I requested a meeting with him. He generously invited us to dinner at his home in Georgetown. The quintessential diplomat worked out an agreement. The foundation would send Norris the monthly stipend, and we would reimburse the foundation.

ℭ

Norris had never been one to shy away from a battle, but he knew there was one battle he would soon lose, the battle against aging. The specter of death did not hold for him the dread that it holds for so many, and he never once expressed the desire to live beyond his usefulness. He looked upon death as a part of life. Possibly his love of animals, plants, trees, and flowers so imbued him with respect for the life cycle, that death for him was as normal a part of life as birth.

CHAPTER 28

"There Comes a Time in a Man's Life When He Must Die"

As for me, already my life is being poured out on the altar, and the hour for my departure is upon me. I have run the great race, I have finished the course, I have kept faith.

II TIMOTHY 4:6,7,8

All sick rooms in the South seemed the same to me, and this room, at first glance, was no different from the many others I had visited. They were uniformly darkened; the closed curtains gave the place the melancholy, mournful feel of death. The centerpiece was the bed with the pale, listless figure lying neatly tucked in. The requisite bedside stand had all the trappings for the ill: the glass of water with a straw, the box of Kleenex, and the hand fan. The fan could be the oddest of accouterments, for often on the front was the local undertaker's smiling countenance, and on the back was his address and telephone number. But in one key way, this room was very different from all others I had visited. In the other sick rooms, the dying had been my patients; in this room, the eighty-two-year-old man slipping inexorably toward death was my father—frail, ill with pneumonia, and barely conscious.

My mother had summoned me from New York the day before, convinced that he would not survive another day. I arrived in the late evening, May 14, 1966, and found my father hot with fever, gasping for air, dehydrated, and barely responsive. I immediately went to the People's Drugstore in Kilmarnock, and though the drugstore had already closed, Ed Layman, the pharmacist, kindly consented to come over and give me the supplies and medications that were needed. The intravenous fluids, antibiotics, and chest percussion worked. Death was denied a victory that night. By morning, his fever had broken, his breathing was rhythmic and gentle, and the stupor had lifted, yet the old ship was listing badly.

About noon, a family friend, Lloyd B. Hubbard, Sr., a businessman and Mayor of White Stone and son of Norris's late colleague, Dr. B. H. B. Hubbard, visited. Norris, who always had enjoyed bantering with Hubbard, did not respond to his comments. He just lay in the bed, prostrate, with closed eyes. Upon seeing the old warrior feeble and worn, Hubbard turned to me and in a plaintive, pleading voice said, "Jimmy, you've got to get your father to a hospital." His visit was brief, and he left with the understanding that I would try to arrange to have Norris admitted.

Later that afternoon, I said to my father: "Lloyd Hubbard visited you today, and he feels we ought to take you to the hospital." My father, irritated that I would consider such an option, turned toward me, lifted his gaunt, weakened body on one elbow, and briefly flashed that familiar steely look of determination. He countered in measured cadence with the resolve in his voice so well-known to me since childhood: "Yes, son, I know Lloyd was here. I heard every word he said! Well, let me tell you, there is no earthly good a hospital can do me! There comes a time in a man's life when he must die, and that is all!"

Three days later, on a crisp spring morning, he asked Theresita to send for their daughter, Alice. She was the oldest of the eight children and the one we sensed my father was really closest to, although he never showed favoritism to any of us. She was teaching school in Warsaw, thirty miles away, but she found a substitute teacher, left her class and rushed to Norris's bedside arriving two hours later. As soon as she entered, he looked up and smiled as his last wish had been granted and uttered weakly: "Thank you for coming, daughter." Then, he closed his eyes—forever.

Facing death, Norris never flinched. Due to my ministrations the prior weekend, his mind remained acute to the end. He knew the score, for over fifty years he had attended so many in similar straits. But he left this life just as he had lived, with courage, fearlessness, determination, dignity, and gratefulness. He had run a remarkable race and he knew it, but modesty would never let him say it.

One looks back on this life and asks: "What did he really do?" My father did not set out to accomplish any specific aim or goal beyond fulfilling a simple promise to his father. It would have been sufficient had he done just that—gotten a medical education, returned home, and made sure that no one would suffer as his father had suffered. But the pragmatic underpinnings of his approach to life honed during his thirteen years of professional preparation would not let him stop with just that. For the rest of his life, wherever he encountered a challenge, he felt he had to rise to that challenge. He had to meet the test. No one ever asked him whether he thought all that he had gone through was worth the effort. No one ever asked him what would he have done differently if he had to do it all over again. No one ever asked him what he considered to be his crowning achievements or most dismal failures. This much is sure: He never once in all his letters to me or anyone else expressed regret about the life he had lived or the choices he had made. Throughout his letters there is one recurring theme—"Fight on!"

During our long conversations and in his letters to me, Norris never spoke of the people he had helped, the projects he had championed, and the battles he had fought. Modesty was as innate to him as breathing. He once wrote to one of his Hampton teachers who wanted to know something about him while he was at Lincoln University:

> You asked me to tell you a little about myself and work. Well, I shall be glad to tell you anything about myself that would interest you. There is so little to me probably after I have told you, there would be a little gain.

This attitude of self-effacement never changed. He did relate to Theresita an experience he had at the National Medical Association meeting in Cleveland in 1957, when a colleague from Red Bank, New Jersey, called him over to a group of men and said to them: "This man is my friend, and I just want to say something: he possesses more magnanimity than any man I have ever known at any time or any place."

Norris touched many lives. The men and women who benefited from his generosity, his exemplary life, his admonitions, his advice, and even his financial help are legion. He was a deeply religious man who carried his religion not on his garments but in his heart. Many of his letters are laced with religious references, such as, "It is heartening to know that God will heal all of our sorrows. Too, he will not make them heavier than we can bear." The latter statement came at the end of his life when he had already suffered so many sorrows: the losses of his parents at an early age, of his only sister, his only niece, one of his children, and the many young patients who fell victim to tuberculosis, infectious diseases, accidents, and violence. Not only had he suffered these personal losses, but also for one so talented and capable to be denied so much because of the color of his skin surely affected his psyche. Yet in all his letters, he never once expressed dismay, and he remained remarkably free of bitterness. He had a big heart, but in that heart, there was no room for bitterness or hate.

Upon his death, Dr. John M. Ellison wrote the family:

Though great the pain of sorrow and deep the sadness, the shadows are lifted and you are consoled when you know and realize not only the length of days but the fullness of life that Dr. Norris lived. His life was so unselfish and fruitful of great deeds and service. Indeed, he was friend to all; no causes for good were alien to his deep interest and sincere patronage. God-fearing, honest, thrifty and open hearted he gave the full measure of his days to make his home, his community, indeed the world, good places in which to live. By these great qualities that under girded his life, he leaves an eternal legacy to all who knew him.

Norris's eternal legacy may lie in his conviction that you can only be constrained if you permit yourself to be constrained, and you can only be contained if you if permit yourself to be contained. Whatever has to be done, must be done well. Finally, there are no limits if with proper education you are willing to make sacrifices, persevere, and fight on.

EPILOGUE

The Northern Neck, the state of Virginia, the United States, and the world are all very different places than they were when Norris lived. Few things have remained the same.

The homeplace that he helped his father buy with his meager savings in 1898 remains in the family. There is no garden, and although the house our family moved into in 1927 and Thornton's house still remain, the office has been demolished. The service station building is now the site of a thriving business. The neighborhood is hardly recognizable from the one on the map included with chapter 10 (circa 1940s). The former school is still a Kingdom Hall of Jehovah's Witnesses. The road is now a dual highway, and Kilmarnock's corporate limits extend far south of the neighborhood. New Saint John's Church, in all its elegance, remains as a beacon.

No one in our family has lived in Lancaster County since 1968. My parents' descendants are scattered in cities across the United States and four continents. Norris would be pleased that his twenty-one progeny (children, grandchildren and great-grandchildren) have acquired over thirty higher education degrees, including four from Hampton and seven from Harvard, and that they hold an eclectic range of occupations. Two grandchildren, both namesakes, are physicians. Morgan Norris Jackson, an internist, graduated from Harvard College in 1969 and Harvard Medical School in 1973. Morgan E. Norris III, a Houston-based, maxillofacial and plastic surgeon, graduated from Virginia Commonwealth University's School of Dentistry in 1985 and from its School of Medicine in 1996.

I return home several times a year. The older people, white and colored, recall Norris with great affection, but the younger people know little about him. The only young person who might have a vague idea of this man is the high school graduate who receives a Morgan E. Norris Scholarship to Hampton University. This is not surprising. In 1985, when Vince Coleman, an African-American and a rookie Major League Baseball outfielder, was asked about Jackie Robinson (see page 291, 1947), he responded that he didn't know anything about Jackie Robinson. My father wouldn't be terribly upset about that response. One of his favorite sayings about life was, "You won't know the difference a hundred years from now." There are lots of things that don't take a hundred years, and as far as recognition or appreciation for one's efforts, he also said, "Son, you don't do something for thanks; you do it because it is the right thing to do."

My mother survived him by twenty-one years. She remained loyal to his vision to the end of her life at ninety-four in 1987. Her deep and abiding respect for him never waned, although he left her little to live on. He had an inconsequential retirement account with Investor's Diversified Services, a mutual fund, but the monthly payout was a paltry sum. During his lifetime, Social Security did not cover the self-employed and individual retirement plans were just coming to the fore.

About six months after my father died, I picked up the telephone to take a call from my mother. She had a desperation in her voice that I never before had heard. The Chesapeake Bank in Lively had just contacted her to call in two loans. Approximately two years before Norris died, he cosigned notes for two enterprising young men that he wanted to help in business ventures. They both defaulted on the payments. Although Theresita knew nothing about the transactions, the bank officer told her in gentlest terms possible that the notes must be paid. I met with the officer at the bank, and an agreement was made so that the loans could be repaid in monthly installments. A disaster was averted, for Norris had left no liquidity to settle the loans. Remarkably, my mother did not rail against him. She was more resigned to his commitment to help young men and women than she was bitter about his decision. She simply asked rhetorically, "How could he commit himself to cosigning notes when he knew he had so little resources?"

On July 31, 1971, a Morgan E. Norris Day was held in my father's honor at the Calvary Baptist Church. One of the featured speakers was Dr. Wendell Russell, president of Virginia State College and son of the late Rev. George S. Russell who was the first principal of the new elementary school that Norris had led the citizens in building. The other speaker was Kilmarnock's mayor from 1970 to 1978, B. Brainard Edmonds, Jr., nephew of Norris's late esteemed colleague, Dr. Jeter Edmonds. Mayor Edmonds and the Kilmarnock Town Council proclaimed July 31, 1971, as Morgan E. Norris Day. The reception was held in a community center designed by Louis Stevenson, an architect and husband of Norris's daughter, Elizabeth. Nearly twenty years later on February 23, 1991, another ceremony was held in Lancaster County when Norris's portrait was added to the portraits of prominent Lancaster County citizens at the courthouse. The other colored Lancaster County citizen whose portrait hangs in the courthouse is Armistead Nickens, who was a member of the House of Delegates in Virginia's General Assembly from 1871 to 1875 and whose ancestors fought in the Revolutionary War.

The Morgan E. Norris Endowed Scholarship Fund at Hampton University was established during the memorial service July 31, 1971, and it is growing—not as fast and as large as it might have grown, but nevertheless growing. Norris would have been pleased about that. He wrote on June 24, 1958, to an old schoolmate: "Probably I have never told you that as a student at Hampton, I hated so much to see students leaving [because of lack of funds] that showed the promise of fine men and women." When his daughter, Alma, whose two sons and three grandchildren are all Harvard graduates, died in 2004, her sons asked that in lieu of flowers, contributions be sent to the scholarship fund at Hampton University. In 2008, I asked each of my father's grandchildren to contribute to the fund to honor the hundredth anniversary of his graduation from Hampton Institute (now Hampton University). Everyone responded enthusiastically.

Norris would rejoice in the progress that this nation and Virginia have

made in the last fifty-plus years. He would be heartened by the improvement in race relations. Yet, he would share the sentiments of that anonymous
colored preacher who said, according to the Rev. Martin Luther King (this is
my best recollection from King's speech in Westchester County, New York,
in 1962):

"Lord, we ain't where we ought to be; and we ain't where we're going,
but thank God we ain't where we used to be."

ભ

The gravesites, on the Tolson property, where the remains of my parents
were placed originally and the adjacent property passed through two owners.
The last owner was a cantankerous old lady. We were not sure that we could
bury our mother at the site, but she reluctantly consented. She refused to
permit our neighbor and family friend, James Moody, to help the family tend
the gravesites and she built a fence between her home and the graves. Tiring
of her objections, the author, with agreement of the family and Calvary Baptist
Church, acquired a site on the hill next to the parsonage lot for a church cemetery. My parents' remains were then interred in the new cemetery.

A sad coda to the lady's fate. The Virginia Department of Transportation created a dual highway along the route and her home was demolished to
make way for the road. She died shortly afterwards.

CHRONOLOGY OF IMPORTANT EVENTS
1861 – 1968

♦ *indicates a date of significance in Norris's life*

1861 United States Civil War began. Eleven states seceded from the Union and formed the Confederate States of America.

1863 January 1 - President Abraham Lincoln issued executive order— Emancipation Proclamation—*"That on the first day of January, in the year of our Lord one thousand eight hundred and sixty-three, all persons held as slaves within any State or designated part of a State, the people whereof shall then be in rebellion against the United States, shall be then, thenceforward, and forever free; ...*

1865 Civil War ended in defeat of the Confederate Armies.

1866 Ku Klux Klan founded.

1867 March 2 - Congress passed first Reconstruction Act.

1877 Reconstruction ended, the last Union troops were withdrawn from the Southern States.

♦ Northern Neck Baptist Association Founded.

1883 ♦ Morgan E. Norris born August 13.

First Negro doctor arrived in Alabama through the efforts of Booker T. Washington.

1884 ♦ John Benjamin Norris, Norris's father, co-founded Little Willie Chapel Church.

1886 ♦ Norris's mother died.

1892   ♦ Calvary Baptist Church (church home of Norris family) and Mount Vernon Church in Lancaster County founded.

1895   National Medical Association founded.

Booker T. Washington gave famed speech at the Atlanta Exposition.

1896   U.S. Supreme Court, in *Plessy v. Ferguson,* reaffirmed separate but equal doctrine.

1898   Spanish American War began and lasted four months.

1900   ♦ Albert Terry Wright and wife, Annie Wright, both teachers, came to Lancaster County.

♦ Sharon Baptist Church founded by Rev. Daniel Tucker.

♦ December - Norris's father died.

1902   Virginia passed new constitution that effectively disenfranchised blacks and poor whites.

Annual capitation tax (poll tax) levied.

Medical Society of State of Virginia wrote new constitution, adding line that membership is limited to whites only.

1904   ♦ Norris entered Hampton Institute.

1905   Northern Neck Medical Association (white) founded.

Old Dominion Medical Association, a group of Negro physicians in Virginia, founded.

1908   ♦ Norris graduated from Hampton Institute and enrolled at Lincoln University.

1910   Abraham Flexner published report on medical education in the U.S. and Canada. Report led to major revisions in medical schools' curricula and the closing of substandard medical schools.

1911   Negro Organization Society of Virginia founded.

1912   ♦   Norris graduated from Lincoln University and entered Howard University's College of Medicine.

1914   World War I began.

1915   National Negro Health Week inaugurated by Booker T. Washington.

Booker T. Washington died.

1916   ♦   Norris graduated from medical school; entered one-year internship at John A. Andrew Hospital in Tuskegee.

1917   Supreme Court ruled segregated housing is illegal.

United States entered World War I.

♦   Norris completed internship and passed Virginia State Board. Starts medical practice in Lancaster County.

♦   Norris commissioned first lieutenant in the United States Army, but was never called to active duty.

White mob lynched William Paige in Northumberland County, a county adjacent to Norris's home county of Lancaster; thirty-six people lynched throughout the South during the year.

1918   April - Piedmont Sanatorium, the first sanatorium in Virginia for Negroes with tuberculosis, opened with forty beds.

♦   June 21 - Norris married Theresita Beatrice Chiles.

November 11 - World War I ended.

Spanish flu peaked. An estimated 300,000 people died in the U.S. from September 15, 1918, through December 15, 1918.

1919   ♦   First of nine children born to Theresita and Norris.

June 4 - Nineteenth Amendment to the Constitution giving women the right to vote was passed by Congress.

1921   ♦ Norris held first surgical clinic in Lancaster County.

1923   February 12 - Veteran's Hospital for Negro disabled soldiers
        dedicated at Tuskegee Institute's Chapel. Vice President Calvin
        Coolidge present.

1924   Virginia General Assembly passed Racial Integrity Act,
        reaffirming the one-drop rule that any person with any
        ascertainable black blood is not white. The act defined the racial
        make-up of a white person, but did not define the racial make-up
        of a colored person.

1926   Virginia passed the Massenberg law prohibiting racial mixing in
        public places. Gov. Harry Flood Byrd declined to veto the bill and
        let it pass without his signature.

1927   ♦ Norris organized the Northern Neck Progressive Association.
        The organization held its first annual Afro-American Fair in
        Brookvale (Lancaster County), Virginia.

1928   Virginia's General Assembly passed an anti-lynching bill.

        ♦ Norris became chairman of the Better Health Committee of
        the Negro Organization of Virginia.

1933   ♦ New Kilmarnock Graded School opened under Norris's
        leadership. It was the first brick school for Negroes in the
        Northern Neck.

1934   ♦ Norris appointed to Board of Trustees, Hampton Institute.

        ♦ The name of the New Kilmarnock Graded School was
        changed to the Morgan E. Norris Graded School.

1938   U.S. Supreme Court ruled that the University of Missouri must
        admit Lloyd L. Gaines, a Negro, to law school or the state must
        provide an equal law school.

1939   Lloyd L. Gaines vanished in Chicago and was never heard from
        again.

♦   Norris led boycott that forced the Lancaster County School Board to provide free bus transportation for the colored students.

1941   U.S. Congress declared war against Japan and Germany.

1942   ♦   Norris and his neighbors successfully petitioned Circuit Court to have the town of Kilmarnock exclude them from the town's corporate limits.

1943   ♦   Norris and colleagues founded the Rappahannock Medical Society.

1945   World War II ended.

1946   U.S. Supreme Court held that segregation on interstate transportation is invalid. Case originated in Virginia by Irene Morgan Kirkaldy, a colored lady from Gloucester County, Virginia.

1947   Jackie Robinson broke the color barrier in organized baseball.

1948   President Harry S. Truman issued Executive Order #9981 desegregating the United States Armed Forces.

President Harry S. Truman introduced a Civil War Plank at Democratic Convention.

Edith Irby Jones became the first colored person admitted to a medical school in the South—The University of Arkansas.

♦   Norris appointed coroner in Lancaster County and became the first Negro coroner in the State of Virginia.

♦   James B. Blayton, of Williamsburg, succeeded Norris as chairman of the Better Health Committee of the Negro Organization Society of Virginia.

1950   Boothe's Bill to end segregation on public transportation in Virginia defeated in Virginia's General Assembly.

1951   Jean Harris, the daughter of a Richmond physician, was the first Negro admitted to a medical school in Virginia (Medical College of Virginia).

1952   ♦   Virginia State Board of Health refused to reappoint Norris
coroner.

1954   Harvey Higley ended segregation in Veterans Administration
Hospitals.

Supreme Court handed down ruling in *Brown v. Board of
Education* declaring educational facilities are inherently unequal
and violate the Fourteenth Amendment.

Medical Society of Virginia voted to drop "white only" clause
from its constitution.

1955   Jean Harris graduated from the Medical College of Virginia.

Supreme Court of Appeals of Virginia upheld the ban on
interracial marriages.

♦   Norris resigned from Hampton Institute's Trustee Board
because of illness.

1959   ♦   Last Afro-American Fair was held in Lancaster County.

1963   November 1 - Fourth Circuit Court of Appeals ruled "separate but
equal" no longer valid.

Supreme Court of Appeals of Virginia struck down the
Massenberg law of 1926.

March 12 - The U.S. Supreme Court left standing the decision of
the Fourth Circuit Court, "separate but equal" no longer valid.

1964   August 18 - President Lyndon B. Johnson signed into law
HR 10041, an act extending Hill-Burton Act for five years;
Amendment by Rep. John Dingell carried the day; the "separate
but equal" clause applied to hospital construction was eliminated
from the bill.

1964   Richmond Academy of Physicians voted to admit Negro doctors.

Title VI of the Civil Rights Act prohibited discrimination on
basis of race, color, and national origin in federally assisted

programs.

♦ Norris effectively ended the practice of medicine.

1965 President Lyndon B. Johnson signed legislation creating Medicare. The National Medical Association was the only national organization of physicians to endorse Medicare.

1966 ♦ May 18 - Morgan E. Norris died.

Supreme Court of Appeals of Virginia again upheld the ban on interracial marriages.

♦ The Morgan E. Norris Graded School closed.

1967 U.S. Supreme Court invalidated Virginia's Racial Integrity Act of 1924 in case of *Richard Perry Loving et al. v. Commonwealth of Virginia.* It ruled that Virginia's laws violated equal protection and due process clauses of the Fourteenth Amendment of the United States Constitution.

1968 AMA ruled that local and state medical societies may not discriminate on the basis of color, etc.

♦ The Morgan E. Norris Graded School building was sold at public auction.

BIBLIOGRAPHY

ARTICLES

Ackerman, S.J. "The Trials of S.W. Tucker." *The Washington Post Magazine* (June 11, 2000): 14.

"AMA Constitution Changed." *JAMA* 206 (1968): 2632.

"AMA vs. Negro Doctors." *Journal of the National Medical Association* 36 (1944): 202.

"AMA vs. Negro Doctors." *Medical Economics* (1944): 130, 132.

"An Appeal to the A.M.A. in Behalf of Negro Physicians in the South." *Journal of the National Medical Association* 41 (1949): 34.

Anderson, Robert J. and Herbert I. Sauer. "Reported Tuberculosis Morbidity United States, 1949-1951." *Public Health Reports* 67 (1952): 1101-1108.

Baker, R.B., H.A. Washington, O. Olakanmi, T. L. Savitt, E. A. Jacobs, E. Hoover, and M. K. Wynia. "African American Physicians and Organized Medicine, 1846-1968, Origins of a Racial Divide." *JAMA* 300 (2008): 306-312.

Bennett, Emily W. "The Work of a Rosenwald Nurse." *Public Health Nurse* 23 (1931): 119-120.

Davis, Ronald M. "Achieving Racial Harmony for the Benefit of Patients and Communities, Contrition, Reconciliation and Collaboration." *JAMA* 300 (2008): 323-325.

Ellison, J.M. "Negro Organizations and Leadership in Relationship to Rural Life in Virginia." *Virginia Polytechnic Institute Bulletin* 290 (1933).
Foster, Charles I. "The Colonization of Free Negroes in Liberia, 1816-1835." *The Journal of Negro History* 38 (1985): 41-66.

Foster, N.M.N. "The Founding and the Founder of Our Society." *Northern Neck of Virginia Historical Society Magazine* 50 (2000): 5915-5918.

Frazer, Walter J. "William Henry Ruffner and the Establishment of the Virginia Public School System 1870-1874." *The Virginia Magazine of History and Biography* 79 (1971): 259-279.

Gover, Mary. "Mortality among Negroes in the United States." *Public Health Bulletin* 174 (1927).

Hutton, Frankie. "Economic Considerations in the American Colonization Society's Early Effort to Emigrate Free Blacks to Liberia, 1816-36." *The Journal of Negro History* 68 (1983): 376-389.

Meier, A. "Toward a Reinterpretation of Booker T. Washington." *Journal of Southern History* 23 (1957): 220-227.

Morón, Alonzo G. "Community Responsibilities of the Practicing Physician." *Journal of the National Medical Association* 42 (1950): 371-377.

Naik, B.J., D.J. Lynch, E.G. Slavcheva, and R.S. Beissner. "Calciphylaxis: Medical and Surgical Management of Chronic Extensive Wounds in a Renal Dialysis Population." *Plastic & Reconstructive Surgery* 113 (2004): 304-312.

"National Negro Health Week Ends." *Journal of the National Medical Association* 43 (1951): 198-199.

"The Negro Medical Doctor and Organized Medicine." *Journal of the National Medical Association* 36 (1944): 202.

"Negro Physicians and the American Medical Association." [Correspondence] *Journal of the National Medical Association* 39 (1947): 222-24.

Phenix, George P. "Sixty-Second Annual Report of the Principal." *The Hampton Bulletin* 26 (1930).

Plecker, M.D., W.A. "Virginia's Effort to Preserve Racial Integrity." In *A Decade of Progress in Eugenics. Scientific Papers of the Third International Congress of Eugenics, New York, August 21-23, 1932*. Baltimore: Williams and Wilkins Co., 1934.

Pole, L.D. "Tetanus." *Virginia Medical Monthly* 48 (1922): 443-444.

"Racisim Rules AMA Policies." *Journal of the National Medical Association* 41 (1949): 34.

Savitt, Todd. "Entering a White Profession: Black Physicians in the New South." *Bulletin of the History of Medicine* 61 (1987): 507-540.

Scott, C. Waldo. "The President's Address Read at the 50th Anniversary Meeting of the Old Dominion Medical Society, Virginia State College, Petersburg, Virginia, June 20-21, 1956." *Journal of the National Medical Association* 48 (1956): 426-227.

Sherman, Richard B. "'The Last Stand': The Fight for Racial Integrity in Virginia in the 1920s." *Journal of Southern History* 54 (1988): 69-92.

Slaughter, James B. "School Desegregation in the Northern Neck." *Northern Neck of Virginia Historical Magazine* 32 (1982): 3615-3652.

Smith, D.B. "Healing of a Nation. How Three Graduates of the University of Michigan Medical School Wrote their Own Chapter in the History of Civil Rights in America." *University of Michigan Bulletin* 2 (2000). http://www.medicineatmichigan.org/magazine/2000/summer/blackhistory/default.asp

"Thomas Foster Wheeldon." In *Virginia Lives: The Old Dominion Who's Who*, by Richard Morton Lee, 1059-1060. Hopkinsville, KY: Historical Record Association, 1964.

Washington, Booker T. "B.T. Washington Wants Justice Done to Negro." *The World*, (August 20, 1908).

West, Earle H. "Robert Russa Moton." In *Dictionary of American Biography*, edited by Raymond W. Logan and Michael R. Winston, 459-463. New York: W. W. Norton & Co., 1982.

Wright, Louis T. "The Negro Doctor and the War." *Journal of the National Medical Association* 11 (1919): 195-196.

Wright, Jr., R.R. "Housing and Sanitation in Relation to the Mortality of Negroes." *The Southern Workman* 36 (1906): 475-80.

Yerushalmy, J., H.E. Hilleboe, and C.E. Palmer. "Tuberculosis Mortality in the United States: 1939-41." *Public Health Reports* 58 (1943): 1457-82.

BOOKS

Alexander, Frederick M. *Education for the needs of the Negro in Virginia.* Washington, D.C. The Southern Education Foundation, Inc., 1943.

American Public Health Association. *Study of Tuberculosis in Virginia; A Report of a Study by a Staff Assembled by the American Public Health Association.* New York: 1952.

Beardsley, Edward H. *History of Neglect: Health Care for Blacks and Mill Workers in the Twentieth-century South.* Knoxville: University of Tennessee Press, 1987.

Behring, Emil von. *Suppression of Tuberculosis, Together with Observations Concerning Phthisiogenesis in Man and Animals.* New York: J. Wiley & Sons, 1904.

Brock, Thomas D. *Robert Koch, A Life in Medicine and Bacteriology.* Madison, WI: Science Tech Publishers; Berlin, New York: Springer-Verlag. 1988.

Buck, James Lawrence Blair. *The Development of Public Schools in Virginia, 1607-1952.* Richmond: Commonwealth of Virginia, State Board of Education, 1952.

Bunie, Andrew. *The Negro in Virginia Politics, 1902-1965.* Charlottesville: University Press of Virginia, 1967.

Brundage, William Fitzhugh. *Lynching in the New South: Georgia and Virginia, 1880-1930.* Urbana: University of Illinois Press, 1993.

Caldwell, Mark. *The Last Crusade: The War on Consumption, 1862-1954.* New York: Atheneum, 1988.Carrington, Thomas Spees. *Fresh Air and How to Use It.* New York: The National Association for the Study and Prevention of Tuberculosis, 1912.

Chafe, William H., ed. *Remembering Jim Crow.* New York: The New Press, 2001.

Cobb, William Montague. *The First Negro Medical Society: A History of the Medico-Chirurgical Society of the District of Columbia, 1884-1939.* Washington, D.C.: The Associated Publishers, 1939.

Conner, Douglas L. and John F. Marszalek. *A Black Physician's Story: Bringing Hope in Mississippi.* Jackson: University of Mississippi Press, 1985.

Cowling, Dorothy N.C., ed. *Historical Notes on the Life and Achievements of Blacks in Lancaster County and the State of Virginia 1619-1974.* Richmond, Va.: Lancaster County African American Historical Society, 1991.

Davies, Pete. *Catching Cold: 1918's Forgotten Tragedy and the Scientific Hunt for the Virus that Caused It.* London: Michael Joseph, 1999.

Davis, Lenwood G. and George H. Hill. *Blacks in the American Armed Forces 1776-1983, a Bibliography.* Westport, Conn.: Greenwood Press, 1985.

Dees, Jr., Jesse Walter, and James S. Hadley. *Jim Crow.* Ann Arbor: Ann Arbor Publishers, 1951.

Dinan, John. *The Virginia State Constitution, a Reference Guide.* Westport, Conn.: Praeger Publishers, 2006.

Dreer, Herman. *The History of the Omega Psi Phi Fraternity, a Brotherhood of Negro College Men, 1911 to 1939.* [Washington, D.C.?]: The Fraternity, 1940.

Du Bois, W. E. B. *The Souls of Black Folk.* New York: Penguin Putnam, Inc., 1995.

Du Bois, W. E. B., ed. *The Health and Physique of the Negro American. Report of a Social Study made under the Direction of Atlanta University; Together with the Proceedings of the Eleventh Conference for the Study of the Negro Problems held at Atlanta University, on May the 29th, 1906.* Atlanta, Ga.: Atlanta University Press, 1906.

Dollard, John. *Caste and Class in a Southern Town.* 3rd ed. Garden City, NY: Doubleday & Co.,1957.

Dormandy, Thomas. *The White Death: A History of Tuberculosis.* Rio Grande, Ohio: Hambledon Press, 1999.

Dubos, René J. *White Plague: Tuberculosis, Man, and Society.* New Brunswick: Rutgers University Press, 1987.

Duke, M. *The Land between Waters: Virginia's Lancaster County: A Short History.* Lancaster, Va.: Mary Ball Washington Museum & Library, 2001.

Dyson, Walter. *Howard University, the Capstone of Negro Education, a History: 1867-1940.* Washington, D.C.: The Graduate School, Howard University, 1941.

Eaton, Hubert A. *Every Man Should Try.* Wilmington, NC: Bonaparte Press, 1984.

Edmonds, B.B. *Kilmarnock.* Kilmarnock, Va.: Little Pebble Press, 1976.

Embree, Edwin R. *Julius Rosenwald Fund: A Review.* Chicago: The Fund, 1928.

Engs, Robert Francis. *Educating the Disfranchised and Disinherited: Samuel Chapman Armstrong and Hampton Institute, 1839-1893.* Knoxville: University of Tennessee Press, 1999.

Flexner, Abraham. *Medical Education in the United States and Canada, A Report to the Carnegie Foundation for the Advancement of Teaching.* New York: Arno Press, Inc., 1972.

Graham, Lawrence. *Our Kind of People: Inside America's Black Upper Class.* New York: Harper Collins, 1999.

Hathaway, Catherine Blake. *When Dabba Was Young: Growing up in a Fine Little Town Called Kilmarnock.* Kilmarnock, Va.: Kilmarnock Museum, 1999.

Hayden, Robert C. *Mr. Harlem Hospital: Dr. Louis T. Wright: A Biography.* Littleton, Mass.: Tapestry Press, Ltd., 2003.

Haynie, Miriam. *The Stronghold: A Story of Historic Northern Neck of Virginia and Its People.* Richmond, Va.: The Dietz Press, 1959.

Hewlett, Richard Greening. *Jessie Ball DuPont.* Gainsville: University Press of Florida, 1992.

Hope, Richard O. *Racial Strife in the U.S. Military: Toward the Elimination of Discrimination.* New York: Praeger, 1979.

Holly, David C. *Chesapeake Steamboats: Vanished Fleet.* Centreville, Md.: Tidewater Publishers, 1994.

Jackson, Luther Porter. *Negro Office-Holders in Virginia, 1865-1895.* Norfolk, Va.: Guide Quality Press, 1945.

Jett, Carolyn H. *Lancaster County, Virginia: Where the River Meets the Bay.* Lancaster, Va.: Lancaster County History Book Committee/The Mary Ball Washington Museum and Library, 2003.

Johnson, James Weldon. *The Autobiography of an Ex-Coloured Man.* New York: Alfred A. Knopf, Inc., 1927.

Jones, James H. *Bad Blood: The Tuskegee Syphilis Experiment.* New York: Free Press, 1981.

Julius Rosenwald Fund. *A Picture-Book about the Costs of Medical Care.* Chicago: Julius Rosenwald Fund, 1932.

Julius Rosenwald Fund. *School Money in Black and White.* Chicago, 1934.

Kennedy, Randall. *Nigger: the Strange Career of a Troublesome Word.* New York: Pantheon Books, 2002.

Kornweibel, Theodore. *Investigate Everything: Federal Efforts to Compel Black Loyalty during World War I.* Bloomington: Indiana University Press, 2002.

Kluger, Richard. *Simple Justice; the History of Brown v. Board of Education and Black America's Struggle for Equality.* New York: Knopf, 1976.

Layman, Ed. *Behind Those Happy Smiles: Growing Pains in the Northern Neck.* Kilmarnock, Va.: Laybank Publishing, 2003.

Leffall, LaSalle D. *No Boundaries: A Cancer Surgeon's Odyssey.* Washington, D.C.: Howard University Press, 2005.

Lebsock, Suzanne. *A Murder in Virginia. Southern Justice on Trial.* New York: W. W. Norton & Company, 2003.

Lewis, David L.,ed. *W.E.B. Du Bois: A Reader.* New York: Henry Holt and Co., 1995.

Lightfoot, Sara Lawrence. *Balm in Gilead: Journey of a Healer.* Reading, Mass.: Addison-Wesley Pub. Co., 1988.

Lindsey, Donal F. *Indians at Hampton Institute, 1877-1923.* Urbana: University of Illinois Press, 1995.

Malval, Fritz, J. *A Guide to the Archives of Hampton Institute.* Westport, Conn.: Greenwood Press, 1985.

National Municipal League. *Coroners in 1953: A Symposium of Legal Bases and Actual Practices.* 3rd ed. New York: National Municipal League, 1955.

Organ, Claude H. and Margaret M. Kosiba. *A Century of Black Surgeons: the U.S.A. Experience.* 2 vols. Norman, Okla.: Transcript Press, 1987.

Oshinsky, David M. *Polio, An American Story.* New York: Oxford University Press, 2005.

Ott, Katharine. *Fevered Lives.* Cambridge, Mass.: Harvard University Press, 1996.

Peabody, Francis Greenwood. *Education for Life; the Story of Hampton Institute.* Garden City, NY: Doubleday, 1926.

Packard, Randall. *White Plague, Black Labor: Tuberculosis and the Political Economy of Health and Disease in South Africa.* Berkeley: University of California Press, 1989.

Parran, Thomas. *Shadow on the Land: Syphilis.* New York: Reynal & Hitchcock, 1937.

Parish, H.J. *A History of Immunization.* Edinburgh: E. & S. Livingstone, Ltd., 1965.

Pearson, Hugh. *Under the Knife, How a Wealthy Negro Surgeon Wielded Power in the Jim Crow South.* New York: Free Press, 2000.

Pfeiffer, Kathleen. *Race Passing and American Individualism.* Amherst: University of Massachusetts Press, 2003.

Picott, J. Rupert. *A Quarter Century of the Black Experience in Elementary and Secondary Education, 1950-1975.* Washington: Picott, 1976.

Pleasant, Mae Barbee Boone. *Hampton University, Our Home by the Sea: An Illustrated History.* Virginia Beach, Va.: Donning Company, 1992.

Quigley, Thomas Bartlett. *Plaster of Paris Technique in the Treatment of Fractures.* New York: Macmillan, 1945.

Reuter, Edward Byron. *The American Race Problem: A Study of the Negro.* New York: Thomas Y. Crowell Co., 1927.

Reuter, Edward Byron. *The Mulatto in the United States.* Boston: Badger, 1918.

Reynolds, P. Preston. *Durham's Lincoln Hospital.* Charleston, SC: Acadia, 2001.

Ridlon, Florence. *A Black Physician's Struggle for Civil Rights: Edward C. Mazique*. Albuquerque: University of New Mexico Press, 2005.

Rise, Eric W. *The Martinsville Seven: Race, Rape and Capital Punishment*. Charlottesville: University Press of Virginia, 1995.

Rom, W.N. & S.M. Garay. *Tuberculosis*. Philadelphia: Lippincott, Williams & Wilkins, 2004.

Rothman, David. *Beginnings Count: The Technological Imperative in American Health Care*. New York: Oxford University Press, 1997.

Rothman, Sheila M. *Living in the Shadow of Death: Tuberculosis and the Social Experience of Illness in America*. New York: Basic Books, 1994.

Roundtree, H. C. and E.R. Turner. *Before and After Jamestown: Virginia's Powhatans and Their Predecessors*. Gainesville: University of Florida Press, 2002.

Rudwick, Elliot. *Race Riot at East St. Louis July 2, 1917*. Urbana: University of Illinois Press, 1982.

Sammons, Vivian O. *Blacks in Science and Medicine*. New York: Hemisphere Publishing Corp., 1990.

Scott, Emmett J. *Scott's Official History of the American Negro in the World War*. Chicago: Homewood Press, 1919.

Schall, Keith. *Stony the Road: Chapters in the History of Hampton Institute*. Charlottesville: University Press of Virginia, 1977.

Schaffer, Howard B. *Ellsworth Bunker: Global Troubleshooter, Vietnam Hawk*. Chapel Hill: University of North Carolina Press, 2003.

Smith, J. Douglas. *Managing White Supremacy: Race, Politics, and Citizenship in Jim Crow Virginia*. Chapel Hill: University of North Carolina Press, 2002.

Smith, Claudine C., and Mildred H.B. Roberson. *Memories of a Black Lay Midwife from Northern Neck Virginia*. Lisle, Ill.: Tucker Publications, 1994.

Smith, Claudine C., and Mildred H.B. Roberson. *My Bag was Always Packed: The Life and Times of a Virginia Midwife*. Bloomington, Ind.: First Books, 2003

Smith, P., and F.W. Wright, and associates. *Education in the Forty-Eight States*. Washington: United States Government Printing Office, 1939.

Smith, Susan L. *Sick and Tired of Being Sick and Tired; Black Women's Health Activism in America, 1890-1950*. Philadelphia: University of Pennsylvania Press, 1995.

Staudenraus, P. J. *The African Colonization Movement, 1816-1865*. New York: Columbia University Press, 1965.

Stowe, Steven M. *A Southern Practice: The Diary and Autobiography of Charles A. Hentz, M.D*. Charlottesville: University Press of Virginia, 2000.

Thorn, Megan. *Roots and Recollections: A Century of Rockywold-Deephaven Camps*. Rockywold-Deephaven Camps, Inc., 1997.

Time-Life Books. *African Americans, Voices of Triumph: Leadership*. Alexandria, Va.: Time-Life Books, 1993.

Tuskegee Institute. *Negro Year Book*. Tuskegee Institute, Ala.: Negro Year Book Publishing Co., 1912.

Ward Thomas, J. *Black Physicians in the Jim Crow South*. Fayetteville: University of Arkansas Press, 2003.

Washington, Booker T. *The Negro in Business*. New York: AMS Press, 1971.

Washington, Booker T. *Up From Slavery*. New York: New American Library, 2000.

Weinberg, Meyer. *The World of W.E.B. Du Bois: A Quotation Source Book*. Westport, Conn.: Greenwood Press, 1992.

Weyers, Wolfgang. *The Abuse of Man*. New York: Ardor Scribendi, 2003.

Woodward, C. Vann. *The Strange Career of Jim Crow*. New and rev. ed.
New York: Oxford University Press, 1957.

Writer's Program, Va. *The Negro in Virginia*. New York: Hastings House,
1940.

CATALOGS AND DIRECTORIES

American Medical Directory. 6th ed. Chicago: American Medical
Association, 1918.

*Chataigne's Virginia Gazette and Classified Business Directory, Lancaster
County Virginia 1888-1889*.
http://www.newrivernotes.com/va/lanc1888.htm

Hampton Normal and Agricultural Institute. *The Fortieth Annual Catalogue*.
Hampton, Va.: Hampton Institute Press, 1908.

Howard University. *Catalog/Howard University. 1912-1913*. Washington,
D.C.: Howard University, 1913.

Howard University. *Directory of Graduates: Howard University, 1870-1963*.
Frederick D. Wilkinson, ed. Washington, D.C.: the University, 1965.

Lincoln University (Pa.). *The Alumni Directory of Lincoln University.
Centennial Edition*. Lincoln University (Pa.): [The University, 1954].

Lincoln University (Pa.). *Lincoln University College and Theological
Seminary Biographical Catalogue*. Lancaster, Pa.: Press of the New Era
Printing Co., 1918.

National Tuberculosis Association. *A Directory of Sanatoria, Hospitals and
Day Camps for the Treatment of Tuberculosis in the United States*. New
York, 1919.

National Tuberculosis Association. *A Directory of Sanatoria, Hospitals and
Day Camps for the Treatment of Tuberculosis in the United States*. New
York, 1931.

National Tuberculosis Association. *A Directory of Sanatoria, Hospitals and Day Camps for the Treatment of Tuberculosis in the United States.* New York, 1934.

National Tuberculosis Association. *Tuberculosis Hospital and Sanatorium Directory: A Directory of Tuberculosis Hospitals and General Hospitals Having Departments for Tuberculosis Patients.* New York, 1938.

National Tuberculosis Association. *Tuberculosis Hospital and Sanatorium Directory: A Directory of Tuberculosis Hospitals and General Hospitals Having Departments for Tuberculosis Patients.* New York, 1951.

DISSERTATIONS

Jordan, Elizabeth Cobb. "The Impact of the Negro Organization Society on Public Support for Education in Virginia 1912-1950." EdD diss., University of Virginia, 1978.

Mullins, Foney G. "A History of the Literary Fund as a Funding Source for Free Public Education in the Commonwealth of Virginia." EdD diss., Virginia Polytechnic Institute, 2001.

Suggs, Henry Lewis. "P.B. Young and the Norfolk Journal & Guide 1910-1954." PhD diss., University of Virginia, 1976.

JOURNALS AND NEWSPAPERS

Journals

Journal of the National Medical Association. Volumes 2-60 (1911-1968).

Virginia Medical Monthly. Volumes 43-47 (1916-1920); 71-82 (1944-1955).

Newspapers

Pittsburgh Courier. Pittsburgh, Pa. 1943.

Herald Statesman, Yonkers, New York. April 1932-March 1933, October 1933- June 1934.

Rappahannock Record, Kilmarnock, Va. 1925-1966.
Richmond Afro-American, Richmond, Va. 1944.

Virginia Citizen, Irvington, Va. 1895-13.

The Journal and Guide. Norfolk, Va. 1916-1917, July 1943 - December 1944.

ONLINE RESOURCES

Gertz, Lindsey Dene. *The Tuberculosis Experience of African Americans in Virginia.*
http://www.faculty.virginia.edu/blueridgesanatorium/

Herbst, Jurgen. *Bibliography of the History of American Education III. From the Revolution to Reconstruction 21. The South.*
http://www.zzbw.uni-hannover.de/HerbstStart.htm

Shenouda, Monica. *The Blue Ridge Sanatorium against the Cityscape of Charlottesville.*
http://www.faculty.virginia.edu/blueridgesanatorium/

U.S. Department of Health and Human Services. Centers for Disease Control and Prevention. National Center for Health Statistics. *VSUS: Historical Vital Statistics of the United States.*
http://www.cdc.gov/nchs/products/pubs/pubd/vsus/historical/historical.htm

ARCHIVAL SOURCES, DOCUMENTS, MANUSCRIPT COLLECTIONS, AND REPORTS

"Abstract of Minutes from the Town of Kilmarnock, Va." November 18, 1935 – October 19, 1942. Typescript.

Combs, M.L., Hoke, K.J., and Smithey, W. R. Lancaster County Virginia High School Survey Report for the Virginia State Board of Education, September, 1927.

Ebenezer Baptist Church, Richmond, Virginia. *125th Anniversary, 1858-1983.*

Forbes, Ella. "Historical Sketch of Lincoln University, Pennsylvania."
Photocopied typescript. Lincoln, PA: Lincoln University, 1988, updated
1994.

*God's Amazing Grace Thru Many Dangers, Toils and Snares. Willie Chapel
Baptist Church, Lancaster, Virginia, 1884-1984.* White Stone, Va.: HS
Printing & Stationery, Inc.

*Historical Sketch of the Willie Chapel Baptist Church, Lancaster, Virginia,
1884-2002.*

Howard University Medical Alumni Association, Inc. *Twentieth Annual
Reunion.* [Program.] Washington, D.C., The Statler-Hilton Hotel. May 31, 1966.

"Information for School Survey of Lancaster County School Board."
Typescript. [1927?].

Jessie Ball DuPont Papers, 1767 (1921-1970) 1982 Finding Aid. Washington
and Lee University. James G. Leyburn Library. Special Collections.
http://library.wlu.edu/research/specialcollections/jessiebd.pdf

John A. Andrew Clinical Society. *The Forty-Fifth Annual Meeting, April
7-12, 1957.* [Program.]. John A. Andrew Memorial Hospital, Tuskegee
Institute, Alabama.

John A. Andrew Clinical Society. *The Forty-Sixth Annual Meeting, April
13-18, 1958.* [Program.] John A. Andrew Memorial Hospital, Tuskegee
Institute, Alabama.

Lancaster County [Virginia] 350th Anniversary Program. 2001.

Land and Community Associates. Charlottesville, Va. "Survey of State-
Owned Properties: Virginia Department of Mental Health, Mental
Retardation, and Substance Abuse." Prepared for Department of Historic
Resources. Richmond, Virginia. March, 1991.

Manning, K. R. "African Americans and the United States Public Health
Service: Evolution of a Relationship." By order of the PHS Order No.
93AF08671401D.

"Minutes of the Lancaster County School Board." Abstracted (Only parts dealing with African-American Schools were copied). Part I: September 19, 1922 – May 13, 1929. Transcribed by Donna Helmuth, March 4, 2005. Courtesy of the Superintendent's Office, Lancaster County Schools. Typescript.

"Minutes of the Lancaster County School Board." Abstracted (Only parts dealing with African-American Schools were copied). Part II: July 9, 1929 – December 13, 1937. Transcribed by Donna Helmuth, March 4 – 17, 2005. Courtesy of the Superintendent's Office, Lancaster County Schools. Typescript.

"Minutes of the Lancaster County School Board." Abstracted (Only parts dealing with African-American Schools were copied). Part III: January 11, 1938 – March 11, 1941. Selected copying from March 6, 1966 – March 13, 1969. With Additional Documents. Transcribed by Donna Helmuth, March 4 – 17, 2005. Courtesy of the Superintendent's Office, Lancaster County Schools. Typescript.

Mount Olive Baptist Church 131ˢᵗ Church Anniversary Bulletin. September 26, 2004.

Morgan E. Norris, M.D., 1888-1966 Memorial Service Programme. Kilmarnock, Virginia. July 31, 1971.

Negro Organization Society of Virginia. *Annual of the Negro Organization Society Incorporated.* Norfolk: Guide Publishing Co., Inc., 1937.

New St. John's Baptist Church, Kilmarnock, Virginia. *94ᵗʰ Church Anniversary, 1910-2004.*

Official Bulletin of The Negro Organization Society, Incorporated of Virginia. Norfolk: H.C. Young Press, 1950.

Oral Histories in the Collections of the Mary Ball Washington Museum and Library, Lancaster, Virginia:
Crosby, William
Gibson, Martha
Grimes, Edith
Norris, Theresita

Pinn, S.B. "St. John's Baptist Church, Lancaster County Virginia, Organizational Structure." July 4, 1868 and "New Era Minutes." September 19, 1875 – June 1888. Transcribed by Donna Helmuth, 2003. Courtesy of the Mary Ball Washington Museum and Library. Typescript.

Richmond Community Hospital 1953 Annual Report. [Richmond, Virginia, 1953].

"Some Milestones of Tuberculosis Control in Virginia." Photocopied typescript. (Probably published by the Virginia Tuberculosis Association, circa 1953.)

Surgeon-General of the Public Health and Marine-Hospital Service of the United States for the Fiscal Year 1909 Annual Report. Washington, D.C.: Government Printing Office, 1910.

Surgeon General of the Public Health Service of the United States for the Fiscal Year 1937 Annual Report. Washington, DC: Government Printing Office, 1937.

The American Lung Association of Virginia Collection (ALAV), MS-3, Claude Moore Health Sciences Library, Historical Collections and Services, University of Virginia.

Thompson, Harry F. and John H. Baker. "Survey of Lancaster County Schools." Compliments of B.H. Baird, Warsaw, Va. Typescript. [1940-1941].

Thompson, Harry F. and Louis E. English. "Survey of Lancaster County Schools." Compliments of B.H. Baird Insurance Agency, Boston Insurance Company, Warsaw, Va. Typescript. [1937?]

Virginia Council on Health and Medical Care. Public Opinion Committee. "Medical Care in Virginia Seriously Inadequate." Public Opinion Report No. 1. Richmond: Virginia Council on Health and Medical Care, [1945].

Virginia Council on Health and Medical Care. Public Opinion Committee. "Our Health Program Expands." Public Opinion Report No. 2. Richmond: Virginia Council on Health and Medical Care, July, 1946.

Virginia Council on Health and Medical Care. Public Opinion Committee. "What's Next in Virginia's Health Program?" Public Opinion Report No. 3. Richmond: Virginia Council on Health and Medical Care, June, 1947.

Virginia Council on Health and Medical Care. Public Opinion Committee. "What is the Virginia Council on Health and Medical Care?" Public Opinion Report No. 9. Richmond: Virginia Council on Health and Medical Care, June, 1951.

Virginia Council on Health and Medical Care. Public Opinion Committee. "Let's Continue Virginia's Heatlh Progress." Public Opinion Report No. 10. Richmond: Virginia Council on Health and Medical Care, October, 1951.

Virginia Health: Annual Report of the Virginia State Department of Health for the Fiscal Year Ended June 30, 1950. Richmond: Virginia State Department of Health, 1950.

Virginia Union University (Richmond, Va.). *Virginia Union Bulletin. Centennial Issue, 1865-1965.* Richmond, Va.: Virginia Union University, 1965.

ARCHIVES AND LIBRARIES CONSULTED

American Museum of Natural History Special Collections

Bedford City County Museum, Virginia*

Clerk's Office, Lancaster County Courthouse, Virginia

Cornell University Library, Rare and Manuscript Collections*

Fisk University Franklin Library, John Hope and Aurelia E. Franklin Special Collections*

Hampton University Archives

Howard University Archives

Hunter College Libraries, Archives and Special Collections

The Lancaster County (Virginia) School Board

The Library of Congress

Library of Virginia

Lincoln University Archives

Mary Ball Washington Museum and Library

MCP Hahnemann University, Archives and Special Collections*

Medical Examiners Office, Richmond, Virginia*

Melvin Sabshin Library and Archives of the American Psychiatric Association*

Messiah Baptist Church Records, Yonkers, New York

The New York Academy of Medicine

The New York Public Library, Humanities and Social Sciences Library

The New York Public Library, Schomburg Center for Research in Black Culture

Richmond Times Dispatch Archives, Richmond, Virginia

The Rockefeller Archive Center, Sleepy Hollow, New York

Saint Luke's Hospital Archives, New York City

Syracuse University School of Medicine Archives*

Tompkins-McCaw Library, Virginia Commonwealth University

Tuskegee University Archives*

Washington and Lee University, James G. Leyburn Library*

Virginia Polytechnic Institute and State University, University Libraries, Special Collections*

University of Virginia, Albert and Shirley Small Special Collections Library*

US Trotting Association Archives*

Virginia Department of Historical Resources*

Virginia Historical Society

Virginia State University at Petersburg. Archives

Virginia Union University Archives*

Site not personally visited but contacted via telephone and correspondence.

INDEX

Note: *Italicized page numbers refer to a chart, map, or photograph.*

Saint Philip Hospital, Richmond, Virginia
   clinics for Negro physicians 260
   death of James "Bozo" Ball 82
   nurses training 74
   polio treatment 132
   tetanus treatment 130
Salk vaccine 131
Sanatorium. *See* Tuberculosis
Sanger, William T. 247, 263
Scattergood, J. Henry 230
Schmeling, Max 72
Scott, Charles W. 211
Scott, C. Waldo *201*, 249, 258
Scranton, Pennsylvania 217
Scrofuloderma *See* Tuberculosis
Seamon, M. C. 172
Sears Roebuck Company 156, 158
Second Civil Rights era (1960s) xix
Segregation in Virginia Public Schools 157
Segregation on interstate carriers 58
Selective Service Act 64
Seventh-day Adventist Church 78
Sexually transmitted diseases 142, 143, 260
Shadow on the Land: Syphilis. (Parran) 260
Shanholtz, Mack I. 248-249
Sharon Baptist Church 88
Sherman, Miss (Correspondence
   Department, Hampton Institute) 45
Shiloh Baptist Church, Reedville, Virginia
   136
Simmons, C. Jackson 171
Slaughter, James B. 137
Smith, Carrie Bean 123
Smith, Claudine 123
Smith, E. Hugh 237-238
Smith, Janie 82
Smith, Major 82
Smith, Rebecca 73
Social diseases. *See* Sexually transmitted
   diseases
the South, colored communities in 71
Spaulding, Charles Clinton 222

Steamboat routes, Chesapeake Bay *111*
Steamboat travel 33, 35
Steuart, George H. 66
Stevenson, Louis 285
Stroud, Effie Jenkins 121, 165
Surgeon General's office 143
Syphilis. *See* Sexually transmitted diseases
Syphax, Burke "Mickey" 265
Syracuse University 216
Syracuse University School of Medicine 216

T
Tappahannock, Virginia 116, 147, 224, 235
Taylor, Jack 98, 240-241
Taylor, Laura 272
Tetanus 130. *See also* Lockjaw.
Tetanus antitoxin 131
Thoracoplasty 207
Thornton, Augustus A. 35, 215
Thornton, Eva Alma
   background 215-216
   death certificate 219
   gender prejudice 216
   passing for white 215, 217-218
   photographs of *197*
   Syracuse University 216-217, 219
   will 219
   work in Pennsylvania 216-217
Thornton, Mary Jane 35, 215
Title of coroner 246
Tolson, Mary 181
Tolson, Rossie 79
Toney, Marcus E. 213, 259-260
Tonsillectomy 151
Towles, Charles 74, 158
Treakle, Coleman 241
Trice, L. L. 174
Trudeau, Edward Livingston 212
Tuberculosis. *See also* Piedmont
   Tuberculosis Sanatorium for Negroes
   anti-microbials 214
   death rates, Negro v. white, graph *211*
   death rates, Negro v. white 213

CPSIA information can be obtained
at www.ICGtesting.com
Printed in the USA
FFOW02n0036290515
13741FF

9 780980 008463